JUDY
HOLLIDAY

JUDY HOLLIDAY

An Intimate Life Story

GARY CAREY

Seaview Books

NEW YORK

00943*4* *Manufactured in the United States of America.*

First edition

14.95 Seaview Books/A Division of PEI Books, Inc.

Library of Congress Cataloging in Publication Data

Carey, Gary.
    Judy Holliday, an intimate life story.

    Includes index.
        1. Holliday, Judy.   2. Actors—United States—
Biography.   I. Title.
PN2287.H613C37   791.43'028'0924 [B]   81–50321
ISBN 0–87223–757–5   AACR2

Design by Tere LoPrete.

CONTENTS

ACKNOWLEDGMENTS

I offer my sincere gratitude to the following, who graciously granted interviews or supplied information for this book: Garson Kanin, Marian Seldes, Howard Teichmann, the late Anita Loos, Morton Gottlieb, Daniel Selznick, Irene Mayer Selznick, the late Max Liebman, Robert L. Green, Joseph Harris, Rex Reed, Cy Feuer, John Greenleaf, and Rita Gardner. Sylvia Regan was most helpful in supplying information about Holliday's family and early years. Norman and Gwyda Kean contributed substantially to the chapter on the production of *Laurette*. Mrs. Cam Walter was of invaluable help in describing the last months of Holliday's life and commenting insightfully on Judy's personality and personal drives.

For earlier projects, I had spoken with George Cukor and Katharine Hepburn, and I have drawn on material from these interviews for this book.

Secondary research was done mainly at the Lincoln Center Library of the Performing Arts and the Film Study Center of the Museum of Modern Art. I wish to thank the staff at each of these institutions for their courtesy and assistance.

I also wish to acknowledge information gleaned from the many books I consulted during the preparation of the manuscript. For information about the Revuers during the period when they were performing at the Village Vanguard, *Live at the Village Vanguard* by Max Gordon (St. Martin's Press, 1980); for information about *Adam's Rib* and *It Should Hap-*

pen to You, Tracy and Hepburn (Viking, 1971) and *Hollywood* (Viking, 1974) respectively, both by Garson Kanin; for background on the stage version of *Born Yesterday*, *"Max Gordon Presents"* by Max Gordon and Lewis Funke (Bernard Geis Associates, 1963); for material about Holliday's Mercury Theatre days, *Front and Center* by John Houseman (Simon and Schuster, 1979); for information about Harry Cohn and Judy's years at Columbia, *King Cohn* by Bob Thomas (G.P. Putnam's Sons, 1967); and for material about Holliday's involvement with the McCarran Commission, *The Journal of the Plague Years* by Stefan Kanfer (Atheneum, 1973) and *Thirty Years of Treason* edited by Eric Bentley (Viking, 1971).

I did not see Holliday when she worked as one of the Revuers. However, I have seen all of her films (with the exception of *Laurette*), and all of her stage performances starting with *Born Yesterday*. Therefore, for the most part, I alone am responsible for the appraisals of Holliday's work presented here, though my perceptions have been appreciably sharpened by conversations over the years with many friends, including Terrence McNally, John Alfred Avant, Pauline Kael, and Richard Corliss, any one of whom may find echoes of their views reverberating in this book.

Finally, I wish to express thanks to my agent, Ray Pierre Corsini, and my editor, Anne Harrison, for their patience and encouragement.

INTRODUCTION

Judy Holliday never wanted to be an actress. "Acting is a very limited form of expression," she once commented, "and those who take it seriously are very limited people."

An unusual comment for a woman who, from the first moment she was "pushed" onto a stage to her last Broadway bow, was to be almost obsessively painstaking in the refinement and perfection of her art. It is an extraordinary comment for a woman who, in a career that was to last little over twenty years, was to win the highest awards of screen and stage: an Oscar for her performance in *Born Yesterday*; a Tony for *The Bells Are Ringing*; and that most impressive of all unofficial accolades, the acknowledgment that she was an "actor's actor"—a performer whose technique is so subtle and so self-effacing that it can only be fully appreciated by the initiated.

But such contradictions were the very essence of Judy Holliday. Running throughout her life is a fascinating counterpoint between what she believed and what she did, what she needed and what she got, what she appeared to be and who she really was. It was not simply a conflict between professional and private images, though that was certainly a part of it. There was a strain of ambivalence and conflict that ran deep in Judy, and it was to be the source of her profoundest struggles and her greatest successes.

Nowhere is this ambivalence more readily apparent than in Judy's attitude toward her professional life. While Holliday was alive, and perhaps even more so today, she was identified in the public mind with Billie Dawn, the most celebrated and glorious dumb blond in screen and stage history. But Holliday was neither blond (except with the help of her hairdresser) nor dumb. In fact, it was Holliday's wit and intelligence, which lay just beneath the surface of all the characters she played, that gave her portrayal of Billie Dawn such depth and brilliance. And yet it was the success of that role that was to ultimately limit Holliday's growth as an actress. And Holliday came to resent it. "I guess I owe everything to Billie," she once said. "But some mornings I wake up cursing her." The more she became associated with Billie, the more she felt she was playing a lie. "I respect my craft," she said later, "but I don't think it can take the place of the real thing."

Only rarely in her films do we get flashes of the "real thing" —the true Judy Holliday. The fact is that Hollywood didn't know what to do with the real thing—Holliday simply did not fit any of the standard molds for film heroines of the Forties and Fifties, and, as this was not a period of daring or great imagination, she was almost invariably cast as a variation of Billie Dawn. Undoubtedly, if Holliday's career had coincided with the present era of filmmaking, when women's roles are not so stereotypically conceived as in the past, she would have found greater latitude in expressing who she really was.

The real thing. The true Judy Holliday. The inner Judy was a mass of contradictions, a nexus of desires and goals all out of harmony. The only child of parents who separated when she was quite young, she was inflicted with a pitiful want of self-esteem; and yet from an early age she set enormously high goals for herself. Basically shy, she could become aggressive and outspoken when fighting for what she thought was right. She was inordinately sensitive about her physical appearance; but she nonetheless allowed herself to be shoved into a career where beauty was a prime ingredient for success, and where her insecurities were certain to be exacerbated by her surroundings. She saw herself, and in many ways acted, the liberated, freethinking woman; and yet in every one of her relationships —with her mother, her lovers, her child—she exhibited powerful maternal and domestic longings. Her sense of self was so fragile that any personal or professional setback could send her into deep depression, and yet she always found the inner strength to forge ahead.

And it is this that makes Holliday such a fascinating and enigmatic woman: For every doubt and reservation that held her back, there was a deeper and stronger urge to push forward. Beneath an outward appearance of timidity and passivity, there was a woman of immense strength and drive. Holliday's life was never simple. She was beset by a host of personal and professional tragedies. But she was a woman who was able, in the little time she had, to pull a considerable degree of happiness and success out of it.

Because Holliday's career was not a long one, it encompassed a very small body of work, and thus her posthumous reputation rests on precarious ground. Despite her Oscar for *Born Yesterday*, she doesn't figure prominently in the books dedicated to "the great movie stars," and her theater career was too sporadic to qualify her for the Broadway Hall of Fame (whose admission requirements stipulate a given number of appearances over a certain number of years). Holliday hasn't been forgotten exactly, but she lives on in a kind of limbo, dimly recalled as Billie Dawn.

Certainly this is not the way she would have chosen to be remembered, but as there have been few attempts to evaluate her career or to place her life and work in the perspective of her times, it is not surprising that most people have decided that there was nothing more to Holliday than Billie Dawn. The facts of her life more than challenge that assumption, however. Holliday's accomplishments were substantial, and she remains an inspiration to the generation of actress-comediennes who have come after her. If she failed to live up to the expectations her initial stage and screen performances aroused—and it would be foolish to pretend she did—it was partly because of her own insecurities, partly because she was too original for the conventional show-business minds of the time, and partly because time ran out just as she was discovering who she really was, just as she was beginning to use that hard-earned self-knowledge as a basis for real creative expression.

She might have had greater fame and fulfillment if she had lived longer. But despite the precarious balance her career and her relationships all seemed to hang in, she did achieve a kind of success in the time she had—not as a star made for Hollywood or a woman destined for happiness, but as a survivor who forged a life for herself out of the strange combination of talent, fear, shyness, doubt, wit, and generosity that was hers.

PART ONE

Yesterday and Before

Chapter One
LOST MEMORIES

Judy Holliday, stage and screen star, found little to say about her childhood as Judith Tuvim. It was not that she was reluctant to talk about those early years, she insisted; simply that whenever she pushed her mind backward, she came up with a blank. "Well, you know what that means," she told an interviewer. "I guess it's pretty obvious that I was unhappy."

While it would be inaccurate to portray Holliday's childhood as an unmitigated tragedy—there was, in fact, much love and security in it—there were many pockets of memory that Holliday preferred not to explore, at least not for the benefit of the lady with the steno pad in her lap. Try as she might, the interviewer could not get Holliday to elaborate any further about her childhood memories. When pushed, Judy started telling funny, wisecracking anecdotes about her past—she had a way of slipping into the role of Billie Dawn whenever it was to her advantage. But beneath the jokes and evasions lay the memory of a time that had been instrumental in making Judy who she was. Throughout her life, indeed, right up until her death, Judy's parents—whether everpresent as her mother was or mostly absent as her father was—were to play vital roles. And it was during Judy's troubled early years that some of her profoundest attitudes and goals— that were to have far-reaching implications not only in Judy's professional life but in the many, often conflicted, relation- ships in her private life—were formed.

But for the interviewer at the time, Judy was not forth- coming. Reticent, highly sensitive, and exceedingly loyal, Holliday cherished her privacy and the privacy of others, and would go to any length to protect herself and her friends from unwarranted public scrutiny. Frequently she either edited her memoirs to cast them in the most attractive light possible or brushed them aside with a general descriptive comment like "I was unhappy."

Rarely was she guilty of a direct lie, however—except about one vital statistic: her age. The very first press biographies list her date of birth as June 21, 1922; and by the time of her death, the date had been advanced to 1923. But the birth cer- tificate in the files of the New York Department of Health shows that Judith Tuvim was born June 21, 1921.

Helen Tuvim, Judy's mother, once told a reporter that she went into labor while watching Fanny Brice in a Broadway revue. She went straight from the theater to the Lying In Hos- pital at 23rd Street and Second Avenue where her only child was born shortly thereafter. Very shortly, apparently, since Judy was born before midnight on the twenty-first, which was the date of the opening night of The Ziegfeld Follies of 1921.

That Mrs. Tuvim was watching Fanny Brice introduce two of her most famous songs, "My Man" and "Second-Hand Rose," just as her daughter was indicating that she was ready to come into the world is an especially pleasing coincidence. Which may be the reason Mrs. Tuvim mentioned the story to the inquiring reporter: While never the stereotypical stage mother, Helen had a definite instinct for the dramatic when it came to presenting Judy to the world.

Helen Tuvim was born in America of Russian-Jewish de- scent: Her father was a manufacturer of epaulets and military braid for the Czar and his guard in St. Petersburg. His wife, Rachel, despised the social inequities and anti-Semitism of Imperial Russia, and in 1888, when she learned that another series of pogroms might occur at any moment, she urged her husband to leave. Rachel often became overwrought when she got on the subject of czarist injustice, but this time her husband paid attention. They joined the mass migration to Ellis Island and, along with thousands of other Russian Jews, found themselves in the teeming streets of New York's Lower East Side. Along the way they acquired a new name. They were now the Gollombs.

The new world proved to be a disappointment. There were no pogroms, but there were anti-Semitism, low wages, exploitation, numbing poverty. To make matters worse, just as the family was starting to make headway, Papa Gollomb, who had found work as a tailor, died, leaving Rachel with four children to feed. A strong woman, she kept her brood alive by slaving at menial jobs. In many ways, Rachel fit the classic image of the American immigrant. She was not going to allow herself to be beaten down by the harsh and unwelcoming new world. She managed, over the years, not only to support her children but to achieve a certain degree of comfort for them. By the time her sons were grown, she was even able to provide an education for them. But the ordeal left its wounds. Always impassioned, Rachel became rabid in her devotion to socialism. She made friends in the community and gathered around her a group of people who shared her beliefs.

One of the Gollomb boys, Joseph, was to become a well-known author and journalist who would number among his friends poet Vachel Lindsay and many theatrical personalities, including the playwrights Bella and Sam Spewack. But Helen was always Rachel's favorite child. Helen grew up under the powerful pull of her mother's strength and passion. And the two women shared many similarities. Like her mother, Helen possessed a volatile temperament; when excited, she spoke so quickly that she often stumbled headlong into a series of malapropisms. Helen also unquestioningly accepted Rachel's political creed, and later was to preside over a kind of salon for aging Debs socialists and their more radical cousins. Whether or not she was actually as committed to the cause as her mother is a matter of conjecture. Though intelligent, she was not especially fond of intellectual pursuits and was rarely seen opening a newspaper. Probably she enjoyed the sociability that was part of socialism: the group meetings and friendliness and sense of being part of a brotherhood. Not a particularly pretty girl, she would have had little opportunity to meet eligible and sympathetic young men outside this circle.

Surprisingly, she caught the pick of the lot. Abraham Tuvim was a few years older than his wife—Helen was born in 1891; Tuvim, in 1884—but he looked much younger. Abe was endowed with a buoyancy and charm that contrasted sharply with his wife's intensity; even in her twenties, Helen seemed matronly, while he was tall and good-looking with sparkling, fun-filled eyes and a dazzling, dimpled smile. People who met him for the first time were frequently surprised that he held such a somber job—a fund raiser for Jewish organizations —but he did the work well and eventually reached prominence in his field.

People were also surprised when Abe married Helen in 1920. There is no accounting for matrimonial taste—but still, everyone wondered what he saw in her. The best answer anyone could come up with was a similarity of political conviction, though Abe never sounded as committed as Helen. But whatever it was that brought them together kept them together for almost ten years, and most of those years were happy ones.

Shortly after Judy's birth, the Tuvim family moved to Sunnyside Gardens in Queens. The area was hailed as a masterpiece of city planning: Roughly seventy acres of barren and mosquito-infested land had been converted into a community of single- and double-occupancy homes and apartment buildings, with a small park situated in the middle of each block.

The layout and architecture were unoriginal, but Sunnyside became a haven for middle- and lower-middle-class families who sought a bit of suburbia but were unable to afford the real thing. It was to be a particularly popular stopping-off place for upwardly mobile Jews.

The Tuvims lived in a modest semidetached house: It was small, but light and airy, and Helen made it look warm and hospitable. Both she and Abe were fond of music and the theater, and professed an enthusiasm for the arts and the higher reaches of culture, no matter what form they took. Abe's work as a fund raiser frequently brought him in contact with celebrities in all fields of the arts—he was always trying to con a magician or a singer or a clown into appearing at a benefit—and through Joe Gollomb, Helen's brother, they also started to move in circles that otherwise would have been closed to them.

One of Uncle Joe's favorite hangouts was the legendary Café Royale at 14th Street and Second Avenue, and often Abe and Helen would drop by when they knew Gollomb would be around to entertain them. For years, the Royale had been the Sardi's of the Yiddish theater; and even then, when most of the Yiddish stars had moved on to Broadway, they continued to return to the Royale for a late-night supper. People like Muni Weisenfreund (later known as Paul Muni) who in 1926 had just had his first big English-language hit in *We Americans*, were frequent patrons.

The Tuvims never got to know Muni very well, but they did become close with one of his *We Americans* coplayers, a young actress named Sylvia Hoffman Regan. "Our relationship was casual at first," Regan remembers, "but a couple of times I was invited to their home for dinner. Helen was very vivacious, running about, making everyone comfortable and cooking really delicious meals. Judy must have been about five at the time, and she was an adorable child, much more outgoing then than she would become later on."

Judy at age five was a plump little girl with straw-colored hair that was fading into mousy brown. She wasn't exactly pretty, but she was pert and pinchable, and she was the apple of her father's eye. He adored her and she adored him. She had charms for Abe that Helen never recognized, possibly because Helen had grown immune to them through familiarity. Judy's mother was always at home, while her father was frequently away on one of his fund-raising tours.

Helen, who loved music and was a moderately gifted pianist, had enrolled Judy in a local ballet school; and whenever the Tuvims had entertained, Judy would separate the parlor portieres and prance in to a recording of "The Dance of the Hours." She anticipated and rejoiced in the gleam of pride in Abe's eyes.

On one occasion, a friend of Abe's brought along his daughter, a little princess with the pouty and porcelain fragility of a Shirley Temple doll. Judy spent most of the afternoon sulking in the shadows of the hallway. No one asked her to go into her pirouettes; everyone was too busy extolling the delights of the rival sweetheart who had never felt the agony of twirling *en pointe*. When the party broke up, Abe took Judy aside and told her not to be disappointed, she had wonderful qualities, she would always be his darling. Then he kissed her, but the kiss didn't seem as sweet as it had in the past.

If Judy needed so desperately to win her father's affection, it may have been because she sensed, young as she was, that Abe was drifting away from her and Helen. Whatever it had been that had brought her parents together was not enough to bind them for all time, and a year or so after Judy's birth the marriage began to fall apart. Not dramatically so—there were no violent scenes. But Judy was an extremely sensitive child, and there were tensions that she must have felt, if not understood.

The denouement came when Judy was six. Abe went to Europe on another of his fund-raising trips, and when he returned, he told Helen he wanted a divorce. Though he never mentioned a specific reason to Helen, it was rumored among his friends that he was involved with another woman.

"When I heard the Tuvims had separated, I wasn't surprised," says Sylvia Regan. "That was the real shock—I felt no surprise. They seemed to be perfectly happy, but when I heard the news I didn't think, Why are they doing this?, but rather wondered about what had brought them together in the first place."

The separation was bitter—Joe Gollomb never spoke to Abe afterward, which is indicative of how Helen accepted the news. She was violently upset. Not unreasonably so, since she was a not terribly attractive, not especially gifted, middle-aged woman who had nothing much to look forward to except a peaceful old age with Abe and Judy. Now that Abe was gone, there remained only Judy, and Judy loved her father first of all.

Second place was not a position Helen could accept. One evening she went into the kitchen, turned on the gas, and placed her head inside the oven. Judy, smelling the fumes, rushed in and dragged her mother away from the stove. Though only seven, Judy fully understood what had happened. She felt responsible for her mother's melodramatic gesture, and she felt responsible for preventing it from happening again. Whether Helen had planned it or not, Judy started to turn away from Abe, whom she blamed for forcing her mother to this, and began to draw close to her mother. She felt she had to protect Helen; instinctively, Judy understood that her mother had no one else who could give her the emotional sustenance she needed.

Abe later claimed that he and Helen had tried to shield Judy from their unhappiness, had tried to make her understand that she was loved despite the rupture in their family relationship. He felt that they had succeeded, but, in saying so, he was guilty either of dishonesty or of self-delusion. Judy felt abandoned, and though there was always to be a surface friendship between father and daughter, she was to harbor an

unconscious resentment toward Abe. Helen did little to dis-
suade Judy from such feelings—in fact, she may have done
a great deal to nurture them; she never had anything good to
say about Abe once they had separated.

Divorce brings out the worst in the best of people, and
the Tuvims were no exception. Every week Judy would visit
Abe, and every week Helen would tell her to ask Abe for the
check. Every week Judy made the request and, without fail,
her father handed over the weekly alimony. When she turned
it over to Helen, it was received with a sharp dig about Abe's
"generosity," one that would be all the sharper if Uncle Joe
Gollomb happened to be around. Helen's family felt Abe
had treated his wife very shabbily indeed, leaving her and his
daughter (so the story went) for a woman who could offer
him nothing more than a couple of afternoons a week.

There were other grievances as well. Abe's alimony wasn't
enough to cover expenses, so Helen started teaching piano—
first privately, and later at the various settlement houses in
the New York area. Since she was out of the house most of
the day, Grandma Rachel moved in less than a year after the
Tuvims' separation, taking over the cleaning, cooking, and
proselytizing.

Once she reached school age, Judy entered P.S. 125 in
Sunnyside, where she scored an impressive 172 on an Otis IQ
test, a score that placed her in the genius category with room
to spare. At age eight, she wrote the annual holiday play, *The
Tucker Family's Christmas*, staging it herself as well as playing Father Tucker; when she was twelve she "composed" a
prizewinning essay, "How to Keep the Streets, Parks and
Playgrounds of Our City Clean and Wholesome"; and in high
school, she was editor of the student newspaper. Since she
was often under the supervision of Rachel, Judy had been
thoroughly indoctrinated in the socialist cause, and until the
early 1950s she was to take a keen interest in public affairs,
often donating her time and talents to various organizations
and fund-raising benefits.

Her intellectual proclivities impressed Helen and Rachel, who gave Judy nearly everything she wanted, provided they approved of her request. "When I didn't get what I wanted," Judy once said, "I was told it was something we couldn't afford. I never had a bicycle or a Girl Scout uniform, but I never really minded. Somehow the explanation that we just didn't have the money for them seemed quite sensible to me."

This was, of course, at the height of the Depression, and Judy was well aware that others were suffering far worse deprivations than she and her family; they at least had a home and enough to eat. But if Judy never missed the bike or the uniform, it's probably because she didn't really want them. If she had been deprived of a book, that would have been a different story. Early on she had developed what she would later term "eye hunger"—an insatiable, almost physical need to devour the printed word. "I've always loved words," she once said. "I ate up all the books I could lay my hands on, and when I couldn't get books, I read candy wrappers and labels on cereal and toothpaste boxes."

While most of her classmates were trying to plow through *Silas Marner,* she was exploring Shakespeare, Shaw, Tolstoi, Schnitzler, and Molière—she even worked at Proust. She received good grades in all but two subjects. One was sewing. "We were supposed to make an apron," she recalled. "I couldn't do it, so my mother made it for me. But she couldn't sew much either and that apron was a sorrowful sight." She also had no head for figures. "I flunked algebra and plane geometry, and had to make them up in summer school. I probably would never have passed geometry except that by mistake they gave the same test twice and I remembered the right answers. I *do* have a good memory."

As a teen-ager, Judy was serious-minded, quiet, somewhat aloof and superior. She had a small circle of friends, kids like herself who took an interest in social conditions and the progress of the arts. They were tolerated because they were smart, but none of them was accepted into the mainstream of school

life. Like many teen-age misfits, Judy tried to compensate by
playing up her idiosyncrasies. "I'm afraid I was horribly stuffy
about social life," she once told an interviewer. "I guess I was
a natural snob. I got a kick out of being different and improving myself and everyone around me. I went out mainly with
boys who would take me to Broadway plays instead of parties.
I was more interested in writing poetry than passing love notes,
and in hearing Bach than dancing to Benny Goodman. I must
have been obnoxious."

Once or twice a month, Judy would spend an afternoon
or evening with her father, who was at this time definitely
involved with a married woman who couldn't, or wouldn't,
get a divorce. It was a messy, painful business, and Abe looked
forward to Judy's visits as an escape from his problems. Judy
was not so eager to see Abe; she continued to harbor feelings
of resentment toward him. Usually they would go to a movie
or a matinee, and to dinner afterward. Often Abe would cook
the meal in his small Manhattan apartment and Sylvia Regan
would occasionally join them. Sylvia had abandoned acting
for backstage work, and in the last few years she had developed
a sisterly affection for Abe.

"What I remember most about Judy at this time—she must
have been about thirteen or fourteen—was her silence," Mrs.
Regan said. "She wasn't sullen or impolite, but she never had
anything to say. I knew she was interested in the theater, and
she knew that I was in the theater, but she never asked me
any questions, never tried to start a conversation. I found that
very strange, though I suppose she was just terribly shy."

Quite possibly, however, Judy's silence was an expression
of the awe she felt at being in the presence of someone connected with the legitimate theater. What Mrs. Regan de-
scribes as shyness and others have called "reserve" was really
a product of Judy's feelings of inadequacy. If her father had
deserted her, Judy felt, then there must be something griev-
ously wrong with her; and she was inclined to think it was

appearance. Though pretty, she wasn't beautiful or striking or original-looking, and being pretty wasn't enough for her. To compensate for this supposed liability, she clothed herself with an armor of adult composure and an air of intellectual sophistication. This outward display was, however, based on an inner conviction that she was special and would make her mark in some way.

By her final years at Julia Richman High School, Judy had already decided she wanted a career in the theater. Not as an actress—she claimed to have no respect for such a frivolous calling and undoubtedly believed she was telling the truth. On some unconscious level, however, she just as undoubtedly did want to be an actress. What held her back was a fear of competing in a business that depended heavily on physical allure. But this was an admission she couldn't make even to herself, so, as a rationalization, she adopted the clichéd put-down of acting: It was, she contended, an interpretive craft, and that wasn't for her; she saw herself playing a creative role in the theater as a writer or director.

People told Judy these were unrealistic goals for a woman, but she disagreed. Women playwrights were a common commodity—not only ladies like Rachel Crothers, who kept churning out such smash Broadway comedies as *When Ladies Meet* and *Susan and God*, but also Lillian Hellman, who was, next to Clifford Odets, just about the most respected American dramatist of the decade. There was also a small group of successful women directors, including Antoinette Perry (after whom the Tony award is named), Eva Le Gallienne, and Margaret Webster, whose 1937 production of *Richard II* had been both a critical and popular success.

On graduating from high school in 1938, Holliday applied for admission to the Yale Drama School, which offered a thorough grounding in all areas of the theater. She was refused admission because she did not meet the minimum age requirement; then as now, Yale's drama division operated at the graduate level. There were plenty of drama schools in the New York area, but most of them didn't begin classes until the fall, and in the meantime Judy felt obligated to find a job to help Helen with expenses. But no one was eager to hire her: She couldn't add or type, had never mastered shorthand. "I tried to learn Pitman, but it was hopeless," she once said. "Too much like arithmetic. I'd sit in class and watch all those silly girls squiggling like mad, and I'd get all confused and upset."

Abe came to the rescue. He called Sylvia Regan, who was now working as press secretary at the Mercury Theatre, run by John Houseman and Orson Welles. He reminded her that his daughter had set her sights on the theater and told her that Judy needed a summer job; was there any chance of an opening at the Mercury? Sylvia mentioned a secretarial position, but Abe said that wouldn't do since Judy had no secretarial skills. However, Sylvia's brother, Arthur, had been working the Mercury switchboard, and had also been helping out with typing and other odds and ends. Sylvia suggested promoting Arthur and hiring Judy for the phone work. She asked Abe if he thought Judy could manage that and he said yes, with training. So that was that. She went to work at $15 a week.

Judy was thrilled. The Mercury was the newest and most discussed of the experimental theater groups, and Orson Welles was Broadway's newest wonder boy. The organization, which was only a year old, specialized in producing plays of classic stature in presentations that were relevant to the current political situation: *Julius Caesar,* as interpreted by Welles and Houseman, became a battle cry against the encroaching wave of fascism. Judy had seen the production and loved it, was excited by Welles and his attempt to create an alternative to Broadway drama. A bastion of "the new theater," the Mercury was located in a bastion of the old: Its offices were in the historic and glamorous Empire Theatre on 41st Street, just across the street from the old Metropolitan Opera.

Holliday's first day at work was a letdown. The Empire's lobby and auditorium were a jewel box of late nineteenth-century theater design, but the suite of offices rented by the Mercury on the mezzanine was dingy and claustrophobic. There was a tiny reception room, presided over by Augusta Weissberger, the general secretary; behind that, a medium-size office for Welles and Houseman; parallel to that, a partitioned-off space for Sylvia Regan and two secretaries. In an airless cubbyhole off the reception room, space had been made for the switchboard and its operator. Judy's post at the telephone cut her off from the mainstream of the office; indeed, in her cubicle she was just as shut off from Mercury operations as she would have been if she had stayed in Queens with Helen.

Sylvia Regan says Arthur taught her switchboard operation in a matter of minutes and that Judy was very efficient at the job. Judy, however, remembered it differently. "Nothing ever terrified me as much as that switchboard. Every time a call would come in, a little thing would flap at me, a buzzer would go off, orange lights would blink like crazy, and I immediately forgot what I was supposed to do. I'd put all the loose plugs in all the empty holes and hope for the best."

Still, she was determined to stick it out because she wanted to attend the Mercury rehearsals and meet Orson Welles. According to Judy, neither event was to occur. "I never got a look at rehearsals. I never saw a play I didn't pay my way to see. I just sat at the switchboard from nine to five and cried."

Once again Judy's recollections do not jibe with the recollections of her fellow workers. Howard Teichmann, a graduate of the University of Wisconsin who joined the Mercury production staff at about this time, says she not only met Welles but also auditioned for him. Welles, says Teichmann, needed a girl for a small part in an upcoming play and Judy asked to audition. "Orson thought she was awful," Teichmann remembers. "He couldn't stop laughing! 'That terrible voice,' he kept saying. And, of course, she did have that silly, high-pitched voice, and at that time she had no idea of how to place it."

This is the first known—and perhaps classic—instance of the Jekyll and Hyde syndrome that ran through much of Judy's career. By most reports, Judy was shy to the point of passivity at this time. And on the surface, it was quite true. But the fact is that Judy *requested* the audition. She was never to display the kind of outward toughness and brashness of many actresses; but when she really wanted something, she would pursue it aggressively.

Moreover, despite her talk, and probably very real dreams, of becoming a director, Judy was already displaying a considerable degree of savvy in recognizing the most practical and likely means of achieving that end. Playing the actress was one way of getting into the Mercury rehearsals. And gaining experience as an actress would certainly help her on the road to becoming a director—you can't direct actors until you know precisely what it is that they do. Beyond this, one guesses that Judy might have been, however unconsciously, testing her own feelings of inadequacy against the opinion of an expert, Orson Welles. But Holliday wasn't Welles's kind of woman, and, as Howard Teichmann says, "Orson didn't know much about comedy; he would have been blind to Holliday's potential."

Judy was never to mention this audition with Welles, and her reaction can only be surmised by her continuing denigration of acting as a respectable trade for intelligent people. Meekly she went back to her switchboard and carried out her chores as proficiently as before. "She had a big smile for everyone," remembers Teichmann, "and she was very cute." On this last point, of course, Judy disagreed. She was still very self-conscious about her appearance. She was at least ten pounds overweight and she looked so immature compared to the glamour girls who swept in and out of Welles's office.

After her audition, Judy had nothing further to do with the Mercury's boy genius, but she did make contact with John Houseman, who was then only slightly less intimidating than he is today—as the imperial *alterkocker* of movie and TV-commercial acclaim.

Judy's first encounter with him occurred one day when she unplugged his call to the Coast three times. He dashed out of his office and chewed her out in words that left her blushing. "I had never heard the words he used before in my life," she recalled. "But I guess he had a reason to talk that way. I kept disconnecting him while he was trying to arrange some big deal."

The Mercury switchboard never stopped ringing, but somehow Judy found the time for additional duties. Every day the mailman left a bunch of unsolicited manuscripts on a table in the Mercury reception room. Since no one ever picked them up, Judy began to leaf through them between calls. "I'd dust them off, read them, and write a neat précis of each one. Nobody read anything I wrote. Nobody had told me to write them. I just did them on my own. Probably they all ended up in the trash."

The job wasn't as fulfilling as she had hoped, but at least it was a job in a field she wanted to explore, and this was sufficent reason for Judy to hang on at the Mercury at a time when millions of Americans were still either unemployed or working at trades that held no interest for them.

Then she got sick. Though she appeared robust, Judy was accident-prone—always breaking bones in bizarre ways—and highly susceptible to disease: She was always the first in class to come down with the measles or the chicken pox. (As a very young child she had developed a very mild case of polio, one that happily left her with no permanent physical disability.) For her, the common cold was a yearlong curse—she was always sniffling and never far away from laryngitis.

During her employment at the Mercury, she came down

with strep throat, was out of the office for several days, and returned before she was fully recovered. When the condition recurred a week or so later, Helen insisted she ask for a short leave of absence. Judy felt her mother was being alarmist, but eventually she requested sick leave, and the Mercury granted it willingly—she wouldn't be paid during her absence, but she would be welcomed back whenever she was ready to resume her duties.

Chapter Two
IN THE VANGUARD

Abe made a small contribution to Judy's vacation fund; but even after his gift had been added to what Helen had set aside from her household budget, the lump sum available for Judy's holiday wasn't lavish. If she had been traveling alone, she might have managed a week at one of the stylish resorts in Connecticut or Long Island, but Helen was going along on the trip; after all, unless she was around to remind her, Judy was certain to forget her bedtime medicine, a home remedy brewed of honey, crushed cloves, and patent cough syrup. "The only way I could get it down," Holliday recalled, "was to think of how Katharine Cornell in *The Barretts of Wimpole Street* bravely swallowed the lager her father insisted she drink. I tried to look as brave as Miss Cornell, but inevitably I gagged at each gulp."

In 1938, when the American economy was still striving to recover from the Depression dumps, people who deserved a vacation but couldn't afford a cottage, or a hotel room at a fashionable spa, went camping. More precisely, they went to summer camps for adults. The brochures and advertisements for these cut-rate resorts promised scenic views, swimming,

canoeing, tennis, basketball, golf, softball, and, once the sun
was down, dancing, entertainment, and romance. Rarely did
the reality live up to the promotional come-on: the "semi-
private bungalows" promised by the brochure frequently
turned out to be a dormitory housing six or eight, with cots
instead of "comfortable twin beds," and whose "hot and cold
running water" was usually cold when it was running at all.
Worse yet, the eligible male guests were all too often the
same creeps who gave you the glad eye on the downtown
BMT.

Such camps existed nationwide, but they were particularly
prevalent throughout New York State—the Catskills and the
Berkshires area were alive with them—and most of the people
who stayed there were from New York City. Many of the
camps catered to an exclusively Jewish clientele, and several
advertised in the *Nation* or one of the other ultraliberal magazines. Possibly, this is where Helen discovered the spot for
her two-week vacation with Judy; an attractive-sounding camp
near the Massachusetts border.

The camp was indeed several notches above its Catskills
competitors. The hot water usually ran hot; and the cabins,
while dilapidated, had been built for two and were free of
leaks, drafts, and ants. The atmosphere couldn't accurately be
described as restful—spontaneous happenings were always announced by a voice that came booming over a loudspeaker—
but few of the other campers were looking for peace and
quiet. Judy was the exception. While everyone else was out
being sportive, she was curled up on a lawn chair, reading one
of the Modern Library Giants she had brought along for
companionship.

Like the other campers, however, when the dinner gong
sounded, Judy allowed herself to be herded into the commis-
sary and, afterward into the "canteen" to watch the dancing
and boozing. She wasn't impressed, and the other guests of
her age gave her a wide berth: There had to be something odd
about a girl who came to camp with her mother as chaperon;

most of the other girls had come there to get away from the
protective and prying eyes of their parents. Judy was aware of
the ostracism, but she rose above it: She was, after all, ac-
customed to taking a superior view of her peers. She liked the
camp, tacky as it was, because she liked nature, enjoyed trees
and flowers and animals, preferred the flora to the camp fauna,
particularly since most of the visiting beasts pranced about in
ways that were decidedly prurient.

On the second day of her visit, however, Judy became interested in some of the group activities. Over the loudspeaker,
the camp's social director announced that after dinner that
night the resident stock company would provide an evening
of light entertainment, and would everyone be so kind as to
take his or her seat in the assembly hall? Judy noticed that
most of the guests immediately scurried off to the canteen,
but she and Helen followed orders and seated themselves on
camp chairs in the first row of what was euphemistically
called "the assembly hall." And what they saw could only
euphemistically be called "entertainment"—a few songs, a
couple of nonroyalty one-acters, a sprinkling of comedy routines (most of them filched from popular radio programs of
the period). The master of the revels was a short, scruffy-
looking guy who could have been a stand-in for any one of the
Three Stooges. He was almost belligerently self-assertive, but
also energetic, spunky, and brimming with intelligence. Judy
decided that here was a person worth cultivating. She hung
around until finally she struck up a conversation with the
camp's funnyman.

His name, she discovered, was Adolph Green. He was from
the Bronx and was a few years older than she—he was twenty,
Judy was seventeen. Like Judy, he was hypersensitive about
his appearance. "I was fat and wildly unattractive," Green recalls. "I was memorably odd-looking. My clothes were shreddy
and ill-fitting. I was matted. But I was terribly polite and terribly shy—except on stage." After graduating from DeWitt
Clinton High School, he had enrolled at New York University,

but dropped out a few weeks later when he realized that what he wanted to learn wasn't being taught at NYU. For a while he supported himself as a runner on Wall Street—that lasted three months—then as a carpet salesman (another three months), and there were a series of other daytime jobs while he played around with little theater groups in the evening.

Every summer he headed for the Catskills to provide the theatricals that passed in the adult camps (in the words of one brochure) as "a midsummer evening's dream of entertainment," and every fall he went back to town hoping to impress Broadway agents and producers with his achievements over the summer. But he never sold what he was peddling, so by winter he was back to marketing carpets or running for Wall Street.

Green and Holliday hit it off from the start. He overcompensated for his shyness by talking a blue streak and wasn't at all disturbed by Judy's reticence—he had enough small talk for both of them. Whenever there was a lull in the conversation, he'd jump in and ask, "Say, what's your favorite Sam de Grasse film?" and if she looked blank, he'd proceed to rattle off all of Sam de Grasse's film credits. Or, "Do you know the verse to 'He Was Too Good to Me'?" and if she didn't, he'd sing it for her. He was funny, sophisticated, a little waspish, a walking encyclopedia of trivial knowledge about the arts, both popular and profound.

Green's verbal dexterity was to awaken a similar, though dormant, gift in Judy, who was discovering within herself a wry, laconic wit. In his presence she also started to shed some of her stuffiness: His eclectic taste, which embraced Khachaturian as well as Kern, broadened her perspective and allowed her to see that there was something of value in life besides social causes and the Modern Library. Green seemed to her just about the brightest, cleverest person she had ever known, but still she wouldn't accept his point of view unquestioningly. The one attitude he couldn't persuade her to reexamine was her refusal to take part in the camp theatricals. His band of players called themselves Six and Company, meaning there were always at least six cast members, with outsiders recruited whenever necessary. She was a backstage person, she insisted; she would be happy to do props or work lights, but she could never consent to making a display of herself in public.

"At first I thought Judy was kind of a drab," Green recalls. "But then I said something that was supposed to be funny—it wasn't really—and she smiled that transfixing smile of hers. That plus those big gazelle eyes made her special, better than beautiful. Also her intensity, which could have been a bore, was quite sweet. The shows we put on at camp were dreadful, and the work she did on them was drudgery, but she performed it as though the world depended on it. Even then, she was a perfectionist."

Adolph kept her so busy that, when it came time for her to return to the city, Judy hadn't finished the third chapter of *Jean Christophe*. Before her departure, she and Green exchanged phone numbers and promised to stay in touch, but Judy was resigned to never hearing from him again. Flash friendships were, as she knew, a hazard of summer camps.

Judy always implied that she did not return to the Mercury after her summer camp experience, but Sylvia Regan, Howard Teichmann, and John Houseman all remember her still working at the switchboard after that summer. If, as seems likely, she did return to her old post, it was only for a few weeks, because the Mercury was then in a financial bind and, after the fiasco of its initial (much postponed) production of the 1938–39 season, *Danton's Death*, the company folded.

Judy's entrance into the world of the performing arts happened more or less by happenstance. One Saturday in September 1938, she was strolling along Seventh Avenue in Greenwich Village. Later when she tried to recreate the sequence of events in her mind, she couldn't recall why she was in Greenwich Village, but she did remember that she was

wearing a white piqué dress. It was spanking new—this was
the first time she had put it on—and damned if it didn't start
to rain, one of those flash September showers that brew up in
seconds and take a half-hour to wear themselves out.

Judy looked for shelter, but there was nothing in sight—
no awning, no overhanging cornice, no movie marquee. Just a
trio of battle-scarred alley cats sniffing around a trash can,
throwing themselves against it, trying to topple it and gain
access to its innards. The first splatter of rain sent the toms
scurrying toward a doorway and down a dark, uninviting stairwell. A plaintive chorus of meows suggested it would be all
right if Judy joined them.

She decided to accept the invitation. She liked cats and,
anyway, she had no choice: If she didn't take refuge, her
white piqué would soon look as forlorn as their bedraggled
coats. She moved cautiously across the doorway, stooped to
pet the first cat, took a few more steps and huddled beside the
second, scuttled down to greet the third, which unexpectedly
hissed and scratched the air with an unmanicured paw.
Startled, she backed off, and suddenly found herself at the
bottom of the stairwell, standing in the doorway of a moderate-
size, dimly lighted room, which at first glance looked like the
kind of place a nice girl should never enter. The ceilings were
low; the walls were a slaphappy collage of travel posters and
magazine photos. The long, triangular-shaped space was lined
with rickety tables, wooden chairs, and a few leather ban-
quettes that might have been pulled off a garbage heap. Ten
or twelve people were seated at tables, some grouped together,
others alone and seeking no company. There were chipped
coffee cups in front of most, and a flask gleamed as it was
passed from hand to hand at one table. The only sound was
the hush of muted conversation.

Judy felt stranded: Should she go forward or retreat to face
the rain and the rancor of the vicious tom? Before she could
decide, a middle-aged man came forward and asked her if she

wanted to sit down. She eyed him cautiously. He was small, his hair was thinning; he seemed harmless, if not exactly respectable. His clothes looked as though they had been thrown on, maybe slept in, but while he seemed too grubby to be a white slaver, one couldn't place faith in outer appearances.

"It's pretty dark in there . . . what kind of place is this, anyway?" Judy asked hesitantly.

"It's a place where artists and poets get together and drink coffee and talk about the things that interest them. Come on in and have a coffee till the rain stops." But then the host, or whatever he was, looked at her again, and since she seemed so young, he added, "Or maybe a Coke." She came in, sat down, ordered coffee—she had heard the stories about aspirin and Coca-Cola.

Just as she started sipping the lukewarm coffee, a customer at the adjoining table got up and spouted a few verses of poetry—nearly as arcane as Rimbaud's "Illuminations," Judy thought, but a good deal shorter, thank God. The other patrons paid no attention, though there was a perfunctory round of applause at the end of the reading.

"Is that meant to be entertainment?" she asked her host. "Is this some kind of nightclub?"

Again the man gave her a sharp look of appraisal. Pretty, in an ordinary way; nice figure, big bones—with bad luck, she'd run to fat in a few years; nothing special about her but the smile—then there was something out of the ordinary, an inner glow. An actress out for a job would certainly know better than to wear that silly white dress, but, then again, actresses were using desperate tactics in these difficult times.

"What are you?" he asked. "An actress? Singer? Comic?"

"Oh, no! I'm not a performer, don't want to be. I want to write and direct."

They began talking, and he explained that his patrons often got up and read parts of their works in progress—poems, novels, whatever. That was, he said, about the only kind of entertainment he was able to afford at the moment. His name was Max Gordon and he was proprietor and manager of the club, the Village Vanguard.

"I'm Judy Tuvim," she said. By then the rain had stopped, and she got up to leave. Gordon asked her to stop by whenever she was in the neighborhood, and Judy promised she would.

And she did. Several times. At every chance she got, she questioned Gordon about his entertainment policy. Eventually she got up the courage to speak what was on her mind. "Look, I've got friends who could put on a show for you— songs, sketches, one-act plays, that kind of thing."

The elite of Greenwich Village bohemia were regulars at the Vanguard, but bohemia's finest wasn't enough to keep the club afloat financially. Gordon wasn't losing money, but he wasn't getting rich, either. He had been thinking about ways to expand the club's audience without sacrificing its individuality. Since he had been fostering poets and writers, what was wrong with fostering other artists—musicians, performers, whoever—as long as they were talented, offbeat, with a slant on life that kept them outside the uptown mainstream? And he had to start somewhere, even if it was at the bottom with Miss Tuvim and her band of summer-camp minstrels.

"Okay," Gordon said, "I'll give it a try. But I can't pay much—maybe five dollars a night, one night a week, this Sunday for a start, and from there we'll see how it goes."

Judy smiled and somehow managed to walk calmly out of the Vanguard without breaking into a run. Once outside, she tore headlong to the nearest pay phone and called Adolph Green. Six and Company, she told him, was scheduled for its New York debut the following Sunday. She would be available to work the lights.

"Are there lights?" Green asked skeptically.

"Well, no," Judy answered.

"Is there a stage?" Green asked.

"Not exactly," Judy replied, "But we'll improvise something."

On the night of Six and Company's debut, the Village Vanguard's regulars were expecting the usual entertainment: four or five half-crocked poets reciting snippets from epics that had been in progress for years, the readings punctuated by a lot of colorful heckling from the audience. The catcalling was always the best and most anticipated part of the show. When Gordon announced that on this evening there would be a different program, the customers started to hoot in disapproval. The howling got louder as the show progressed. What had seemed passably amusing in the Catskills was devastatingly unfunny on the stage of the Vanguard. When it was all over, Gordon shook his head sadly. Judy gazed at him with damp, soulful eyes. Though crushed, she was not to be put off so easily. "Oh, Mr. Gordon, this was just a warm-up. . . ." She went on pleading and cajoling until Gordon caved in. "Okay, next week, maybe it'll be better."

Green knew without being told that he needed sharper material and better talent if things were to improve the following week. He threw out some of the sketches, discarded two or three cast members, and brought in Alvin Hammer, a goofy-looking redhead with more than his share of freckles who was the same age as Green and came from a similar background. For a time Hammer had worked days as a clerk in the garment district so that he could perform at night in little theater groups. Recently he had been doing pretty well—ten bucks a show—performing monologues at fraternal organizations and neighborhood nightclubs in Queens, the Bronx, and suburban Long Island. Green had heard some of his routines: They were clever; some were even original.

At the second performance, the level of disapproval dropped to a continuous murmur of barely decipherable obscenities. A definite improvement, Judy thought. "It's better," Max Gordon had to agree. "Better—but not good."

Before the third week, Adolph cast aside another member of Six and Company and called on another friend, Betty Comden. The two had met during his brief stay at New York University and had stayed in touch ever since. What brought them together was an offbeat sense of humor that no one else found quite as amusing as they did. There were other similarities: Both were Jewish and native New Yorkers. But Comden's background was somewhat more elevated than Green's. Her mother was a former high-school English teacher; her father a successful lawyer. She had grown up in a fashionable section of Brooklyn, where she had attended a local Ethical Culture school and, later, the then highly respected Erasmus Hall High School in Flatbush. Nourished on a Saturday-matinee diet of opera, concerts, and the best of Broadway, she had gravitated naturally toward the drama department of New York University, though originally she had planned to major in English literature. Unlike Adolph, she stayed at NYU for the full four years, and at the time he called to ask her to appear at the Vanguard, she had had some experience working in borough theater groups and had even played a small part in a subway-circuit production of the 1937–38 Broadway hit *Having a Wonderful Time.*

Today Betty Comden is a handsome, glamorous woman, but in 1938 she was at best what the French call a *belle laide;* her nose was too large (later it would be pared to conventional standards) to qualify her as a beauty, but she had her own distinction. Cool, reserved, poised, she stood out from the crowd not only by her appearance but because of her sly and unexpected sense of humor. There was something especially intriguing about a woman who was both witty and attractive—like Constance Talmadge or Carole Lombard or Ina Claire or Lynne Fontanne. This was in the back of Green's mind when he asked Comden to come down and see what was happening at the Vanguard.

Comden liked what she saw, and the Vanguard denizens thought she was swell when she appeared as part of Green's troupe. Even Max Gordon agreed that the act was looking up. But there was still room for improvement. Comden was of the same opinion. What was needed was someone with musical talent. Adolph, Alvin, and Betty could all sing on key, and they all played a little piano—as a matter of fact, Comden played quite well, thanks to childhood piano lessons. All three were musical, but none of them was particularly gifted as a musician. They needed someone who could help them with the technicalities of scoring and writing the songs and musical material that were needed to add diversity to the act. Comden came up with a possible candidate—John Frank. He had worked his way through NYU singing with a group called The Peasant's Quartet. He played piano, mandolin, guitar, and, in a pinch, the viola da gamba. Furthermore, he had a wife and baby and was in desperate need of any easy cash he could pick up.

Frank accepted the invitation to join the group, which was now nearly complete. Except for Adolph, the original Six and Company had vanished, and Comden was the only woman in the troupe. This was an imbalance that everyone agreed must be corrected. They needed another girl to offset Betty, someone not quite so aristocratic, not so brunet, someone who was outwardly ordinary but inwardly special, a girl with a secret flair. No one could think of a likely prospect except, maybe, Judy.

"You got to be kidding!" she screeched. They insisted that they were serious. She demurred again: She had no training, no experience in cabaret performing, she was certain to make a fool of herself. She really didn't want to do it, but, out of loyalty to the group, she agreed to go ahead, with the understanding that the arrangement was strictly temporary: She would drop out of the act as soon as they found a replacement, which would, she hoped, be soon.

On the night of her debut, Holliday was terrified. Unlike

Betty, Adolph, and friends, she had no training or experience in performing before a live audience, except for the partisan gatherings at the annual school play. She was to be a chronic sufferer of severe stage fright, and she was physically ill both before and after her first appearance at the Vanguard. In between she looked green and desperate, all too clearly wishing she were anyplace except where she happened to be.

Part of the problem was that Judy was performing material that wasn't suited to her. She was singing a couple of Bea Lillie songs, and, being a middle-class New Yorker, she couldn't assume the Belgravia dottiness that came naturally to Lillie. But even later, when her material was more congenial, she would often curl up in a corner of the Vanguard storage room, crying and bemoaning the inadequacies of her performance.

"At first, she was really quite bad," Betty Comden remembers. "She was nowhere. But she'd sit in that closet between shows, mulling and thinking, and then suddenly one night she'd pull it all together. It was truly phenomenal; in a matter of a few weeks she picked up what the rest of us had learned over a period of years."

Originally, Judy slaved at refining her performance out of an obsession with perfection: Whatever she did had to be done as competently as possible. She was always to be her own harshest critic, but when, in her own opinion, she showed definite signs of improvement, she had to admit she rather enjoyed performing. It was nothing she cared to pursue as a lifelong goal, but as an interim assignment it wasn't all unpleasant.

There were, however, many evenings when it wasn't much fun. These occurred when the Village Vanguard regulars came out in full force to heckle Green and his upstarts. Foremost among them was the bohemian, left-wing poet Max Bodenheim, a gaunt, shabby-looking man with bloodshot eyes. An apostle of the cult of Saint Hair-of-the-Dog, he was always working off one hangover while building up to the next. But,

drunk or semisober, Bodenheim had a caustic tongue. At the
end of each sketch, he'd cackle and dismiss what he had seen
with a choice piece of profanity. The Vanguard mummers
learned to ignore Bodenheim's taunts and eventually came to
enjoy the invention and wit behind them—all except Judy.
She was never to reach the level of self-confidence that would
allow her to see Bodenheim's abuse as a backhanded compliment—cursing people was his way of encouraging them and
pushing them along. Before every show, she'd send out a spy
to see if the poet was at his usual table. If the report was
negative, she'd sigh with relief; if positive, she'd turn ashen
and head for the john.

After a very few weeks, the group decided they would have
to write their own material. One of the reasons for this decision was financial—they had to pay royalties for published
works, and that was an expense they couldn't handle; Gordon
was still paying them only $5 each for a night's work. Also, as
Max kept telling them, they needed original material, and
since they couldn't afford to hire a writer, they were forced to
do the work themselves.

Several times a week they'd meet at a coffee shop on Sheridan
Square. Betty, equipped with a long yellow pad, would jot
down any feasible idea thrown out for discussion, and would
call the group back to order whenever their imaginations became too feverish.

Adolph was the worst offender in this area. "Too special,"
Betty would reprimand. "Remember, Adolph, Zita Johann
isn't exactly a household name."

When the scrawls on Comden's pad looked like they might
add up to the beginning of a sketch, the group would walk
down the street to the Vanguard, where they'd improvise
variations on the original idea until they had settled on something that might please even Max Bodenheim.

The group's sketches were joint efforts, so much so that
later no one could remember exactly who had done what. "I
had a friend who taught me four, five chords on the piano,

and I wrote all kinds of things on the basis of those few chords, judiciously arranged," Betty Comden recalls. "John Frank really could play the piano, and we used to sing melodies at him and he'd play them back." The act was, Comden says, a testament to "the tremendous nerve and courage of youth."

After a few weeks of performing together, the group had gained enough confidence in their future to give some thought to finding a name for themselves; Six and Company wouldn't do—they numbered only five, and there was no need for additions. For a couple of weeks, they were advertised as The Vanguarders, but that suggested the avant-garde, which sounded pretentious, and also identified them almost exclusively with Gordon's club. Someone—none of them ever remembered who—came up with the Revuers. Nobody liked it much, but it stuck.

Judy was so pleased with the Revuers' progress that she started to invite friends to drop by the Vanguard and watch the show. Sylvia Regan remembers: "Judy came into my office and told me she and some friends were doing this little revue on weekends, and would I come by and see it. Well, naturally, I said yes, and of course I did stop by, bringing along some friends whom I had warned in advance that this was a way of doing a favor for a girl I liked—you know, the kind of excuses you make when you're going to put people you know and respect through an evening of hell. So we got to the Vanguard and sat there, sipping oversweet lemonade, feeling miserable, and then the show started. What a revelation! The lyrics and sketches were sharper and wittier than anything you could have heard on Broadway at the time, the music was more than adequate, and the five of them were so bright, so talented, so clever that the lemonade started tasting like champagne."

As they rose to prominence, the group was frequently asked to perform at benefits for supposedly worthwhile causes, many of which, it would later turn out, were promoted by Communist-front organizations. But a good cause was a good

cause, no matter who was backing it, and the Revuers gave
unstintingly of their time and talents. All members of the
group were inclined politically to the left—as indeed were
most theater people of the 1930s—but Judy was perhaps
slightly more active in expressing her allegiance than the
others: She was frequently to be noticed marching in parades
and joining demonstrations.

Little of this political engagement spilled over into the
Revuers' act, which was frequently compared to *Pins and
Needles*, the famous revue sponsored by the International
Ladies Garment Workers Union, which was to run for over
a thousand performances on Broadway. Comparison was later
also made to the European cabaret tradition of political satire.
The first comparison is better than the latter, but both are
misleading. The Revuers' humor could be described accurately
as topical, but their material was rarely drawn from the front
pages, and the treatment lacked that abrasive, often grotesque
edge that is a chief characteristic of the cabaret style.

The Revuers' style of satire was liberal without being committed. It was good-natured, and was inspired mainly by the
entertainment pages of the papers. The Revuers poked fun at
movies, radio, and Broadway; and since they were addicted to
the absurdities they ridiculed, there was always a core of affection beneath their sketches. Here one senses Comden and
Green as the controlling personalities in the quintet of collaborators, if only because so many of the musicals they were
later to create for Hollywood and Broadway were show-
business spoofs.

One of the most popular of the early Revuers sketches depicted a meeting of the Joan Crawford fan club. The clan has
gathered to sing the praises of Miss Crawford, but the hosannas are interrupted by an apostate who has fallen under the
spell of Sonja Henie. (The skit was written while Crawford
was appearing in *Ice Follies of 1939*, a film that critics compared unfavorably to the Henie extravaganzas.)

Another early favorite was a parody of the Mickey Rooney–

Andy Hardy comedies, with Alvin Hammer as Hardy/Rooney. Alvin/Andy kept mugging and upstaging his family and friends until in desperation they stuffed a napkin in his mouth and tied him to a chair; then Judge Hardy (John Frank) went into *his* song and dance.

A third sketch presented variations on the potion scene from *Tristan and Isolde*. First it was shown as a typical Met production of the 1940s: Green, a very short Melchior, wafts bad breath at Betty Comden, fitted out *à la* Flagstad or Traubel— no waist, enormous bust, and cow horns on her helmet. (Only a purist might notice that the Revuers had confused Isolde with Brunnhilde.) Then the same scene was depicted in the style of various contemporary dramatists. In a Noel Coward vignette, Comden approached Green and said, "My name's Victoria Marden. I adore you." Green turned and handed her a highball glass. "Extraordinary how potent cheap liquor can be!" In the final segment of the sketch, Green and Comden came on wearing Clifford Odets trench coats. "What are you doing here?" he asked. "I'm waiting for Lefty," she gasped. Green gave her the Group Theatre treatment. "Don't wait for that guy. What you need is a man—me—Moe Rappaport." Then, handing her a flask, "Here, drink dis."

From here to the movie parodies of "The Carol Burnett Show," "Saturday Night Live," and "Fridays," there is but a short step. The Revuers were mining their own vein of comedy, rather than Americanizing a foreign form like the *Pins and Needles* revues or the European-inspired cabaret artists of the period. Their satire was clever, sometimes as sharp as a tack, but it derived more from George S. Kaufman, the sketches of the *Follies* and the *Scandals*, the short stories of Lardner and Perelman than from the caustic black humor of Berlin and the Continent.

The Revuers got one of their biggest laughs on their entrance. In single file they backed onto the playing area of the Vanguard, looking over their shoulders with apprehension at the audience. This was, of course, a burlesque of the cheery welcome that began every star act, as Adolph Green explains. "You see," he says, "if people started throwing things at us, we would be in an ideal position to walk off the stage with dignity." At the time of their first appearance, they wore outdoor clothing, as though they might be waiting for the uptown IRT. The men wore tatty raincoats and fedoras; Betty looked spiffy in a fox jacket; Judy wore an indescribable garment made from the skins of what furriers euphemistically describe as "unknown animals." There may have been a satiric point behind this apparel, too, but originally it was adopted for practical reasons: The Vanguard was freezing, and the Revuers had to find some way to stay warm until they got into the performance and the adrenaline started to flow.

The winter of 1938–39 was unusually cold—weeks and weeks of record low temperatures, and finally, in January, a blizzard that all but immobilized the city. Inside the Vanguard, the Revuers could see their own breath, and Comden and Frank, after their alternate turns at the club's ancient upright piano, checked their fingers for frostbite. More than once the only customers were a few stray drunks and Judy's old friends, the tomcats, which still used the Vanguard as a refuge in foul weather.

Eventually the temperature rose and business began to pick up at the Vanguard. The Revuers had started to catch on. At first their reputation grew through word of mouth; then there were squibs in the gossip columns; and finally, brief, always flattering, notices from the night-life reviewers. By the spring of 1939, the group had built a substantial cult following. They were chic. They had been discovered by the Right People.

Among their earliest fans were Lillian Hellman, Emily Kimbrough, and a large group of *New Yorker* contributors— S.J. Perelman, John Cheever, Irwin Shaw, and William Shawn. Tallulah Bankhead, toting her own flask, became a regular, as did John Houseman, who quickly forgot Judy's inefficiencies at the Mercury switchboard and became, for a while, a close friend.

Judy and Betty also had a small group of stage-door johnny admirers, included Reeves McCullers, the husband of novelist Carson McCullers. When they left the Vanguard, he was often waiting for them, always a bit in his cups, and would follow them to the bus stop, babbling about how he had not yet decided which of the two was the more attractive. He was harmless, the girls agreed. Life upon the wicked stage, as Oscar Hammerstein had written, wasn't all it was cracked up to be.

Once or twice, one of the targets of a Revuers sketch turned up to see how he was treated, most notably Robert Morley, that Humpty-Dumpty of an English actor, who was then appearing on Broadway in *Oscar Wilde*. Morley came down to the Vanguard to check out Green's impersonation of his performance of Louis XVI in the film *Marie Antoinette*. The place was so crowded that Morley had to deposit his considerable girth on the bottom step of the Vanguard entrance-way, but he laughed happily and later told Max Gordon that the act had been "positively enchanting."

By this time, the Revuers' performance schedule had been raised to two shows, five nights a week. They had prepared four entirely different shows, each a miniature musical revue, centered around a connecting theme—Hollywood, advertising, magazines, newspapers; on the fifth night, they presented a potpourri of all their sketches. Gordon had raised their salary, which allowed them to hire a pianist who took over whenever Comden and Frank were both needed on stage. They were also able to afford a combination stage manager and lighting technician, a young man named Julian Claman.

In the summer of '39, Gordon finally obtained a liquor license, moved in a bar, and started serving mixed drinks. This proved to be a mixed blessing for the Revuers; the bar, though minuscule, encroached on the already severely cramped performing area. But the customers definitely approved of this and other renovations, and soon the *New Yorker* was telling its readers that the Vanguard was "a nice little spot to visit" though "the cellar ambiance often becomes a trifle claustro-phobic." The article went on to mention that the club had recently changed its entertainment forces. "The Revuers, who we heard are moving uptown, have been replaced by a band of strolling Calypso singers. . . ."

What the *New Yorker* had heard was right: The Revuers were indeed moving uptown, and on a very grand scale.

Chapter Three

REVUERS' LUCK

In the later 1930s, New York City was teeming with night-clubs of all sizes and varieties, with an "after-dark" spot for every conceivable taste and pocketbook. At the top of the heap there were such café-society *boîtes* as the Persian Room in the Plaza Hotel and the Waldorf's Starlight Roof, where the prices were exorbitant—a $1.50 *table d'hôte* supper *plus* a $1.00 cover charge—and formal attire was *de rigueur* on the dance floor. For skating fanatics, there was the lavishly produced ice show at the Iridium Room at the St. Regis—here, too, the dance floor was restricted to those wearing black ties and floor-length gowns. Tourists and tired businessmen on expense accounts applauded the Gay Nineties Revue at Billy Rose's Diamond Horseshoe; Latin-American aficionados congregated at La Conga (featuring Desi Arnaz on the bongos); people who felt uneasy about traveling to Harlem could enjoy (in the words of *Stage* magazine) "the exotic sepia entertainment (some of it served up *au naturel*)" at the Kit Kat Club in the heart of Broadway. Last came the countless smaller and less fashionable clubs, like the Vanguard, which *Stage* or the *New Yorker* would occasionally deign to sanction with varying degrees of condescension.

One of the newest and most elegant of the after-dark spots was the Rainbow Room, located on one of the top floors of the RCA Building in Rockefeller Center. "A vast and lofty place," wrote the *New Yorker,* and the description actually fell short of the mark. When the room first opened, you couldn't get through the front door unless you had a pedigree and were dressed like Astaire and Rogers. Yet, despite hosannas from all the nightclub reviewers and an expensive advertising campaign, the club failed to build a clientele. Its stepsister, the more intimate Rainbow Grill, located on the same floor of the RCA Building and run by the same management, was doing quite nicely with Marlynn and Michael, a dance team who invited customers onto the floor and awarded a split of champagne to the couple who won the warmest round of applause. But next door, the vast and lofty main room kept looking vaster and loftier as increasingly fewer tables were filled each evening. Talent wasn't the problem— the Rainbow Room initially booked only the best—but once the best failed to bolster business, the management, in desperation, drifted toward novelty acts: first puppets; then a table-tennis exhibition and competition; finally, the Revuers.

As soon as they had started attracting attention at the Vanguard, the Revuers had been courted by some of the finest agents in the business, and eventually they signed with the highly respected Ruth Morris of the William Morris Agency. In terms of prestige representation, they could have done no better, but what first seemed to be a stroke of luck turned out as a curse in disguise. Such paradoxical twists of fortune soon became so familiar to Judy and company that they coined a phrase for them: Revuers' Luck.

In the spring of 1939, Ruth Morris asked the Revuers to audition for John Roy, the manager of the Rainbow Room. Roy was impressed, but wanted to see the group perform before an audience and asked them to make "a guest appearance" at one of his nine o'clock shows. The evening was a nightmare. To get on the Rainbow stage, the Revuers had

to march down a staircase with shallow steps, and in the
middle of their entrance, eyes sparkling at the audience, one
of them stumbled, and the rest came within inches of collid-
ing with one another. They never quite managed to regain
their composure. Roy, however, overlooked the *faux pas* and
booked the group as the Rainbow's opening attraction for the
fall 1939 season.

There was extensive publicity preceding the Revuers' appearance at the Rainbow Room, and the subsequent reviews
were more than respectable. But Adolph Green correctly
sums up the outcome of the engagement in two words: "We
bombed!" The negative public response was a stunning blow
for the Revuers, and yet in hindsight it seems almost to have
been inevitable. First, because the group prided themselves
on "deflating the pompous," and the Rainbow patrons were
conspicuously conservative and stuffy: They weren't about to
laugh at their own peccadilloes. Next, because the Revuers
shared the bill with Jack Cole and his dancers, an ensemble
that specialized in a lavish and ludicrous style of choreog-
raphy usually found only in tourist-trap musicals or the orgy
sequences of biblical spectacles. Normally this was the kind
of act that would have sent the Revuers into a paroxysm of
parodistic inspiration, but as Cole and his kootch dancers
were temporary teammates, they stifled their laughter and
gagged the muse. Worst of all, the Rainbow Room proved
to be too palatial a setting for their kind of act. What had
seemed fresh and intimate at the Vanguard looked undernourished, even a trifle amateurish, in such grandiose surroundings, particularly when compared, as it was at every show, to
the gaudy glamour of the Cole troupe. Certainly, the Revuers
would have felt more at home in the smaller Rainbow Grill,
but Michael and Marlynn still held the franchise on that
space.

In the next year or so, the Revuers would again be booked
for equally unsuitable engagements, and always with the same
result: Revuers' Luck. They did a stint at Loew's State and

later at the Radio City Music Hall, where they took part in a between-the-movie revue called "The Magazine Rack." Their turn included one of their most popular sketches, a burlesque of self-help columns. Judy played a housewife overwhelmed by the advice she finds in the monthlies: *Parents* has already succeeded in making her a mother; *Popular Mechanics* tells her how to construct a pot that will turn an omelet into a hard-boiled egg; *Esquire* gives her helpful hints on how to turn her loser of a husband into a top-level executive; *Fortune* advises her on the proper investment of her pin money. In the vast reaches of the Music Hall, the sketch made no impact, but the Revuers stayed there for ten weeks, only because the stage show's run was dependent upon the success of the accompanying feature film, and *Escape* (starring Norma Shearer and Robert Taylor) was one of the big hits of 1940.

These setbacks taught the Revuers that their talents were most successfully showcased in Manhattan's more informal cabarets—places that catered to a clientele that went out not to be noticed by the society columnists but to watch the entertainment. They learned that they appealed mainly to the knowledgeable, hep, slightly offbeat side of the New York night-life scene. There were long and profitable stays at Spivy's, at Le Ruban Bleu, at both the downtown and uptown editions of Café Society. Thanks to the publicity department of the Morris Agency, they received royal treatment from the press. *Life* gave them a four-page spread; *Vogue* glamorized them in a full-page, prominently placed photograph; the night-life reviewers for *Cue* and *PM* became devout admirers. For sixteen weeks they had their own half-hour radio show on NBC's experimental "blue network," for which they created another of their famous sketches, a takeoff on the celebrity-for-a-day-type interview. Judy played a reporter trying to get a story out of the decrepit Ambroise Mippy, once renowned as the inventor of the shoehorn. Their reputation continued to grow among the cognoscenti to such a degree that a small record company asked them to put a few of their routines on disc. The first (and only) releases were prominently displayed in Doubleday and Liberty Music Shop windows, but no one bought them except a small band of devoted fans.

And so it went. Every tiny triumph was inevitably followed by a tiny defeat. Between Manhattan engagements, the Revuers, for economic reasons, occasionally were forced to accept an out-of-town engagement, and always regretted it. Whether it was Long Island, Philadelphia, or Florida, they always flopped; their humor, like asparagus or caviar, was too rarefied for provincial taste. They had suspected as much: A year earlier when they performed at one of the cabarets on the grounds of the 1939 New York World's Fair, they were cold potatoes, and that was Flushing Meadows, only twenty minutes (so the Fair brochure claimed) from Broadway. No doubt about it, they weren't for Rainbowers or suburbanites or American provincials.

Still, some good did come from the job at the Fair. It provided material for another famous sketch, in which a number of celebrated New York landmarks castigate fickle tourists who have deserted them for the spectacle in Flushing Meadows. First came a lament from Grant's Tomb (Green), then the cry was taken up by Cleopatra's Needle (Comden), the Empire State Building (Frank), and Rockefeller Center (Hammer), the agitation mounting until the Statue of Liberty (Judy) waves her torch menacingly and predicts, "I'll still be here when Flushing is a dump again!"

Today the sketch seems mild, but in the 1940s when financiers had backed the Fair in hope of turning Flushing Meadows into a marketable piece of real estate, it had genuine pertinency, and was to become one of the most admired of the Revuers' sketches.

*   *   *

The Revuers had been working nonstop for almost two years and it seemed time for a vacation. They went their separate ways, with Judy choosing Woodstock, a fashionable artists' resort in upstate New York. Judy chose Woodstock because she had heard that it was filled with interesting people, and while the primary reason for her holiday was relaxation, she was not adverse to the idea of making new acquaintances, maybe even forming a romantic attachment. So far her love life had been pretty much a blank, and now that she had passed her twentieth birthday, the lack of an emotional commitment stronger than friendship began to weigh heavily on her mind. The days when she could pretend to herself that she was above such matters were over, but the insecurities that had made her shy with boys in high school lingered on. She still had no great confidence in her physical attractiveness; the psychic wound incurred at the time of Abe's desertion was not yet healed.

Complicating the problem was the fact that many men found Judy nearly as intimidating as she found them, particularly men of her own age. She was, after all, something of a minor celebrity; she was highly intelligent; she wasn't one to pretend a man was fascinating company when in truth he was a crashing bore. The men who did attract her were often older—and therefore usually otherwise engaged, or troubled by sexual hang-ups, or determined to fulfill their own ambitions before becoming seriously involved with a woman. And, of course, this was the start of World War II: Many eligible men were either overseas or about to ship out.

Nevertheless, Judy's holiday was a total success, though in a somewhat unorthodox fashion. Shortly after she arrived in Woodstock, she met and became friendly with a woman who here will be called Tessa. She was a bright, attractive, and vibrant woman about ten or twelve years older than Judy. She was Jewish, chauvinistically so, and politically way to the left, "a parlor pink" at the very least.

But there was a less somber side to Tessa: She had an individual sense of humor, possessed a gift for witty repartee, and, though not professionally involved in the theater, she was knowledgeable about show business and the popular arts. Judy was immediately drawn to her, and soon the two women were embarked on a full-fledged romance.

This homosexual episode was an isolated incident in Judy's life, but it was one of some duration—a year, perhaps some months longer. Her friends now describe this interlude as a "learning experience" or a form of "self-exploration," and feel it would be misrepresentative to give it undue prominence. As far as is known, it was a relationship Judy accepted without any feelings of guilt or shame; she slipped into it apparently without any breast-beating or soul-searching. While this may seem strange, it should be remembered that many girls of Judy's age have a brush with homosexuality, particularly girls who, like Holliday, move in freethinking or artistic circles. In the theater world of the Thirties and Forties, there was no stigma attached to homosexual or bisexual behavior —a goodly portion of the first ladies and gentlemen of the American and English stage were known to be (in the slang of the period) "double-gaited."

For neither Tessa nor Judy was the physical aspect of the relationship the most important. Tessa was not an especially sexual person; and Judy, in committing herself, was undoubtedly reaching out for warmth, affection, and companionship. At the end of their vacation in Woodstock, she and Tessa rented a roomy, sunny apartment in the Village, filled with animals and plants, both of which Judy adored. Tessa's idea of making coffee was to throw a heap of grinds into a pot of water, so Judy did most of the cooking and in time became expert in preparing home-style meals. Both liked to entertain, and there was an easy flow of guests, both invited and uninvited.

One frequent caller was Helen Tuvim. Judy had been living with her mother when she met Tessa, and when she announced that she was moving out, Helen became distraught. Her distress had nothing to do with Tessa—consciously or not, she failed to grasp the significance of her daughter's romantic alliance. She felt she was being abandoned for the second time—first Abe, now Judy. To comfort her, Judy said she could drop by at any time, and soon Helen was spending as much time in her daughter's apartment as in her own. She developed a genuine fondness for Tessa, possibly because Tessa made no fuss over Helen's intrusion into her life with Judy. And Helen was easy to like—she was nervous, but sweet-natured, unobtrusive, content to stay in the background or to withdraw when she sensed her presence was a nuisance.

The sexual side of Judy's relationship with Tessa died out as soon as Judy realized, apparently through casual experimentation, that she liked men as bed partners better than women. In fact, in time, she discovered that she liked men very much, and was quite open about her sexual appetite (though never vulgarly so; she wasn't a conversational exhibitionist like Tallulah Bankhead, but her freedom in owning up to her desires made her a precursor of the liberated women of today, according to her friends). She never went to any great lengths to hide the nature of her relationship with Tessa (except to the press), even after the sexual attraction behind the alliance had faded away.

After Judy and Tessa ceased to be lovers, they remained close friends—that side of the relationship was to endure and grow until Judy's death. In time their feelings for each other would take on a sisterly, then a mother-daughter coloration, which was, one suspects, the primary source of their initial attraction.

At the end of 1940, when Judy was living with Tessa, the Revuers returned to the Village Vanguard. It was a warm homecoming, and the troupe was enthusiastic about Max

Gordon's renovations: They no longer had to dress in the
rest rooms—they now had two cubicles all to themselves; and
when they made their entrance, they came through a velvet
curtain—a bit worn, perhaps, but better than the piece of
cheesecloth they had formerly draped over the hallway off
the men's lavatory. For this occasion, the Revuers created
several new sketches, one of which was greatly admired by a
New Yorker critic: "One of the most engaging of their
sketches concerns two members of a girl trio lamenting in
harmony the defection of a colleague, who has thoughtlessly
got married and left them without anybody to carry the
melody."

Despite fine notices and the warm feelings engendered by
a return to familiar surroundings, the Revuers weren't especially happy about this engagement. Over a year had passed,
and they had come full circle—here they were back where
they started, at the Vanguard. They had made a sort of name
for themselves, yes; but they were still in the same groove.
The failure to break into the big time was particularly aggravating to Comden and Green, who often slipped into the star
image they were developing for themselves and who desperately wanted that final burst of fame and success that
always seemed about to happen, only to fizzle out at the last
moment.

Judy was diffident. She was proud of what she had accomplished as one of the Revuers, but she didn't really hanker
after what Betty and Adolph wanted, and she was content
to let them take the limelight. While she enjoyed performing as one of the Revuers, she still wasn't intrigued with the
prospect of spending her life on stage. She wanted to write
or direct, and the best part of being one of the Revuers was
that she got a chance to do a little of both—everybody contributed to the creation and staging of the act. So she was
perfectly willing to leave the glamour and image stuff to
Adolph and Betty—that kind of nonsense held no interest
for her. Certainly not after she saw the photograph *Vogue*

had published of the Revuers posed in their World's Fair skit. Judy's nose looked bigger than Comden's, and she exuded as much allure as a mannequin in a Lane Bryant window.

All the Revuers were distressed at their lack of progress during the previous fourteen months. They realized they had to break new ground or turn stale, and they all pretty much agreed that the new ground should be Broadway. A couple of months before, they had appeared, along with Gene Kelly and other promising "new faces," at Westport, Connecticut, in a slapdash summer-stock musical revue, and their performance had brought them nibbles from several theatrical producers, who invited them to think about writing and starring in a Broadway show. The offers, however, were always tentative and none of them led anywhere until the spring of 1941.

While still at the Vanguard, the Revuers were invited to join the cast of a new musical, *My Dear Public*. The show was the creation of Irving Caesar (best known as the lyricist for "Tea for Two" and "Just a Gigolo"), who had been trying to get it into production since 1935. Based on what was then regarded as a novel concept—a musical about the making of a musical, featuring a show within a show—it was to be a precursor of such backstage extravaganzas as *Me and Juliet*; *Say, Darling*; and *A Chorus Line*. (It was also derivative of the Busby Berkeley song-and-dance films of a few years earlier.) For some reason, the concept seemed too outré to attract Broadway money in the late 1930s, and Caesar went through a hellish number of rewrites and auditions before raising the backing for the show.

Initially, the Revuers weren't overjoyed by their parts in *My Dear Public*—they would be playing themselves, as members of the company of the play within the play, and would be billed in the program as "The Revuers." But they would be free to write their own material, and the originality of Caesar's idea appealed to them, so they agreed to join the

show. Unfortunately, as they came to realize during rehearsals, not much of Caesar's concept found its way into
the finished product. The run-throughs were a shambles, and
the show was coming apart at the seams as Caesar kept trying
to make revisions to suit the tastes of his producers and
moneymen, all of whom had conflicting ideas about how the
musical should be developed.

On March 1, 1942, the Revuers boarded a train for New
Haven along with the other members of the *My Dear Public*
company, including Cora Witherspoon, Mitzi Green, Tamara
Geva, and Smith and Dale (the vaudeville team that was
the model for Neil Simon's *The Sunshine Boys*). Spirits were
low, though the Revuers kept reminding themselves of how an
out-of-town flop could turn into a Broadway hit. Judy looked
glum, but Adolph hummed a few bars from "Forty-Second
Street," and they both broke up. The next day there was a
full dress rehearsal, and the following night the official opening. The first-nighters were not enthusiastic. Neither were the
critics. *Variety* stated bluntly: "It's going to require time and
the utmost skill in cultivating this one into a click show."
There was, however, a special commendation for the Revuers, whose "one big sketch" was "a stand-out." For the
show, the team had created a spoof of Shubert operettas
called "A Night in Philadelphia (With a Chorus of 600—
Six Hundred Beautiful Girls—600)."

The New Haven opening party for *My Dear Public* would
have been very melancholy except for the presence of Adolph
Green's friend, a young musician named Leonard Bernstein.
They had met at an adult camp in the mid-1930s and
immediately recognized each other as kindred souls when
they discovered that each could identify a Prokofiev symphony after hearing the opening three measures. Back in
Manhattan, the two roomed together for a while, and later
Bernstein would stop by the Vanguard. After closing time,
he'd sit down at the piano and there'd be an impromptu
concert, covering everything from "Honky-Tonk Train" to

Ravel's "Ma Mère L'Oye." Judy and Bernstein hit it off
immediately and were to stay close friends until her death.

At the party in New Haven, Bernstein lifted the sour mood
by taking over a piano and playing a medley of Irving Caesar
songs. Caesar started singing along, with Mitzi Green, Betty,
and Adolph providing a backup chorus. Even Judy joined in
on the harmony—that was her forte; she never could carry
the melodic line without straying from pitch. Caesar was so
taken with Bernstein that he was instrumental in getting the
young man a job at Harms, Inc., then the most prestigious
of the American pop-music publishing houses. This opportunity was to have important repercussions for Judy, since it
was through his work at Harms that Bernstein met a man
whom he would later introduce to Holliday and whom she
would subsequently marry.

After five days in New Haven, *My Dear Public* moved to
Boston, where the reviews were, to put it kindly, mixed. One
critic astutely noted that "the main trouble lies in the fact
that [the musical] never makes up its mind whether it wants
to be a book show or a revue." Elliott Norton, the highly
respected reviewer for the Boston *Post*, thought the book
should be discarded in favor of the plotless revue format.
Norton again singled out the Revuers for praise, calling their
major number "a corking good burlesque of the cornier kind
of operettas."

Judy was downcast over the show's poor reception, and
found distraction through a flirtation with one of her fellow
cast members. During rehearsals, she had become infatuated
with John Buckmaster, an English actor who had first come
to this country in 1936 to appear with his mother, Gladys
Cooper, in a play titled *Call It a Day*. He had stayed on to
play Alfred "Bosie" Douglas to Robert Morley's Oscar Wilde
—Morley was married to Buckmaster's sister, Joan—and then
branched out into cabaret performing, where he became
noted as a specialist in "the silly-ass school of English Comedy." Good-looking in a languorous, very upper-class British

manner, Buckmaster was sophisticated, talented, a clever conversationalist, and quite intelligent—all qualities Judy appreciated in a man. He was touched by Judy's puppylike adoration, impressed by her talent and sensitivity, and delighted by the originality of her mind. A strong attachment developed, but Buckmaster was, for all his charm, emotionally unstable—he was prone to mental breakdowns and eventually spent many years under institutional care—and his relationship with Judy was shadowed by his private devils from the outset. She cared deeply for him, but there was little she could do to help a man who was already showing signs of schizophrenia.

The affair with Buckmaster had nearly run its unhappy course by the time of the demise of *My Dear Public*, which came in swift order. From Boston, the show was scheduled to move to New York and its Broadway premiere, but the producers decided to keep it on the road for another week of out-of-town warm-ups. Next stop: Philadelphia. Along the way there had been some tinkering with the script and one major cast change (Joy Hodges replaced Mitzi Green), but Philadelphia reviews were the worst of the lot. The day after the opening, a closing notice was posted backstage. The show was to go into cold storage while Caesar did a complete overhaul of the book. Six months later it did open in New York at the 46th Street Theatre with an entirely new cast. The reviews were tepid and the run short—fifty-five performances.

The Revuers shrugged it off philosophically. They had come out unscathed, with a portfolio of admiring out-of-town notices and one good sketch for their nightclub act. It was just another case of Revuers' Luck.

Chapter Four

HOLLYWOOD DREAMS

After the fiasco of *My Dear Public*, the Revuers had no choice but to go back to the nightclub circuit. They played a long and successful engagement at the Blue Angel, a cabaret that Max Gordon had recently opened on East 56th Street. The Angel was much smarter than the Vanguard, a tastefully appointed, spacious room, but not so large that it overpowered the intimate appeal of the Revuers. The group stayed there for several weeks and received love-letter reviews from all the New York critics.

Then they went on the road, and there they would remain for most of the latter half of 1942 and nearly all of early 1943. Judy traveled from one dreary engagement to the next, a routine that became more depressing with every passing day. The makeshift meals, the hotel existence, the suburban audiences, the bus and train rides between dreary cities that merged together as one nameless, gray blob—it was a deflating, joyless way to make a living. Judy felt as though she were on a treadmill, speeding along for days and weeks, only to end up where she had started. They were all feeling that way, and they began talking about splitting up the act and seeing what was out there for them as individual performers.

Then, when they were performing in Toronto, someone approached them with what looked like a way of getting ahead with some real momentum. Their savior presented himself as a Hollywood "scout" working for a friend who was about to go into production with a movie that demanded fresh and original personalities—"kids" just like the Revuers. The "scout" didn't talk money or contracts, but he made it sound as though all that would be a cinch once they arrived in Hollywood—traveling expenses paid, to be sure, by themselves. The "kids" were not unaware that the offer had as many holes as a pound of Swiss cheese, but they persuaded themselves that it was worth a try. Anything was better than another year on the boondock circuit.

There was one defection. John Frank had been feeling unwell for some time, and decided his health would not permit him to go on with the traveling for much longer. The other Revuers accepted his withdrawal with sympathy, though none of them realized how ill Frank really was. He had leukemia and was to die only three years later.

So there were only four Revuers on the train headed for Los Angeles in the late summer of 1943. There were, however, five passengers: Though they had lost a partner, they had gained a chaperon—Helen Tuvim. Judy's mother nearly swooned when she learned of the impending trip to the West Coast. She had borne up bravely when Judy had left home to share an apartment with Tessa, had stifled complaints while her daughter was on the road, but a transcontinental separation was more than she could endure. Judy was all the family Helen had, and, as Alfred Kazin points out in his autobiography, *New York Jew*, the sense of having "no family" carried an engulfing sense of isolation for many Jewish immigrants and their first-generation American descendants. The compulsion to maintain familial bonds, Kazin concludes, can become a form of bondage for the children of the next generation, and certainly at times Helen was an aggravation for Judy. It was not, however, an aggravation she took measures to eliminate, as she undoubtedly shared Helen's strong belief in family cohesion.

Judy's friends accepted Helen's presence with equanimity. She wasn't bossy or bothersome; she asked nothing beyond the privilege of walking in her daughter's shadow, a path she followed with a quiet, self-effacing dignity. Sometimes she was guilty of checking Judy over, constantly worrying about her health and eating habits, but most mothers are guilty of such demonstrations of overprotection.

The five-day train trip to California was uncomfortable, both physically and psychologically. The weather was sultry; the air-cooling system inefficient; Helen kept worrying over the nutritional value of the railroad meals; Hammer spent most of his time sleeping; Adolph buried his head in crossword and Double-Crostics magazines. Judy entertained herself by playing the prophet of doom. "A disaster," she'd murmur. "This whole stupid trip is going to wind up a disaster." Always inclined toward the negative viewpoint, Holliday had also acquired enough show-business savvy to recognize that the odds were decidedly against the Revuers in this instance.

Betty Comden was inclined to agree. A year earlier she had married Steven Kyle, later to become a well-known designer of fabrics and household articles, and if Kyle had not been drafted overseas, she probably would not have come along. Like Judy, she felt the Toronto offer would become a wild-goose chase once they reached Los Angeles.

The two women, who had become quite close over the past few years, tried to pass the time by reading, but neither could concentrate and soon they were reduced to playing double solitaire and a moronic card game called pisha-paysha. Judy adored playing cards, poker later becoming one of her favorite pastimes. Occasionally Adolph would drop by their compartment for a few rounds of a mind-twister he had invented: He'd quote the first and last lines of a movie, and from this information the other players were to identify the film. The game wasn't so much a competition as a chance for Adolph to display his trivial erudition. Alone among the group, Green remained resolutely cheerful, dreaming of how he would soon be meeting Rafaela Ottiano or one of the other bit players who were his movie favorites.

Arriving in Los Angeles, the Revuers checked in at the Roosevelt Hotel, located in the very heart of Hollywood. The epitome of elegance during the 1920s, the Roosevelt had lost much of its standing and glamour over the years, but still it was a link with the golden era of moviemaking: The Garden Court Apartments, where D. W. Griffith once lived, were nearby; and just down the block was Grauman's Chinese Theatre. Adolph was in seventh heaven, and even Judy felt slightly giddy as she measured her shoe against Chaplin's and Pickford's footprints in the courtyard of the celebrated pagoda of film fantasies.

That wave of euphoria vanished as soon as they learned that the movie they had come to the Coast to make had been called off. Worse still, their Toronto contact had nothing else to offer them. And worst of all, he implied they were daft to have come all the way to California without a firm commitment. Judy cursed Adolph for stranding them in the land of perpetual sunshine. "Why doesn't it rain?" Judy wailed. "Why doesn't the weather cooperate?" Adolph refused to be cast as the villain. They hadn't been shanghaied to Los Angeles, he pointed out, and, furthermore, they were melodramatizing. Something was bound to turn up. "Soon, I hope," Judy said, looking with distaste at her cartons of tepid fried rice and egg foo yong (the Revuers' main source of sustenance during their stay at the Roosevelt). They had only pennies left above the cost of the train fare needed to get them all back to New York.

Something did turn up, but it wasn't what any of them wanted. The West Coast branch of the Morris Agency got them a booking at the Trocadero. Once again they were back on the nightclub treadmill, but, as Adolph patiently explained, this engagement had real possibilities. Their salary was handsome—$1,000 a week—and the Troc, as the club was known to its habitués, was a favorite hangout for movie executives—all the big bosses went there with their tootsies, and sometimes they had eyes for the entertainment as well. Every performance would be an opportunity for them to be "discovered" by a Mayer or a Cohn or a Zanuck.

Assured of the Trocadero booking, the Revuers began looking for an apartment, preferably one with a short lease. They finally settled on one located above a realtor's office on Wilshire Boulevard, not far from the La Brea tar pits. The centerpiece of the flat was an intricately structured bamboo bar in the "family room." "It looked like a prop left over from *Red Dust*," recalls Betty Comden. Behind an alcove, there was a sunken boudoir—two steps leading to a tiny chamber with a curtained bed. The other rooms were barely furnished except for cots, a few wicker chairs, and collapsible cardboard closets, the kind used by movers for transporting clothes. There was also a tar-covered "terrace" that offered a panoramic view of traffic-jammed Wilshire Boulevard.

Since the public transportation system in Los Angeles was then, as today, possibly the worst of any major city in the United States, the Revuers also found it necessary to invest in a car if they were to get from Wilshire to the Trocadero, located across town on Sunset Boulevard, in time for their first show. Green badgered his friends into buying a decrepit limousine, a battle-scarred relic of the silent era, which ate up gas but was, Adolph contended, "a memento of Hollywood history."

The Los Angeles press gave the Revuers' debut at the Trocadero sensational reviews, and soon studio scouts and producers stopped by to appraise the act. There were some nibbles of interest, even a couple of definite offers. But they weren't the kinds of offers that had been expected. Everyone loved the act, but everyone also thought it too special for mass movie appeal. No one wanted the Revuers as a team— the offers were all for Judy. She, however, wanted no part of a deal that did not include her friends. Loyalty was to be one of her outstanding traits—she was unfailingly loyal to her friends, and she expected them to show the same considera- tion for her. Though at this time she recognized that the Revuers had not much further to travel as a team, she wouldn't be responsible for breaking up the act unless it was to every- one's advantage, not for her benefit alone. And anyway, she didn't want to stay in Hollywood; she was ready to hitchhike back to New York.

Judy's continual refusals of contracts and screen tests were misinterpreted by the Hollywood talent corps, who presumed she was holding out for more money. Offers were flourished with increasingly attractive financial arrangements, but still she said no. Even when Betty and Adolph and Hammer urged her to accept, she continued to refuse.

Finally a compromise was achieved. Judy signed a contract with Twentieth Century-Fox with the assurance that she would initially appear as one of the Revuers, and that if this first screen appearance was a success, the rest of the troupe would also be placed under contract.

They were rushed into a Fox musical called *Greenwich Village*, a production that had been plagued with bad luck since its conception. Originally it was to star Alice Faye, but she got pregnant; then Betty Grable was to take over the lead, but she, too, got pregnant; next came June Haver, who sprained an ankle during dance rehearsals. So finally the part fell to Vivian Blaine, who was the newest addition to the Fox list of female musical stars. Don Ameche played the male lead, a hick composer who comes to the big city to make his mark, which eventually he does when Blaine sings one of his songs at a Greenwich Village bistro. The supporting cast included Carmen Miranda, William Bendix, the DeMarcos and the Step Brothers. The Revuers were added to bring a note of much-needed authenticity to the film's background.

Under the supervision of a second-unit director, they shot two of their nightclub sketches—one was their spoof of Shubert operettas—and also appeared on the periphery of several other scenes. But in the release print of the film, both numbers had been cut, and the Revuers had vanished except for a brief scene in which Comden, as a hatcheck girl, hands Ameche his fedora. No one was particularly surprised to learn that Fox wasn't picking up its option for the Revuers. The studio was, however, keeping Judy under contract.

Judy was genuinely distraught. She insisted she would break the contract unless Fox kept her friends on the payroll as well. "I won't break up the act!" she sobbed. Adolph and Betty tried to argue her out of any feelings of disloyalty and betrayal: The act had fulfilled its promise and had been surviving on borrowed time; the moment had come for each of them to go his own way; they were all capable of looking out for themselves. But Judy couldn't get over the awful wrong of what had happened: She, who had never wanted to be a performer, had been chosen over her friends, who wanted nothing else. She appreciated the generosity behind their encouraging words, but also knew that, no matter what they said, they must be hurting.

Ultimately, Judy was persuaded that she was legally obligated to Fox and that any defection might lead to a court battle, which she was in no position to afford. She remained, however, distressed over the predicament of her friends, who seemed uncertain about what to do next. She also sensed that at least unconsciously Comden and Green did harbor feelings of resentment, and probably she was right—this was perhaps the starting point of the uneasy, not always friendly, relations between Judy, Adolph, and Betty in later years.

At the time, there can be no question that Comden and Green were upset by their dismissal. A few days after the insult, they showed up at Sylvia Regan's office in Hollywood.

Two years earlier, Regan had written a moderately successful Broadway play, *Morning Star*, and was immediately brought to the West Coast as a Twentieth Century-Fox screenwriter. From time to time she had run into the Revuers on the Fox lot, and she knew what had happened with *Greenwich Village*; the picture had been written by her friend and occasional collaborator Walter Bullock.

"Betty and Adolph walked in, very down-at-the-mouth," Regan recalls. They told her about Judy's contract and said that they, too, wanted to stay on in Hollywood and had received a couple of one-picture deals from Monogram and one of the other poverty-row companies.

As they had come seeking advice, Mrs. Regan felt free to tell them what she thought without mincing words. "I don't think either of you have any future in pictures," she said. "You aren't pretty enough." She went on to say that perhaps they could establish substantial careers as character or supporting players, but that this probably wasn't what they wanted and certainly wasn't what they should aim for; their gift was writing, and writing was the path they should follow. "Go back to New York and write a show," she suggested.

Later, Regan and her husband, composer Abraham Ellstein, were walking along Wilshire Boulevard on their way to the Brown Derby for dinner. Just outside the restaurant, they met Adolph, looking glum and slightly scruffy, and insisted he join them for the evening. During the meal, he reported that Betty had gone back to New York but he was still undecided. He kept hoping something might turn up in Hollywood.

Betty had rushed back to New York as soon as she learned her husband was about to get a ten-day furlough. Adolph followed her not long after his dinner with the Ellsteins at the Brown Derby. When his train pulled into Grand Central, Betty was there to welcome him, waving a placard that read, ADOLPH GREEN FAN CLUB. (This greeting would later be recreated for *The Band Wagon*, one of the best of the Comden-Green film musicals.) Alvin Hammer remained in Hollywood and worked successfully for a time as a supporting player in a wide variety of pictures, his most visible and highly praised appearance occurring in A *Walk in the Sun* in 1946. But shortly after the Revuers broke up, Hammer decided to leave the Wilshire Boulevard apartment for bachelor quarters.

Judy stayed on with only Helen as company, but initially she had no time to brood over her solitude—she was too busy at the studio as the experts appraised her chances for stardom. She was given a softer makeup, a more flattering hairdo, and a new name. Tuvim sounded too Jewish, so she was redubbed Holliday, the latter being a translation of her Hebraic family name.* Judy liked the change—it was, in fact, just about the only thing that happened to her in Hollywood that she *did* like.

Shortly after Judy was overhauled by the Fox glamour experts, she was informed that Darryl Zanuck, the head of the studio, had asked to meet his newest starlet. Zanuck had the reputation of exercising *droits de seigneur* over his indentured lady players, and before Holliday was ushered into his office, she was checked out for imperfections and a pair of falsies were artfully hidden in her bodice. Zanuck was sitting behind his desk when she entered, and he wasn't bad-looking except for that gap between his two front teeth —"the passion pit" it was called in certain Hollywood circles.

Zanuck started telling Holliday of how he had created many Hollywood stars, of how she now belonged to Twentieth Century-Fox, and therefore, by implication, to him. Then he rose from behind his desk and started toward her. Holliday stood her ground. "Well," she said, reaching into the front of her dress, "I guess these belong to you, too!" She threw the falsies in Zanuck's face and ran from the office.

Despite this piece of effrontery, Holliday was swiftly put to work by Fox, though in a very minor capacity. Her first

* Toyvim is the most common transliteral spelling of the Hebrew word for holidays. In Yiddish it is *yontovim*.

assignment was *Something for the Boys,* a war musical about a poor southern belle who turns her plantation into a residence for soldiers' wives. It was supposedly based on a Cole Porter–Ethel Merman stage musical, but the resemblance was in title only. The film starred Vivian Blaine, Perry Como, Michael O'Shea, and Phil Silvers. Judy met none of them. She played a welder in a defense plant—a one-line part. Her big scene required her to raise her welder's mask and say, "I once knew a girl who got carborundum on her teeth, and it turned her into a radio receiver set." (This line was virtually the only thing that remained from the original plot, and it was—believe it or not—a succinct summary of the Broadway script.) On the first day of shooting, the director told Holliday: "Look, we don't want to waste much time on this. Say it fast." On the first take, Holliday spat out the line so rapidly that she sounded like Danny Kaye performing one of his patter songs. The director glared at her. "Now, ah—what's your name?—Judy—yes, well, Judy, you've got the idea: fast, but *intelligible*, please!"

Her spirits rose when, a few weeks later, she was cast in a class production, the film version of Moss Hart's air force pageant, *Winged Victory*, which was still running on Broadway. This time out, she had a fair number of lines and scenes: Along with Jeanne Crain and Jane Ball (two other Fox hopefuls), she was one of a trio of war brides rooming together while their husbands were serving overseas. Of the three, Holliday alone managed to project a semblance of authenticity, but the studio perhaps would have preferred a more plastic expression of dutiful sweetness and simplicity. After *Winged Victory*, Jeanne Crain was promoted as a "Star of Tomorrow"; Holliday was to be shelved and forgotten.

For the next six months, Judy was idle. Her nights were spent reading and her days sunbathing on her tar terrace or at the beach. Like many transplanted New Yorkers, Holliday was at first enchanted by the glorious California sunshine; but after months of cloudless skies, she started praying for rain—anything to break the monotony. She was never to care much for California or for most of its denizens.

As a minor contract player, she had little contact with the higher echelon of Hollywood society, but she did attract the attention of a few second-rank executives, at least one of whom tried to get her into bed by listing his impressive group of friends. Whenever they were together, there would be a series of phone calls, and he would explain the interruptions by saying, "That was Cary" or "That was Marlene." Judy decided she had had enough when he hung up and reported, "That was Yehudi." She gave him a withering glance. "Well, Yehudi to you, too!" she called as she sailed out of the apartment.

She did find a small group of kindred souls in Hollywood, most of them transplanted New Yorkers. One was her former Mercury Theatre boss, John Houseman, who was then working at Paramount as an executive producer. Another was Nicholas Ray, later to become famous as the director of *They Live by Night, Rebel Without a Cause,* and *Johnny Guitar.*

Ray was at the time working at Fox as an assistant director on the production of *A Tree Grows in Brooklyn.* Like Judy, he was something of a misfit in the insular world of the Hollywood studio. Handsome, highly intelligent, outwardly macho but inwardly sensitive and gentle, Ray had arrived at his current position through a roundabout, somewhat checkered route. After a few years as a Frank Lloyd Wright scholarship student, he had migrated toward the stage, working in various capacities—actor, writer, director, stage manager—for several radical theater groups in the Thirties. Just before coming to Fox at Kazan's invitation, he had worked for the "Voice of America" radio program when it was under the supervision of John Houseman.

Judy saw Ray as a possible oasis in the midst of the Los Angeles desert—where people snuggled up in bed with *Variety* instead of a good book, and seemed to take an interest in world events only insofar as they affected international film grosses—and he was drawn to her for similar reasons. They met one another most likely through Houseman or possibly just on the lot, and began seeing one another seriously several months after her arrival in Hollywood. It was a meeting more of minds than bodies. Ray had grown up in a house dominated by female relatives; and as an adult, his need for women was emotional rather than physical. He was, in the opinion of many friends, latently (possibly even covertly) homosexual. The weave of Ray's psyche was a good deal more tangled than was readily apparent. Given to violent shifts of moods, alternately taciturn and maniacally verbose, beset with subtle sexual hang-ups, he was unpredictable and yet exuded a definite fascination for the many women who loved him, sometimes married him, nearly always with unhappy results.

Judy was intrigued by Ray, but she was wise enough not to take him quite as seriously as he took himself. She had a sense of humor and he didn't, which gave her an edge over him: She realized he tended to dramatize his sense of psychic discomfort. The affair blew up during their stay in a Malibu beach house they had borrowed for a long weekend. Morose from too much soul-searching and tequila, Ray suddenly suggested they end it all by drowning themselves in the Pacific. Judy wasn't sure this was the best of solutions, but if he wanted to play A Star Is Born, she was willing to give it a try. They waded out into the water until they were immersed to their waists, and then, as she expected, Ray suggested they go back to the house, have a drink, and reconsider.

After this charade, the romance ended, though Judy and Ray were to remain good friends. This was, however, a bad time for Holliday. Fox wasn't doing much about keeping her busy, so she found herself sitting day after day on the beach and brooding about what she wanted to do with her life. Sensing that Judy was depressed, Helen kept urging her daughter to drown her sorrow in food, and Holliday complied. Soon she was ballooning in size. She told herself she had big bones and could carry the pounds; but when she caught a glimpse of her profile in a mirror, she wasn't so sure. Still, there were no other ways of killing time except eating, reading, sunbathing, and mulling over her career. She was collecting what was for this period (and considering her rank) a handsome salary—$400 a week—but if Fox couldn't find any use for her talents, she was determined to forgo the money and request a release from her contract. Comden and Green, she knew, were working on a Broadway musical. Maybe if she got back to New York she could work with them in some capacity.

As it turned out, she didn't have to ask for leave—the studio informed her that it would not be picking up its option on her services. The news came as a blow to Judy's pride. While she was eager to leave Fox, she hadn't expected to be booted out. The curt dismissal left her overwhelmed by a sense of futility: A year out of her life, and she had nothing to show for it except a suntan, an extra chin, a failed romance, and a heightened insecurity about her abilities as an actress.

But at this time Judy was resilient. She had retained her belief that someday, somehow she would make her mark, and she was able to spring back quickly. It was a characteristic that she was to retain throughout most her life, at least in terms of career. After every setback, there would be an intense period of depression. But it was usually of brief duration and she generally was able to snap back quickly and move on. You went on with your life; you didn't gloat over the triumphs, or despair over the disasters, you simply got on with it. That was pretty much Judy's attitude when she returned to New York in 1944. But she wasn't at all certain about what the next step should be.

Chapter Five

BEST SUPPORTING PLAYER

On her return to New York that fall, Judy immediately came down with a severe case of influenza. Still, it was a wonderful homecoming, she later recalled. "Just like every other New Yorker, I was in bed with aspirins and Kleenex and honey with lemon. It was blissful. I felt part of things again. And I lost all the weight I had put on in California."

Judy didn't know what she would do with herself now that she was back in New York, didn't much care in these first days of release from the land of perpetual sunshine. She and Helen had taken a small apartment on the West Side; the rent wasn't high, but, still, it was more than they could afford. Despite the healthy salary she had earned at Fox, Judy hadn't managed to put much aside—she wasn't good at handling money, as she freely admitted. Whenever she went out, she spent whatever she had in her purse, whether it was fifty cents or fifty dollars, and usually on books or records or frivolities. Pretty soon, she and Helen were in debt, and they took to using the back stairs to dodge the creditors lurking around the front elevator.

Judy spent these first weeks in New York catching up with

her friends. Tessa was waiting to greet her, though by this time the romantic side of their relationship had subsided. Betty and Adolph were eager to fill her in on the details of the musical they were writing in collaboration with Leonard Bernstein and Jerome Robbins. Called *On the Town*, the show was an expansion of the popular Bernstein-Robbins ballet *Fancy Free*, and it was just about to go into rehearsal with Comden and Green, Nancy Walker, Alice Pearce, and Sono Osato playing leading roles. Things were looking rosy, Adolph told Judy; M-G-M had already paid a very generous $250,000 for the film rights, and if the musical was a hit, he and Betty might well be returning to Hollywood in a style to which they would soon become accustomed—Beverly Hills, not the La Brea tar pits.

Adolph said nothing about Judy's becoming involved in the production—though there were at least two roles she might have played—and Judy took this rather badly. She felt excluded, then resentful, and finally guilty because she realized her initial reactions were selfish. Betty and Adolph were her friends, after all, and she should wish them well. But their success, while still unproven, was a bitter reminder of her own failure in Hollywood.

John Houseman, who happened to be in New York at this time, realized that Judy was at loose ends, and, to offer her a chance to think things out, he invited her to spend two weeks at his home in New City. She spent her time there puttering around the garden, scribbling away at song lyrics, short stories, and poetry, but her efforts, she felt, were not good enough to be sent out for publication.

She was back in Manhattan for the opening of *On the Town* on December 28, 1944. Virtually everyone was captivated by its gaiety and ingenuity, with the exception of Louis B. Mayer and a band of M-G-M executives who left the Adelphi Theatre with glum faces and the firm resolution not to lose more money by producing a film version of the musical. (It was not until five years later that the studio reversed itself and placed *On the Town* on its production list.) But the entire Broadway community fell instantly in love with *On the Town*, and Comden and Green were swiftly welcomed into the inner circle of the theatrical elite.

Judy loved the show, but she couldn't help feeling jealous of her friends' triumph: They had made it as both actors and authors of a Broadway smash, while she seemed destined to be remembered as nothing more than a former Revuer. Betty and Adolph were, however, never less than gracious, and, expansive with the first flush of success, Green invited Judy to lunch at Sardi's on West 44th Street, a favorite hangout for stage celebrities. As a Hollywood never-was, Judy felt uncomfortable about appearing in such exalted surroundings, but she did dearly love Sardi's cannelloni, and she allowed appetite to take precedence over pride.

All during the meal, well-wishers stopped by the table to congratulate Adolph on the success of *On the Town*, and later, as he was retrieving his coat from the checkroom, Herman Shumlin walked through the front door. One of the most highly regarded of Broadway producers and directors—he had staged all of Lillian Hellman's plays to date—Shumlin paused to tell Green how much he had enjoyed *On the Town*. "You remember Judy, don't you?" Adolph asked, looking anxiously about to see what had happened to her. She had tried to fade into the background—this was, after all, Adolph's scene; she was, at best, just a supporting player. But when Green called her name, she stepped forward and smiled tentatively at Shumlin.

As it happened, Shumlin did indeed remember Judy. At Lillian Hellman's insistence, he had gone downtown to see the Revuers at the Vanguard, and later had become one of their fans. He asked Judy what she had been doing. Before she could answer, Green said, "Judy's been in Hollywood, making some pictures for Zanuck."

Shumlin appraised her for a split second, and then said, "I'm casting a play at the moment, and there's a part that might be right for you. If you'd like to audition, stop by my office on Forty-second Street anytime this week."

As they walked out of Sardi's, Judy turned to Adolph and said, "No, don't ask—the answer is no! I'm not going to do it." Green, however, was determined she would audition for Shumlin. She wasn't an actress, she protested, certainly not a stage actress; the only real acting she had ever done was on screen in *Winged Victory*, and look what that had led to—a kick in the backside and kiss Hollywood goodbye. Anyway, she didn't want to be an actress or even a Revuer; if she was going to make it in the theater, it would be as a writer, maybe later as a director.

She almost worked herself into a tantrum, but Green paid no attention. Like many of her friends, he believed that she secretly did want to succeed as an actress—if only to prove to herself that she did have the required skills and talent— and that it was nothing more than depression and a sense of inadequacy that kept her from owning up to this ambition. Green gave her good advice: Leave the writing and directing till later, he said authoritatively; take the opportunity that's offered now. Tessa and other friends argued along the same lines, and eventually Judy allowed herself to be coerced into visiting Shumlin's office—if for no other reason than that she needed the money.

She got the part. The play was tentatively titled *The Lonely Leave*, an adaptation of Frederic Wakeman's best-selling novel, *Shore Leave*, about three navy pilots on a four-day rest-and-recreation holiday after months in the South Pacific. Wakeman's novel, in the words of one critic, "pulls no punches in its presentation of civilian selfishness and chicanery in exploiting the boys who have come back and its dry digs at the Paper Navy," but the stage adaptation concentrated almost exclusively on the pilots' romantic misalliances during their vacation at the Mark Hopkins Hotel in San Francisco.

Holliday was cast as Alice, a pro, semipro, or maybe just a dumb blond who agrees that rest and rehabilitation for service

boys should begin between the sheets—the script was am-
biguous about the exact nature of Alice's professional status.
Still, it was a flashy part. Alice had all the zingy lines and
was the only really colorful character in the play. It was, in
fact, a dream role for a supporting actress.

During rehearsals, however, the role was a daylong nightmare for Judy. The cast for *The Lonely Leave* included
Richard Widmark, Dennis King, Jr., Jayne Cotter (later Jayne
Meadows), Paul Ford, and a number of supporting players
with substantial theatrical experience behind them. In such
company, Judy felt like an amateur. Except for *My Dear
Public*, she had never worked on the stage, and she didn't
know how to build a role or project it beyond the footlights.
Her voice was high-pitched and white in tone, so it did not
carry well; it came across the stage as a barely audible whine.
As late as the final run-through in New York prior to the
tryout tour, Judy was having problems with projection. The
rest of her performance was there, but would anyone hear it?
Comden and Green were concerned, but not nearly as apprehensive as Judy, who commented: "You can't see me for
dust." Normally a rough and tough director, Shumlin was
also worried, but he constantly reassured Holliday even while
chastising her for inaudibility, and never once did he consider
replacing her.

His faith was rewarded when the play—now called *Kiss
Them for Me*—opened at the Locust Street Theatre in
Philadelphia. The local reviews were poor to mixed, with
Holliday alone being singled out for special commendation.
"Capital!" wrote the Philadelphia *Inquirer* of her performance. And the out-of-town critic for *Variety*, while predicting
a brief run for the play, forecast an unlimited engagement
for the former Judith Tuvim. "Judy Holliday, out of Hollywood, scores a decisive triumph as the moronic, but devastating nitwit. She's going places." The *Variety* reviewer went
on to say that though Alice was "just another of those stereo-

type tarts with a heart of gold," Holliday's performance was "terrific . . . warm, sweet, exquisitely tender and humorous at the same time."

There was a flurry of second-guess alterations during the pre-Broadway engagements, but the New York reviewers greeted *Kiss Them for Me* with as little enthusiasm as their out-of-town brethren. They described it as a pleasant show that raised but failed to deal incisively with the subject of the disparity between the experience of soldiers and the civilians they had left behind. The play never really came to life until Holliday appeared, wearing a scarlet dress with Joan Crawford shoulder pads and purple pumps, a bunch of artificial posies nesting in her mousy blond hair. Judy got laughs out of lines that weren't all that funny. According to one critic she broke up the house by asking one of the pilots, "Do you ever read *Fortune?* It costs a dollar."

Kiss Them for Me ran for over fourteen weeks, always in the red, even moving from one theater to another (an expensive procedure, even in the 1940s), but it never really caught on. The people who came to see it came mainly for Holliday, but there weren't enough of them to keep the show alive for more than 111 performances. *Kiss Them for Me* closed on June 23, 1945.

Throughout the run, Judy was plagued by throat trouble. The problem, she believed, was caused by the vocal tone that she assumed to characterize Alice—that high-pitched, nasal whine which delighted audiences and critics. Actually Alice's voice was not so very different from Holliday's own sound, which was light, white, tentative, and breathy. But there was enough of a difference to assume that the false voice was the source of irritation of Holliday's vocal chords. Wisely Judy decided to seek professional help in alleviating the problem and went about learning the proper way of placing her voice to produce the desired result without continuous damage to her throat. She was pleased with her vocal coach, Vernda

Bennix, but Holliday's throat problem continued to trouble her until the closing of *Kiss Them for Me*, and was frequently to recur during later stage appearances.

This ailment was about the only sour note in Judy's brief but happy engagement in her first Broadway show. *Kiss Them for Me* gave her a name that stage producers and their staffs stored away in the front of their memory banks for future reference. And while it was still far from being a household name, she had been featured in interviews and pictorial layouts in several New York papers. But Holliday didn't place much stock in this kind of achievement: Every year there was a bright, up-and-coming star who fizzled out and was forgotten a season or so later. Her success built up her confidence as an actress, but acting still wasn't a profession she took seriously. She didn't sell it short, but it couldn't compare with writing a memorable book or play or song. Next to such achievements, her moment in the sun seemed paltry indeed. Five years on, who would remember Judy Holliday as Alice in *Kiss Them for Me*? She was excited when she won the prestigious Clarence Derwent Award as best supporting player of the 1944–45 season, and thankful for the $500 prize money that came with it, but nonetheless she wondered where it would all lead.

At first, as Judy had feared, it seemed to lead to nothing, at least not to anything that she found attractive. There were roles she might have accepted, but they were inferior copies of Alice, and she didn't want to be limited to playing dumb blonds. In all her early interviews, her intelligence and creativity were stressed by reporters who seemed surprised to discover that Alice was an acting job and not just a piece of self-impersonation. But Judy's attempt to liberate herself from *Kiss Them for Me* got her nowhere. The only alternative to playing Alice again was going on the road with the touring company of a Broadway hit, and she didn't want that. Having seen so much of the country as one of the Revuers, Holliday was reluctant to set off on another grand tour. In fact, she preferred starving in New York to earning her dinner on the road.

And starving, or something close to it, became a way of life for Holliday during the next few months. The Derwent prize money didn't last long, and soon Judy and Helen were again coming and going via the back staircase while creditors lined up at the front door. Judy was too proud to ask support from her friends, though they were willing to help. Her social conscience also prevented her from accepting welfare when she knew that others required charity more than she, a woman who could take care of herself and wasn't desperately in need of help from friends or father or Uncle Sam.

Betty Comden recalls that frequently Judy would join a party of theater people at a steak house across the street from the Adelphi Theatre where *On the Town* was playing. Occasionally she would order a Taipai sling or a "Bounty" julep—though never much of a drinker, she had at this time a taste for exotic cocktails—but usually she requested nothing more than coffee. She watched as her companions ate, and then, as they were finishing their supper, she'd turn to the waiter and nonchalantly ask if the leftovers could be wrapped up for her dog. No one thought of snickering at this subterfuge: It was too gallant and courageous to seem ridiculous— even though Judy, all the while she sat drooling over the table scraps, was wearing a mink coat bought on a wear-now-pay-later installment plan.

Fancy clothes were never a passion with Judy, but she needed a warm coat, she liked to look nice, and appreciated quality goods. The purchase of the mink was, according to Betty Comden, characteristic of Judy, who was always something of "a gambler." For all her insecurities and setbacks, Judy kept betting on herself, and she retained faith in her ability to make something of herself in one field or another. Maybe songwriting—she had a gift for words, and she thought some of the lyrics she had written were pretty good.

At the end of 1945, it did seem as though there would be

a break in Judy's streak of bad luck, but in the field of acting, not writing. She was asked to audition as standby and possible replacement for Betty Field in *Dream Girl*, one of the big hits of the new season. It was a job with definite possibilities: Field was highly susceptible to viruses and, since the opening of the play, had missed several performances. To relieve the pressure of a physically demanding role, the producers were considering the possibility of having the standby play the role at matinee performances. Judy was intrigued. Georgina Allerton, the play's heroine, was a literate young woman who managed a bookshop, a sensitive soul with a brain as well as a libido, a character who had absolutely nothing in common with Alice of *Kiss Them for Me*.

Judy auditioned for Elmer Rice, the author, and for members of the Playwrights' Company, the producers, and came away feeling pleased and confident. True, Rice had looked dour throughout the reading, but dourness, she had been warned, was Rice's everyday expression. At the end of the audition, one member of the production team had told her she had "gone over big" and should be expecting to hear from them soon.

Days passed, weeks passed, and nothing happened. The obstacle, it seems, was Rice; he had written the part for Betty Field—they were then married—and he couldn't see anyone else as Georgina. Though the producers told him it was commercially unfeasible, he really wanted the show shuttered whenever Field couldn't appear, and he was reluctant to sanction a replacement for his wife even for a single performance.

Judy knew none of this, and the blow of not winning the part seemed like a personal affront. Her professional status was becoming ludicrous: The Derwent Award money was nearly gone; the scroll that went with it was collecting dust on Helen's mantelpiece; and here she was, almost twenty-five, wearing mink and living off steak bones. It would have been funny if it weren't so terribly depressing.

Then, in January 1946, as depression was beginning to deepen into despair, Judy got a phone call from her agent. "Max Gordon wants to see you Monday morning at nine sharp."

Judy was puzzled. "If Max wants to see me, why doesn't he call himself?" she asked.

"You got the wrong Max," she was told. "This is Max Gordon, the theater producer. He's got a show out of town, *Born Yesterday*, and there's trouble with Jean Arthur. They're looking for a replacement. They want a name, but, Judy, this looks good."

Judy said she'd be there at nine Monday morning. The theatrical columns of the New York papers had been filled with the rumors about the problems with *Born Yesterday* and its star, Jean Arthur, who, according to Shubert Alley gossip, wanted out. Judy wasn't sure she wanted in; replacing Arthur was an awesome assignment, and, according to what she heard, *Born Yesterday*'s female lead was just another variant of Alice. That didn't appeal, nor did the scuttlebutt that the *Born Yesterday* team was looking for a star replacement for Arthur. Small chance, she told herself, but nonetheless she decided to give it a try.

Chapter Six

BORN YESTERDAY

The new Max Gordon of Holliday's life was a veteran Broadway producer responsible for such hits as *The Band Wagon,* *Dodsworth, The Women, My Sister Eileen,* and *Junior Miss.* This Gordon was a highly proficient merchant of "literate" stage entertainment, but in the early Forties he seemed to have lost his touch as one flop followed another. The best scripts were no longer coming his way, so when Garson Kanin, a Hollywood scriptwriter and director, submitted his first play, *Born Yesterday,* the producer stayed up all night reading—and laughing. The script had problems: It got weaker as it went along, the third act resolving the initial complications in a singularly sanctimonious fashion; and the whole plot became predictable after the first few pages. Still, the premise was intriguing and the dialogue bounced along until it bogged down in the social significance of the final act.

Gordon asked for revisions, but otherwise he told Kanin he would be delighted to produce the play. As soon as the author had agreed to refashion the script, contracts were signed. Then Kanin announced that the play had been written for Jean Arthur, and that Arthur was ready to return to Broadway after a fifteen-year absence, at $2,500 a week plus a percentage of the gross receipts. She also demanded certain other perquisites, including approval of the stage manager and press agent; final say on billing, advertising, and photographic material issued by the management; and finally, a hairdresser, chauffeur, and car, to be provided gratis by the producer.

Gordon demurred, not so much because of this list of Olympian prerogatives—that kind of nonsense was expected of a Hollywood star; what put him off was Arthur's reputation for being unreliable. Kanin insisted that Arthur was misunderstood—that while a trifle eccentric, she was not difficult. He had written one of her most popular Hollywood films, *The More the Merrier* (1943), and throughout the production, she had been an angel, he said. After several heated discussions, Gordon gave in. "Well, you're the author and director of the show," he told Kanin, "so if you want Arthur, okay, you got her." But he was uneasy about the decision.

Problems started with the first rehearsals. Arthur, changing lines, suggested rewrites at each run-through. She didn't feel comfortable with the role. A gifted comedienne with a distinctive voice and a brilliant, idiosyncratic sense of timing, Arthur had always stayed within a very limited range of characterizations: reporters and other bright, white-collar workers; young women of capability, wit, and abundant intelligence; girls who protected their femininity and soft hearts with a veneer of aggressive cynicism. Not since the earliest years of her career had she played anyone remotely like Billie Dawn in *Born Yesterday*.

Kanin's play, a variation of Shaw's *Pygmalion*, tells the story of Harry Brock, a junkyard tycoon, who goes to Washington to pull off (with congressional aid) an international swindle. He brings along his mistress, Billie Dawn, an ex-showgirl who is one tough cookie, hard as a diamond and as bright as a ten-watt bulb. When her uncouth behavior shocks

polite Washington society, Brock hires a *New Republic* writer
to smooth the rough edges and provide her with a conversational knowledge of world events. Predictably, Billie turns
out not to be as dumb as she looks. She and the writer fall
for each other, and, between clinches, he wises her up to
Brock's corrupt manipulations of the democratic process. By
the final curtain, Billie has scotched Brock's deal and shed
her minks and diamonds for the horn-rimmed glasses she's
bought to read the *Washington Post*. And, of course, in this
case, men do make passes at girls wearing glasses. Billie winds
up with Mr. *New Republic*.

Born Yesterday gets weaker as Billie gets smarter, but Jean
Arthur felt comfortable only with the latter section of the
play. She wasn't sexy in a blatant or obvious way, as Billie
had to be in the opening scenes, and was reluctant to fake it.
Furthermore, Kanin's comedy was farcical as well as romantic
and satiric, and Arthur had no experience in playing farce and
wasn't sure she could manage it. Rather than try, she kept
pushing the part toward more congenial ground.

As the days passed and Arthur continued to fight the role,
Gordon started urging Kanin to find a replacement. Kanin
refused—he insisted Arthur would eventually come through
with flying colors. Gordon didn't press the point, but privately he felt that Kanin, in deciding to direct *Born Yesterday*
himself, had taken on more than he could handle. The second
and third acts still needed considerable rewriting, and there
were indications that the actor playing Paul Verrall, the
New Republic writer, wasn't up to the part and would probably have to be replaced. All that, and Arthur, too, was too
much to expect one man to handle.

When the show opened in New Haven on December 12,
1945, both the play and Arthur's performance were still un-
focused. The reviews were mixed, as they were when the show
opened in Boston a week later. Elliott Norton wrote in the
Boston Post: "Mr. Kanin has to make up his mind here and
now whether he means *Born Yesterday* to be a rousing, rowdy

comedy with rumbling undertones of social protest or just a funny farce. . . ." The problem began, Norton noted accurately, with Billie's transformation, a change that "ripped the play in two," the second half gradually subsiding into the kind of "sentimental nonsense you might find in a B movie." After a few mild words of praise for Arthur, he went on to rave about Paul Douglas, a radio sports commentator who was making his professional stage debut as Harry Brock.

Two days after the Boston opening, Arthur informed Gordon that she had a bad cold and a sore throat, but would be able to perform that evening. She continued to play Billie until the Wednesday matinee of the next week. That morning her doctor reported that her cold had turned into a viral infection of the throat and intestinal tract, and that she would be unable to return to the show until it opened in Philadelphia the following Tuesday. Mary Laslo, Arthur's understudy, played Billie for the rest of the Boston run, but no one felt she was ready to take over the role on a permanent basis—Miss Laslo least of all. (She was to remain in the show as "a manicurist.")

Though the doctor had implied that Arthur would be returning to the play, Gordon did not believe it. Neither did the Broadway community. Rumors circulated that she was quitting the show, and not because of illness but because she felt she couldn't handle the part and was aggravated at being overshadowed by Paul Douglas. If she did leave the production, it was predicted that she would be replaced by Ruth Gordon, Garson Kanin's wife, but Miss Gordon immediately squelched that rumor: She was, she announced, giving up acting for a time so that she could concentrate on her new career as a writer. Her second play, *Miss Jones* (later retitled *Years Ago*), was scheduled to go into production only a few weeks after the opening of *Yesterday*.

In the three-day interval between the Boston closing and the Philadelphia opening of the show, Max Gordon and Kanin returned to New York. Kanin was to concentrate on

rewriting the third act while Gordon interviewed replacements for Arthur in the probability that one would be needed.
A leading contender was June Havoc, who auditioned for
Gordon. She gave a professional reading and certainly possessed the brassy come-on the part required. Havoc, however,
had just opened on Broadway in S. N. Behrman's *Dunnigan's
Daughter,* and while that show looked as though it would
quickly expire, there could be legal problems if the actress
withdrew before the end of the run. Gordon decided to go
on with his search.

He asked friends and business associates for suggestions.
Several people mentioned Holliday, describing with high
praise her work in *Kiss Them for Me.* Gordon hadn't seen
the show, but did remember what had been said about
Holliday's performance, and immediately got in touch with
Judy's agent to arrange an interview the following morning.

Gordon was so excited by Judy's audition that he at once
pushed her into a cab and sent her off to read for Kanin. The
playwright hadn't seen *Kiss Them for Me,* but he had heard
of Holliday. Mainbocher, the costume designer for the show,
had watched several performances, shaken his head sadly,
and told Kanin to find a replacement. "Get Judy Holliday,"
he suggested.

Kanin was impressed by Holliday's reading, but was still
not ready to replace Arthur until Arthur decided to voluntarily withdraw. A few days later, as if on cue, a representative
of Miss Arthur called with the information that the actress
would not be opening in Philadelphia the following night;
worse still, she was leaving the show for good. Her viral condition had become exacerbated, and she was now suffering
from hyperinsulinism, a periodic lowering of the blood sugar.
Gordon didn't believe this tale of woe, and discounted her
physician's confirmation of the serious nature of her ailment.
But he didn't much care. Despite all the difficulties that were
bound to arise with her withdrawal, he was almost relieved to
see her go.

The first obstacle to overcome was the Philadelphia opening. It would have to be postponed, of course—but not for long; the engagement was sold out, and every canceled performance would mean a massive refund at the box office. Could Holliday be up in the part by, say, Saturday?

Judy was too stunned by what was happening to answer coherently. Without really thinking, she echoed, "Saturday."

"Okay," Gordon said, "we'll start work tomorrow in Philly —that'll give us three full days of rehearsal before the opening on Saturday. Now go home, pack your bags, and, for God's sake, start getting your lines down."

Arriving in Philadelphia, Judy was to spend the next three days dashing between a hotel room in the Bellevue-Stratford Hotel and the Locust Street Theatre just up the block. When she wasn't on stage rehearsing, she was being cued on her lines. The work went on around the clock. Occasionally she was fed a sandwich or a carton of chop suey, but later she could remember consuming nothing except coffee and Dexedrine. Two old friends who happened to be in Philadelphia gave Judy all their support. John Houseman and Nick Ray were in town with *Lute Song*, a Mary Martin musical— Houseman was the director; Ray, his assistant—and whenever they could steal an hour from their own show, they coached Judy on her lines.

Looking back on those three days, she saw only a blur, could recall no feeling more definite than the awful effort of extending herself beyond the point of exhaustion. One of her few concrete memories of this period was, ironically, of something that probably existed only in her imagination. She told an interviewer that she knew June Havoc was waiting in Philadelphia to take over if she failed; but this was unlikely since Havoc was performing on Broadway in *Dunnigan's Daughter* at that time.

Though the recollection is inaccurate, the sentiment behind it is expressive of the tensions, insecurities, and pressures Holliday must have felt at the time—it was in a sense a hallucination brought on by the fear of failure. Judy knew that Gordon and Kanin were staking a great deal on her making an immediate hit as Billie Dawn. *Born Yesterday* had built up a $20,000 advance ticket sale in New York—a large sum for that period—mainly on the strength of Arthur's name. All advance ticket buyers were entitled to a refund if Arthur didn't appear, and some of them were already standing in line for their rights. The demand would certainly grow if the word from Philadelphia was negative about Arthur's replacement. If she did bomb in Philadelphia, which was a real possibility, Judy realized that Gordon and Kanin would have no choice but to replace her immediately with a star. They couldn't afford to play for time while she gradually worked her way into the part. Judy was a slow study—the lines came easy, but she had to inch her way into a characterization—and there was no time for mistakes, reflection, or experimentation.

Holliday wasn't at all sure she'd be ready for the Philadelphia opening. The part of Billie Dawn was long and complicated, involving not only pages and pages of dialogue but also a great deal of complex stage business that demanded intricate timing. There was, for instance, the gin rummy game between Billie and Brock at the end of the first act: It had to look spontaneous, but each movement required meticulous blocking and orchestration. Then, too, there was the problem of Billie's transformation from party girl to anti-Brock lobbyist. As Arthur had recognized, and as Holliday was coming to realize, the change that overtakes Billie in the middle of the second act was abrupt, simplistic, and unconvincing. There might be a way to bridge the gap, but as yet Holliday wasn't sure what it could be.

At the final run-through, Judy was in a state of semihysteria. She was in control of herself before every entrance; but after she left the stage, she broke down and wept uncontrollably. Between scenes, she spent most of her time standing over or sitting on the toilet. When she was called for her next entrance, she was calm, but again burst into tears when the scene was over. The pattern repeated itself during each of the three acts. The run-through was a disaster, but realizing that Holliday was operating on raw nerve ends, Kanin told her to go back to the hotel, get some sleep, and try to relax before the opening the following evening. Judy did her best to follow the prescription, but she was too keyed up to do more than go through the motions.

For the Philadelphia premiere, *Born Yesterday* had not only a new Billie Dawn but also a new third act and a new Paul Verrall—Gary Merrill had taken over the part of the reporter during the final performances in Boston. Merrill was a real improvement, but Kanin's revisions still were not entirely satisfactory; the second half of the play was always to coast on the goodwill built up by the earlier scenes. Holliday was better than anyone had dared hope—she was funny and her teamwork with Douglas was brilliant. For the first time, the production really came together, really looked like a hit, and was greeted by a prolonged ovation at the final curtain. One of the first to hug and kiss the somewhat stunned and bewildered Holliday was Ruth Gordon, who said something sentimental about theater clichés and how they had a way of coming true. And it *was* true: Judy had gone out there a virtual unknown and come back looking like a star.

The only person with reservations about Holliday's performance was Holliday herself. "That Saturday night, I was deeply ashamed of my performance," she confessed. "Oh, the laughs were there, all right, but I knew I should have been better. I fell back on all the tricks I knew for getting laughs. It was a cheap, easy way to go at the part because I hadn't time for anything else."

Following the Philadelphia run, the show was supposed to move to New York for the Broadway opening, but Gordon decided to keep it out of town for another week of polishing. While the comedy was playing at the Nixon Theatre in Pittsburgh, Kanin (with some help from his friend, George S.

Kaufman) kept revising the script, while Judy concentrated on refining her portrayal of Billie Dawn.

In the script, Billie is described as "stunningly beautiful and stunningly stupid," and as Holliday was neither, her performance was bound to be a paraphrase of Kanin's original conception. But, as sometimes happens, the paraphrase was better than the original—at least it made dramatic sense. The problem with *Born Yesterday* had always been the dawning of Billie Dawn: If she was all that dumb, how did she become so smart by the end of the play? Judy's solution was to suggest from the outset that Billie was self-absorbed, under-educated, cynical, but never stupid. Holliday's Billie was a smart broad who had learned that the only way to keep yourself in mink and diamonds was to be born beautiful and act dumb. Holliday's Billie was a latter-day Lorelei Lee, one with little affection or gratitude for the "creeps" who keep her. One of the earliest indications of her latent intelligence is her disdain for Brock, whom she treats as the overgrown bully he is.

Holliday's only obeisance to Billie's alleged stupidity was her assumption of the stereotyped dumb-blond voice—high-pitched, nasal, slightly harsh, and very similar to the voice she had used as Alice in *Kiss Them for Me*. There was no attempt through makeup, hairdressing, or costume to suggest the more obvious allures of a stunningly beautiful showgirl. Unlike the film version, where she is tarted up *à la* Jean Harlow, the stage Billie Dawn was a nice-looking woman (with a striking resemblance to Jean Arthur) with dark blond hair, a conservative wardrobe, and few of the manner-isms of the party girl in a typical Hollywood B movie. Billie's erotic appeal was suggested by an emphatic jiggling of the hips and backside, nothing more. It was, considering what most actresses would have done with the part, a subtle piece of characterization, but many critics found it highly suggestive. Judy defended the walk as a legitimate piece of realistic observation: "I think Billie is the kind of girl who *would* let her hips swing loose."

Born Yesterday finally opened in New York at the Belasco Theatre on February 4, 1946. The reviews the next morning were entirely affirmative, ranging from mild approval to open euphoria. There was praise for Kanin, for Merrill, and, most of all, for Holliday and Douglas, who shared equally in the acting honors. Neither took precedence over the other, and neither received paragraph upon paragraph of glowing accolades, as might be expected. The acting was discussed in surprisingly terse fashion. Still, there was no doubt that Holliday had turned in one of the top performances in a season rich with memorable appearances by such stars as Gertrude Lawrence (*Pygmalion*), the Lunts (*O Mistress Mine*), Bobby Clark (*The Would-Be-Gentleman*), Katharine Cornell (*Candida*), Ethel Merman (*Annie Get Your Gun*), Marlon Brando (*Truckline Cafe*), and Laurence Olivier and Ralph Richardson in a series of Old Vic productions.

Technically, however, Holliday did not become a star on the opening of *Born Yesterday*. Stardom then was harder won than it is today, and had been achieved only when an actor saw his or her name above the title of the play in which he or she was playing. That status was not granted until an actor or actress in question had built up a substantial following that would buy tickets for anything in which he or she appeared.

Holliday's name was not placed above the title of *Born Yesterday* until late in the run, when Douglas and Merrill had left the show for Hollywood and when the play's continuing survival depended largely on the tourist trade, all cosmopolitan theatergoers having seen it at least once. By then, the honor was richly deserved. Holliday stayed with *Born Yesterday* until late May 1949, an endurance test that seemed remarkable at the time and, today, when major actors demand limited runs of sixteen to twenty weeks, seems ex-

traordinary. Even the most disciplined actor begins to feel
stale after playing the same role for a year, but somehow
Judy managed to stay fresh for a very long time. Shortly after
the 537th performance, Brooks Atkinson of *The New York
Times* wrote that she still seemed to be "inventing those
[clever] lines extemporaneously."

The question remains, however, as to why she wanted to
go on playing a role that offered so little room for growth or
exploration after its first difficulties had been hurdled. There
are any number of answers, starting off with salary. Dazed
though she may have been at her first meetings with Gordon,
she was clearheaded enough to wangle a very good deal for
herself. There were none of the perquisites given Jean Arthur
and she never expected to get the same wages. But what she
did receive—about a thousand dollars a week—was more
than she had ever earned before, and gave her, for the first
time in her life, a sense of financial comfort.

There was also the difficulty of finding a new vehicle. She
once said she read over five hundred scripts during her three-
year stay with *Born Yesterday*, and all offered her roles that
were inferior variations of Billie Dawn or Alice in *Kiss Them
for Me*. She wasn't ready to settle for typecasting—not yet.

Nor was she driven to consolidate her success as Billie
Dawn with another Broadway triumph. *Yesterday* marked the
beginning of one of the happiest periods of her personal life,
and she didn't really need variation or professional challenges
to feel fulfilled. Once again, she was in love. She was now
seeing David Oppenheim, a clarinetist with the New York
Symphony Orchestra, which gave three concerts a week at
City Center on West 55th Street and was acclaimed for its
avant-garde repertoire and the theatrical presence of Leonard
Bernstein, its junior conductor.

Bernstein had met Oppenheim when both held minor
posts at the Harms Publishing Company in the early Forties.
They became friendly, and one night after dinner at a Green-

wich Village chop-suey joint, Bernstein had taken Oppenheim to see the Revuers, later introducing him to Adolph,
Betty, and Judy. It was a pleasant encounter, but nothing
came of it as Oppenheim was soon to get greetings from
Uncle Sam. He remembers that during his tour of duty he
was leafing through a copy of *Life* that featured as "play of
the week," a pictorial recreation of *Kiss Them for Me*. The
photographs of Judy caused a rush of warm recollections,
and he decided he would look her up when he got back to
New York.

At the time he became a civilian, Holliday was appearing
in *Born Yesterday*. Oppenheim wasn't sure she'd remember
him, but he pushed his way backstage, using Bernstein's
name, and Judy acted as though she hadn't forgotten their
initial meeting. Their second encounter was really no more
intense than the first, except that each felt an itch of interest,
a prickling of compatibility. Oppenheim was very good-
looking—one of Judy's friends recalls him as being "a real
dish"—and terribly charming: Another friend depicts him
accurately as being the embodiment of that elusive quality
described by the German word *gemütlichkeit*. He was also
amply endowed with intelligence, wit, talent, and ambition.
Not content with being a promising concert performer and
soloist, he also wanted to be a composer, and had reams of
unpublished music to show for it. All these were qualities
Judy admired, and, as a bonus, David seemed emotionally
stable, unlike some of the earlier gentlemen in her life. He
also shared her passion for food, particularly Italian and
Chinese, the real stuff, not the Americanized fare that was
served up in the pizza and foo-yong palaces in the Broadway
area. So their first dates took them to Chinatown, where they
gorged themselves and discovered they shared another trait—
a tendency to overweight.

Judy had no formal education in David's field, but she was
well informed about all types of music. And while David had

no practical knowledge of the theater, he had a genuine interest in all areas of the arts. Each found the other's work stimulating. Politically, he was nearly as liberal as Judy, and they almost always agreed on national and world events. Compatibility led to attraction and then to a proposal, which was promptly accepted.

Though she moved in artistic, freethinking circles, Judy was not at all averse to the idea of marriage: When she made a commitment to someone—as she did really for the first time to David—it was a total commitment, requiring the most intense form of loyalty. Besides, she wanted children, and the late 1940s were not a period when unmarried women—even actresses—bore children out of wedlock. The post–World War II era was, in fact, a repressive period for women, a period when women were being urged to return to their rightful place at the kitchen stove after playing around on the picket lines of the Thirties and the war factories of the early Forties. Significantly, Judy's political activities began to diminish around this time; soon she was to become a passive rather than an active liberal, though she would campaign for Henry Wallace, the Progressive candidate, in the presidential election the following fall.

They were married on January 4, 1948, in the parlor of Helen Tuvim's apartment in the West Seventies. A civil ceremony was conducted before a fireplace, the mantelpiece of which was a shrine of Holliday memorabilia—school pictures, stage protraits, and the scroll that had come with the Clarence Derwent Award. Afterward, Helen served cake, sweet wine, and champagne to a small gathering of guests, including Judy's father. (Abe was one of Judy's greatest fans and had continued to see his daughter on an irregular basis throughout this period, but rarely did he meet with Helen, who would never forgive her former husband for his desertion.) Helen was fond of David; and David, though well aware of his mother-in-law's possessiveness, felt kindly toward Helen, who became a regular guest in the Oppenheims' household.

After the marriage, David and Judy moved into a rambling seven-room apartment in Greenwich Village, just off Washington Square. It was the top floor of an old red-brick building, with garbage cans and stray cats providing the only exterior landscaping. There was no elevator—visitors had to climb five steep flights of stairs to reach the Oppenheim apartment. The living room was predominantly olive green with splashes of vivid purple provided by upholstery and throw pillows. The rooms were furnished with cast-off furniture and bibelots, some quite good, which the couple had refurbished or restored; Judy and David were devotees of junk and secondhand stores long before thrift decoration became fashionable for the well-to-do. The only sign of high living was a soundproof study, and this was a necessity: Oppenheim needed space to rehearse without disturbing the neighbors.

Despite their theatrical careers, the Oppenheims led a quiet, almost prosaic life for the first years of their marriage. He would meet her at the theater; they'd have a late supper; she'd walk the dogs—a mutt named Lifey and a ginger-colored spaniel, Muffin—and then go to bed. They had decided to pool resources and collaborate on the creation of a musical or maybe a radio show, which would star Judy, and before lunch they'd hash over ideas. When David went off to rehearsals, Judy would read or shop until it was time for her afternoon nap. After a light dinner, she'd leave for the theater and David would go about his own business—performing, rehearsing, or just mooning around until it was time to pick up Judy at the stage door. On Sundays, they did what other couples do—movies, *The New York Times* (Judy wouldn't get out of bed until she had completed the crossword puzzle), friends, country excursions. They were hunting for a Connecticut or upstate house for holidays and vacations, but no realtor was able to come up with a property that was both attractive and within their means.

Two weeks a year, Judy went off to Miami or the Caribbean while her understudy or the touring-company Billie Dawns replaced her on Broadway. Business fell off when she was away, picked up on her return: No one wanted to see a substitute Billie Dawn when, by waiting a week or so, he could see the genuine article. By this time, there were two touring companies of *Born Yesterday* traveling across America, and the play was beginning to enjoy international success with its presentation in London under the management of Laurence Olivier. In England, the comedy was a success without Holliday—but there, or anywhere else, it has never worked quite so well as when Holliday was onstage as Billie, though the role has been played by everyone from Mary Martin to Sandy Dennis. Holliday *was* Billie Dawn, just as Marlon Brando was Stanley Kowalski, or Katharine Hepburn the Tracy Lord of *The Philadelphia Story*. Anyone who dared follow them was bound to seem either an impostor or a mimic.

And herein lies perhaps the best explanation of why Holliday stayed with *Born Yesterday* for so long. By going on with the show, she was establishing her patent on the rights to Billie Dawn against all Hollywood claimants. The film rights to the play had been sold to Columbia Pictures, and dozens of actresses had been considered for the role of Billie on screen. Some were stars, a few were Holliday's vacation replacements. Anyone who might conceivably have suited the part had been tested—everyone except Judy. But Judy was determined not to be passed over again in favor of Jeanne Crain or some other studio sweetheart. In the past, Judy had been passive, sometimes even self-destructive, in furthering the course of her acting career. But Billie Dawn was really her creation, she was proud of what she had accomplished, and she was ready to fight for what was hers.

Determination alone, however, would not be enough to win over Harry Cohn, the head of Columbia Pictures, who had bought the rights to *Born Yesterday* with Rita Hayworth in mind. He had yielded on that piece of casting, but he couldn't work up much enthusiasm for Holliday. She might be okay for Broadway, but nobody would ever be able to convince him she'd be anything more than a washout on screen, and she hadn't a clue as to how she could convince him otherwise. What she did have, though, was a group of influential friends, all of them conspiring to find a plan whereby Cohn would have no alternative but to choose Holliday as the original and only Billie Dawn.

PART TWO

···———●◉●———···

The Hollywood Years

Chapter Seven

COURTING HARRY

The seemingly insurmountable obstacle between Holliday and the film role of Billie Dawn was Harry Cohn, a man who would play an important part in Judy's life for the next ten years. Cohn was the boss of Columbia Pictures, a studio he had lifted from poverty row to almost first rank. If there was ever such a creature as the prototypical Hollywood mogul, it was Cohn: He was tough and crude, the kind of boor who scratched his privates in public and once ascribed the secret of his success to his behind. According to a famous anecdote, he told a group of studio executives that he had a foolproof test for the popular appeal of a picture. "If my fanny squirms," he said, "it's bad. If my fanny doesn't squirm, it's good." Herman Mankiewicz, the author of *Citizen Kane*, digested this and then murmured, "Imagine—the whole world wired to Harry Cohn's ass!"

Though he was the constant butt of jokes, Cohn had better taste and more intelligence than he was given credit for, and he could also be very charming when it was to his advantage. When it wasn't, he could be loud and vulgar, and he always drove a tough bargain—so much so that many

Columbia actors and writers made something of a game of outsmarting their boss.

One of the chief practitioners of this sport was Garson Kanin, who used Cohn as the prototype for the Harry Brock character of *Born Yesterday*. Kanin had worked at Columbia as a scriptwriter in the early Forties, and he had come to know Cohn very well, liking him one day, detesting him the next. Once, he had gotten the better of Cohn during the negotiations for *The More, The Merrier*, a screenplay he had written for Jean Arthur (one of Columbia's top stars), but Cohn made him pay for his brief triumph during the negotiations for his next film. In both cases, it was a power play for authority; and when Kanin lost in the final round, he retaliated by making Cohn the villain of his comedy. The portrait, as caricatured as it was, was nonetheless so realistic that no one in Hollywood missed the resemblance—except Harry Cohn. There were other private references as well. In conceiving Billie Dawn as a role for Jean Arthur, Kanin was merely underlining the joke, since Arthur's relations with Cohn, though never of a sexual nature, were as prickly as those between Brock and Billie in the play. *Born Yesterday* can, in fact, be read on two levels: It is both a farce about Washington chicanery and, subtextually, an exposé of Hollywood politics.

Cohn, however, saw neither himself nor Hollywood in *Born Yesterday* when he attended a performance of the comedy shortly after its Broadway opening. He enjoyed it immensely and started negotiating for the film rights. All the studios were bidding for the play, but Cohn swept them off the board by raising the stakes to a cool million for a ten-year guarantee on all rights (TV, musical, and so on), after which Kanin would regain total control of his property. The price and the conditions were record-breakers for the time, and the other studio moguls disapproved of Cohn's lavish expenditure. Cohn probably needn't have gone so high, but he was overly sensitive about heading a company that was not quite on a par with M-G-M, Paramount, Warners, and Fox, and he was always looking for ways to outclass his rivals.

Of course, having paid a pot of gold for the property, he was determined to have it made as he (and his fanny) saw fit. And that meant with Hollywood stars in the two lead roles. The night he had seen the play on Broadway, Paul Douglas was two sheets to the wind and gave a listless performance; and Holliday was definitely not Cohn's idea of the kind of girl who could ever make it big in the movies. "Yeah, she's great," he told Kanin. "Great for the stage, but a dud for the screen." Cohn thought she looked mousy and fat. Judy was quite thin at this time, but Cohn apparently liked ladies with razor-thin profiles. Two years earlier he had discovered Shelley Winters and told her to lose weight. As she then weighed under 110 pounds, she asked: "Where should I lose it, Mr. Cohn? From my elbow?"

Cohn bought *Born Yesterday* for Rita Hayworth and Humphrey Bogart. Bogart owed Columbia a commitment, but he passed on this property. That left Cohn with Hayworth as Billie Dawn. Hayworth was a Columbia star; her career had been carefully nurtured by the studio and Cohn, and she had a lot of professional know-how. With a lot of coaching and skillful direction, she might have pulled off the stunt of playing Billie Dawn—though in none of her other screen performances does she show a glimmer of a sense of humor. Still, the part would undoubtedly have been hers if she had not decided to marry Aly Khan and retire from the screen—temporarily, as it turned out.

Once Hayworth had defected from Columbia to the Riviera, Cohn started scouting for another Billie Dawn. For a while there was talk of Lucille Ball, but she had never really made it as a major movie attraction. Marie Wilson, the quintessential dumb blond—her breasts were ten times as large as her squeak of a voice, which seemed ten sizes larger than her pea brain—who had made a huge hit as radio's "My Friend

Irma," was eventually disqualified because of her lackluster performance in films during the 1930s. (Interestingly enough, when there was talk of Wilson playing Billie on screen, there was an offer for Holliday to play Irma for the movies.)

Discarding Wilson, Cohn shifted his search from the upper reaches to the ranks of supposedly up-and-coming personalities. Over thirty-five actresses were considered and at least ten were given screen tests, including Jean Hagen, Jan Sterling, and Cara Williams (all of whom had played Billie in one or another of the *Yesterday* road companies), Marie MacDonald, Gloria Grahame, Barbara Hale, and Celeste Holm. (There is a long-standing story that Marilyn Monroe was also tested, which may well be true since Monroe was briefly under contract to Columbia in 1948.) Kanin kept insisting that Holliday was the perfect Billie Dawn, but Cohn wouldn't give an inch on his position that Holliday was destined to prove a loser as a film star.

Kanin didn't have time to argue the point any further—he had other things on his mind. With his wife as a collaborator, he had written a screenplay for Katharine Hepburn and Spencer Tracy, which was then nearing the preproduction stage. This script, eventually titled *Adam's Rib*, was the story of Amanda and Adam Bonner (Hepburn and Tracy), two lawyers who become, respectively, the defense attorney and prosecutor in the trial of Doris Attinger, a dumb and frumpish Bronx housewife accused of trying to shoot her husband, who has been carrying on with a two-bit floozy.

One night, as the Kanins and Tracy and Hepburn were discussing possible casting for the supporting roles, someone suggested Holliday as Mrs. Attinger. No, Kanin said, it's too small a part. Small, but colorful, Hepburn argued, and it could be built up. "Yes," Kanin answered with mounting excitement as he began to see the possibilities of Hepburn's suggestion. He dearly loved Holliday, and here was a chance to allow Cohn to see what Judy could do on screen. If she came across in *Adam's Rib*, Cohn might give her a second

look for *Born Yesterday*. It was a crazy idea, but, when dealing with Cohn, a touch of craziness could be an advantage.

Holliday was on sick leave from *Yesterday* when she received the *Adam's Rib* script. A few days earlier, getting out
of a cab, she had somehow managed to close the door on her
hand, and she was now forced to wear a sling. Still, with only
one hand at liberty, she managed to read the script in record
time, and with equal speed decided to pass on it. Her friends
were perplexed. From what she told them and from what
they had heard, *Adam's Rib* sounded literate and destined to
become an important picture. "Yes," Judy replied, "that's true,
but it's not for me."

Kanin was sure Judy's rejection had been prompted by the
relative unimportance of the role, and promised to build up
the Doris Attinger part once she agreed to play it. But Judy
wouldn't agree. Hepburn called her and cajoled, but she
didn't get anywhere with Holliday, either. Finally, after much
badgering, Judy opened up and gingerly explained why she
had rejected the part. Doris Attinger was described as overweight. She didn't like that. She didn't have to go any further—Kanin immediately caught on to what was distressing
her.

In the past couple of months, Judy had put on a lot of
weight, and though she had been dieting, she hadn't succeeded in shedding the excess pounds. One night, as she had
been putting on her first-act costume for *Born Yesterday*, she
had burst the seams of the dress. She'd made a lame excuse
about how the dress must have shrunk in cleaning, and her
maid had smiled noncommittally. Hearing about the incident
a day later, Kanin had kiddingly sung, "Judy's bustin' out all
over." But instead of accepting the ribbing good-naturedly,
Holliday had started to cry, which surprised Kanin, who had
not realized how deeply sensitive Judy was about her weight.

Naturally, Judy didn't remind Kanin of this incident when
he called her about *Adam's Rib*. He told her the part could
lead to *Born Yesterday* on screen, but she asked how playing

a fat, slovenly Bronx housewife would help Cohn envision her as the one and only Billie Dawn. When Kanin finally got the point, he promised to delete all references to frumpiness, and add to the script a final scene in which Doris Attinger would be glamorous and, hopefully, svelte. With this assurance, Judy agreed to play the part.

Although Holliday had informally agreed to appear in *Adam's Rib*, a legal obstacle had to be overcome before she was free to join Kanin and company: Contractually, she was committed to *Born Yesterday* for another three months. Since she had stayed with the show for so long, however, Max Gordon was willing to release her on two weeks' notice. In gratitude, Judy extended him a favor: As *Adam's Rib* was to be shot partly in New York, she promised to play Billie Dawn on stage each night while shooting the film by day. Though she would be working almost twenty hours a day, she was determined to stay with the play until it was time for her to leave for the Coast.

On the first day of filming, Judy woke almost paralyzed with terror. Her initial brush with movie acting had left her insecure about her ability to master screen technique. She wasn't a spontaneous performer—"I have to do something five or six times before it starts to be right," she once said—which started her off with a definite liability. At this time, film production schedules allowed for only a few perfunctory run-throughs before the camera started turning. Furthermore, in working with Hepburn and Tracy, and director George Cukor—who had worked with Garbo, the Gishes, all three Barrymores, Laurette Taylor, Harlow, Crawford—she was stepping into a whole new ball game, one that rightfully frightened her.

Cukor, Hepburn, and Tracy were all known to be difficult, each quite intolerant of any view that failed to match his/her own. And together they could be quite cliquish, excluding any member of the production team who failed to measure up to their standards. A few years earlier, Tracy and Hepburn, while working on *Sea of Grass*, had treated Elia Kazan, their director, like an unwanted pledge for a posh fraternity. Cukor had been gracious and encouraging when he directed Judy for her scenes in *Winged Victory*, but that had been one of his meat-and-potatoes assignments—a film, Judy felt, that interested him as little as the people who appeared in it. She doubted whether he even remembered her.

Holliday was only half right. While it was true that Cukor took no special pride in *Winged Victory*, he did indeed remember working with Holliday, and had been mightily impressed by her performance in *Born Yesterday*. On the initial day of shooting on *Adam's Rib*, he was ready to extend every consideration to put her at ease. She was the kind of actress he liked: She was always line-perfect, she hit her marks, she made no fuss. Instinctively, she knew where the laughs were and she went straight toward them; she didn't worry about camera placement and she didn't delve into arcane discussion of character motivation. She did what she was supposed to do—read the lines as written—and left the rest to him. She was thoroughly professional from the outset.

Judy's opening scene, filmed at a New York City police precinct in Greenwich Village, was an account of Doris Attinger's first interview with her attorney, Amanda Bonner (Hepburn). It was a lengthy, crucially important dialogue (in terms of plot and characterization), with the brunt of the conversation carried by Holliday—the Hepburn character acting mainly as a "feed." Cukor decided to shoot the scene in one continuous take, the camera placed behind Hepburn's shoulder and looking steadily at Holliday. By doing this—and it was a relatively unorthodox method of filming at the time—Cukor was allowing Holliday to "flow" with the role, to sustain and build up a character as she might on stage.

Nonetheless, when Judy sat down opposite Hepburn for the first take, she was almost frozen with fear and nervousness.

Fortunately, the near-immobility that often goes hand in hand with a state of severe tension was not inappropriate to what Doris would have been feeling, and so what Holliday was suffering personally became a telling piece of screen impersonation. After the first take, Cukor said he was more than satisfied with the results, but that it would be necessary to shoot again, this time from another angle, favoring Hepburn. "Forget it, George," Hepburn interrupted, "the scene is fine and it should belong to Judy, anyway." A few reaction close-ups of Hepburn were shot for editing purposes; otherwise, the sequence appears in the film pretty much as it was originally photographed.

After this incident, and all through the New York shooting, Judy's confidence began to rise—she realized that Hepburn, Tracy, and Cukor accepted her as a peer, though there was little after-hours contact between them. After three weeks, it was time for the company to move to California and for Holliday to leave *Born Yesterday*. When that moment finally arrived—May 24, 1949—it struck her with more force than she had ever anticipated. "I didn't think much about it until [that final] night," Holliday recalled. "But a bouquet arrived from my husband just before my first entrance, and I began to cry. I managed to dry the tears and get on, but [I went on crying] all evening." The other actors choked up, too; and at the end, a star-studded audience gave her a standing ovation.

Still somewhat shaken by her separation from Billie Dawn, which had provided a professional security blanket during the previous four years, Judy left for the Coast with her mother. Because of his concert schedule, David was unable to accompany her, a disappointment for both of them, but their separation promised to be short: Holliday's remaining work on *Adam's Rib* was expected to be completed in three to four weeks. During this period, Judy and Helen stayed at the Chateau Marmont, a residential hotel on Sunset Boulevard, much favored by New York actors and writers. From the outside, the Marmont looked like a tacky replica of a French manor house, but the rooms were comfortable and nicely furnished, there was a tiny swimming pool in the rear, and the prices were moderate. Judy and Helen splurged a bit and took a bungalow next to the pool. Every morning a studio limousine picked Judy up and drove her to Culver City and Metro-Goldwyn-Mayer where the interior scenes for *Adam's Rib* were being shot.

Though its glamour days as "the Tiffany's of American studios" were almost over, M-G-M was still kingpin of the Hollywood dream factories, and many of the great stars of movie history could still be seen strolling the lot: Hepburn, Tracy, Astaire, Garland, Turner, the two Taylors (Liz and Robert), Ava Gardner, Walter Pidgeon, and Mickey Rooney. Judy loved roaming around the lot between scenes and gazing at the M-G-M Olympians, and at least one of them was over-whelmed by Holliday's unexpected appearance outside one of the sound stages.

Because of a rather overly fanciful plot twist, Judy, Tom Ewell (playing Doris's unfaithful husband), and Jean Hagen (Mr. Attinger's "friend") were required to appear in drag for one scene. Hair slicked back with Vaseline, sporting a match-stick moustache, and wearing a double-breasted pinstripe suit, Judy started to stroll the labyrinthine streets of M-G-M during a lunch break. Turning a corner, she nearly collided with Greer Garson, the Queen Mother of the Metro lot, who yelped in horror at the androgynous stranger who accosted her from nowhere. Judy was enormously amused by Garson's re-action; she was never to dwell on anecdotes from her past, but this was one story she did enjoy telling to her friends in later years.

Everyone concerned with *Adam's Rib* was excited by Judy's work, including Judy. Bolstered by the unflagging support of Cukor and Hepburn, Holliday began to recognize her abilities as a screen actress. As shooting progressed, the gossip columns in the Hollywood trade papers started carrying "inside" re-

ports about how Judy was stealing the picture from Hepburn
and Cukor. Though Judy realized that this was part of the
Kanin-Hepburn-Cukor conspiracy against Cohn, and also
valuable publicity for the picture, she knew that such prin-
cipled and exacting professionals would never have stooped
to such a ruse unless they genuinely believed in her talent.

Though there was indeed some hype behind these reports
(no one was ever able to succeed in stealing a picture from
two such potent screen presences as Hepburn and Tracy),
Holliday did, in fact, come very close to pocketing top acting
honors for the picture. A lesser actress might have played
Doris Attinger as a caricature, but Judy brought to the part a
gentle wit and surprising delicacy, and thereby provided the
film with most of its originality: The Hepburn-Tracy battle-
of-the-sexes routine, though written and acted with sleek and
energetic professionalism, was by this time starting to lose
some of its freshness.

Several weeks before *Adam's Rib* opened to glowing reviews in New York during December 1949, Holliday had been
promised the screen role of Billie Dawn. While she was in
Hollywood, she was tested at least three times (once wearing
a dress borrowed from Hepburn) before Cohn surrendered—
with reservations: She had, he made it clear, won by default
and not because of any inner conviction on his part that she
was the best possible choice. "If only that cunt Hayworth,"
he could still be heard muttering, "hadn't married that fucking
Moslem playboy!"

Holliday was, of course, thrilled when she learned the good
news, but her elation didn't fuddle her brain when it came to
discuss business. Though she insisted she had no sense when
it came to handling money, Judy was extremely tough on all
matters relating to salary and contracts, and on this occasion
her intransigence almost cost her the part. Her agent started
negotiations by insisting on a one-picture deal. This was Judy's
idea: If she was going to be an actress, she would be a New
York actress—she wanted to get out of California and return

to her husband, friends, and Broadway as quickly as possible. This, however, was the era of the seven-year contract, and Cohn was equally determined to sign her only on his terms. On the off-chance that she did make a success in *Born Yesterday*, Cohn felt that Columbia should share in the rewards and profits that would inevitably ensue from that success. He would accept nothing less than a seven-year, exclusive contract.

After days of heated transcontinental conversations, a compromise was reached. For the next seven years, Judy would make one picture a year for Columbia (the first being *Born Yesterday*); after that annual commitment had been fulfilled, she was free to pursue whatever outside activities she chose— stage, radio, TV, anything except film. As a bonus, she was given some say over what pictures would be assigned to her, though Cohn retained veto power over any selection that set his behind atwitter.

Though a compromise, the contract was something of a victory for Judy since such concessions had been granted to only a handful of stars. The privileges she had been extended should have bolstered her morale, but had the opposite effect. By the time she was scheduled to leave for California and Columbia for the filming of *Yesterday*, she was again experiencing the flashes of anxiety and doubt that had besieged her before *Adam's Rib*. And whatever confidence she was able to muster vanished immediately when she met face-to-face with Harry Cohn.

Chapter Eight
ANOTHER YESTERDAY

As *Born Yesterday* was not to start shooting until the spring of 1950, Judy had several months to relax in New York City. She caught up on some of the new Broadway plays, particularly those that had people she knew in the cast: Alice Pearce was supporting Carol Channing in the musical version of *Gentlemen Prefer Blondes*; Maureen Stapleton was appearing in an ill-fated Arthur Laurents play, *The Bird Cage*—once or twice a month, Stapleton threw an all-ladies poker party, which occasionally Holliday and Tessa attended. She went to the opening night of Max Gordon's new comedy, *Metropole*, and consoled him the next day when the show closed ignominiously after only two performances.

She and David went to many concerts and liked to close out the evening at a jazz club—they had a gang of musician friends who fascinated Judy; she loved their crazy sense of humor and the colorful way they talked. So far, Holliday's success had done little to alter the Oppenheims' mode of living. She could still move around the city without being accosted by strangers seeking autographs; they still had a listed telephone number and never received crank calls. Judy continued to haunt the bargain shops without the salespeople jacking up prices because they recognized her as a celebrity.

Neither as a guest nor a hostess did Judy like big, flashy parties. When she entertained, it was usually for a small cluster of close friends, and often when musicians were invited the evening would end with an impromptu jam session, Judy frequently joining in with some skat vocalization. On one of the rare occasions when she did throw a huge cocktail bash—this occurred some years later—someone walked off with her mink coat. "Taking an ashtray or some silver as a party favor I could overlook," she said, "but filching a fur coat is definitely bad manners."

One of Judy's favorite pastimes was eating. She wasn't really a glutton; the problem was her metabolism, she'd explain: She had only to look at a plate of pasta to gain five pounds. Throughout *Adam's Rib*, Judy had dieted zealously, and while she did manage to slim down a bit, Kanin had to keep reminding her that the glamour scene was still to be shot and that perhaps another inch off the waist and hips was needed before she was ready to push Dovima or Dorian off the cover of *Vogue*. Every time Kanin launched into his lecture, Holliday bit viciously into a carrot or celery stick, and as a result she looks quite trim in *Adam's Rib*, though there are a few telltale close-ups where her face seems a trifle fleshy.

Once the picture was completed, Judy went back to feasting on fattening foods, and soon she had put back most of the weight she had lost. Just before she set out to the Coast for *Born Yesterday*, she returned to a regimen of vegetable broth, poached eggs, cottage cheese, and liver, but she was still well above her ideal weight when she boarded the plane for Los Angeles.

Once again she was traveling without David, though he hoped to join her in a couple of weeks. Judy asked her mother to come along as companion again, and Helen was, of course, delighted to accept. Judy was equally delighted to have her: Helen could be fussy and a nuisance at times, but she always tried to make herself useful, and Judy knew she could always count on her for moral support. On this trip, Holliday would be staying in California for three to four months, so she was hoping to find a small house that would be available on a month-to-month rental basis; in the meantime, she and Helen would stay at the Chateau Marmont.

She arrived at Los Angeles Airport about four hours after the scheduled arrival time—at around 11:00 P.M.—looking world-weary and very rumpled. Her traveling costume, a pearl-gray flannel suit that wasn't particularly well designed or tailored to start with, had lost whatever chic it originally possessed somewhere over the Grand Canyon. Waiting to greet her was a Columbia press representative, who said Mr. Cohn was still waiting in his office to welcome her officially to the studio. Tired and very conscious of her sartorial disarray, Holliday begged for a postponement, but the attaché suggested that it would be best not to disappoint Mr. Cohn. Helen and luggage were sent off in a cab to the Marmont while Judy climbed into the back seat of a studio limousine.

At this time it took well over an hour to get from the L.A. airport to Columbia, located at the intersection of Sunset and Gower in the heart of Hollywood. Every minute of the trip added to Judy's fatigue, and by the time they drove onto the lot she was nearly immobilized from lack of sleep. "This used to be known as the cabbage patch," said her companion. "It's sure come a long way since then!" The statement demanded an affirmative response, but the best Judy could do was to nod and smile in wan agreement. Outside Cohn's office, she felt as though she might faint, but the studio rep grabbed her under the elbow and murmured, "Steady!"

This was the moment she had been dreading. Her only other exposure to a studio mogul—Darryl Zanuck—had been a case of unhappy first impressions, and she was all the more apprehensive knowing Cohn was called "White Fang" because of the vituperation he heaped on new contract players.

Still, she was determined not to give him the upper hand in this meeting. She would be friendly, but firm.

Somehow she managed to pass over the threshold of the holy of holies, and there, across the room, seated behind an imposing oak desk, was God Cohn—a surprisingly benign-looking deity, Holliday observed. He wasn't all that tall—beefy like a Buddha, but no King Kong mogul. He didn't seem all that intimidating, but as yet she had not established eye contact. Cohn hadn't glanced up when she entered the room; he just kept ruffling through a pile of papers strategically placed on his desk. The press representative cleared his throat and said, "Mr. Cohn, this is Miss Holliday." Judy beamed and stuttered something not entirely coherent about how much she appreciated Cohn's consideration in staying up so late to welcome her. . . .

Cohn raised an eye from his papers. Then he acknowledged Judy's presence by a piercing, head-to-foot glance of appraisal. For a moment their eyes locked. Judy kept smiling nervously, but there was no visible sign of response from Cohn. Returning to his papers, he commented to no one in particular, "Well, I've worked with fat asses before."

Judy was too stunned to be angry—anger would come later. Before she had time to think of a reply, the press representative had whisked her out of the office and was driving her to her hotel. Still in a state of shock, Judy was silent during the trip while Cohn's assistant floundered around looking for some excuse for his boss's boorishness. He was embarrassed and excessively apologetic; he kept insisting that Cohn hadn't meant to be insulting, but was merely advising her to lose weight before production started.

Judy was too distraught to sleep. As she lay awake rehashing that evening's events, she veered between feelings of hostility and humiliation. If Cohn wanted some buxom caricature for Billie, she'd withdraw in favor of Marie Wilson. Either he'd take her the way she was or he could start extradition proceed-ings for Rita Hayworth, who—rumor had it—was now almost as overblown as the Blue Mosque. But by morning, she had admitted to herself that this was nothing more than self-destructive fantasizing: The weight had to come off.

And it would come off—but every bite of unbuttered kale, every sip of sauerkraut juice, would taste even less appetizing because they had been prescribed by the Great Boor Cohn. In the four weeks before shooting, Holliday was to shed almost fifteen pounds, but she still looks plump in *Born Yesterday*, noticeably more so than in *Adam's Rib*. Possibly she might have lost more if Helen hadn't urged her to "eat, darling" lest she "waste away to nothing." In order to protect Judy from Helen's temptations, Jean-Louis (costume designer for *Born Yesterday*) cinched in the waists of her dresses and fitted the bodices with a tightly boned inner structure. "If she was even an ounce overweight," he recalled, "she would have gasped with pain every time she sat down."

Jean-Louis, best known for the deftly engineered, "semi-transparent" costumes Marlene Dietrich wore in her stage and nightclub acts, and for Rita Hayworth's strapless black satin gown in *Gilda*, was amazed when Holliday expressed little interest in the design or fitting of her costumes. He assumed that she was indifferent about her appearance, but this was only partly true. Clothes, Judy often said, were low on her list of priorities, but in fact it depended to a great extent on her weight. When heavy, Judy avoided thinking about how she looked; but once she trimmed down, she immediately started riffling the pages of *Vogue* and *Harper's Bazaar*. Even at her most svelte, however, she never would have gravitated toward the Jean-Louis line of clothing, a cross between haute couture and Frederick's of Hollywood. She preferred softly tailored outfits—no spangles, frills, or décolletage. It was not an unfashionable look for the time, but often as not Judy seemed to have reached into the closet and picked the first thing that came to hand. She was always well groomed, but never particularly stylish or glamorous.

After Cohn's vicious remark at their first meeting, Judy didn't dare make any suggestions about how she should be made up for the part or for publicity stills; she let Cohn, the Columbia experts, and Jean-Louis decide. Her hair was frizzed, bobbed, and bleached to a platinum hue, with not entirely pleasing results: She emerged from the Columbia hairdresser's looking like a cross between Jean Harlow and Harpo Marx. Decked out in Jean-Louis's trousseau for an expense-account whore, Judy felt gaudy and much less appealing and individual than she had been as Billie Dawn on stage. She had been conventionalized into the stereotypic, comic movie tramp.

Judy hated the whole glamour regimen that was such an essential part of filmmaking. Every day she had to be at the studio two hours before shooting so that the cosmetic magicians could get her in shape for the camera. From seven to eight they worked on her hair, and from eight to nine the makeup artists added contour and emphasis to her face. Every third day, her hair had to be rebleached. "I couldn't do that as a steady thing," she later told a reporter. "I like living too much for that!"

Otherwise she was quite pleased with the progress of the film. George Cukor was directing, and the script was much the same as the Broadway play, though it had been opened up to make room for a few travelogue shots of Billie gazing in awe at famous Washington monuments. William Holden, who was then one of Hollywood's hottest leading men, was set for the expanded (but still undernourished) role of Paul Verrall. And as Brock, Cohn had personally selected Broderick Crawford, who the year before had won an Oscar for best actor in Columbia's *All the King's Men*.

Kanin had urged Cohn to sign Paul Douglas; but Cohn, remembering Douglas's boozy performance on Broadway, would not give in on this point, even though Douglas had made a sensational screen debut in Joseph L. Mankiewicz's *Letter to Three Wives* the year before. Judy wasn't particularly disappointed when Douglas was placed out of the running:

She was not, in fact, especially fond of her former Broadway costar. Four years earlier, not long after the opening of *Born Yesterday*, she and a friend had been passing a Broadway newsstand when they happened to notice a magazine featuring Douglas on its cover. "Schmuck!" Judy exclaimed. "Two more weeks out of town and I wouldn't be sharing billing with that ham!"

What Judy was implying was that if she had been granted more time to work on her performance prior to the Broadway opening, she would have wiped Douglas off the stage. It was not typical of Holliday to be so ungenerous to a fellow actor, particularly one as proficient as Douglas, but the target of her animosity was Douglas the man, rather than Douglas the actor. He was closer to Harry Brock than he'd ever admit, Judy felt: tough-talking, hard-drinking, thickheaded, so boisterously masculine that he seemed to have grown up in a locker room. He was the epitome of everything she most despised in a man.

As an alternative choice, Crawford was agreeable to everyone—indeed, prior to Douglas, he had been a serious contender for the role on stage. Crawford, however, wasn't thrilled about the role; like Holden, he felt the men in the film would be overshadowed by Billie, particularly since Billie was to be played by Holliday. Judy became aware of the problem, and confronted Crawford and Holden about it. "It's a wonderful script," she said, "and there are lots of opportunities for everyone." To convince them, she suggested they rehearse the play with Cukor and stage an abbreviated performance for the Columbia employees. This was done, with Cohn's reluctant approval, and the result was as Judy had planned: an enormous success for everyone involved.

During the shooting of *Born Yesterday*, Judy's professional love affair with George Cukor intensified. In 1950 Cukor was a portly and bespectacled gentleman about to celebrate his fifty-first birthday. He was noted as "a woman's director," a label he despised, but one that is warranted because of his

extraordinary empathy for the glamour and romantic misalliances of the women who move through his films. Flaubert
once said, "Emma Bovary, c'est moi!" and one imagines
Cukor watching Garbo in *Camille* or Hepburn in *Bill of Di-
vorcement* and *The Philadelphia Story* or Jacqueline Bisset in
Rich and Famous, and experiencing the same sense of identi-
fication. An oddity among Hollywood directors of this period,
Cukor was cultured, well read, and a connoisseur in many
fields—painting, rare books, good food, graceful living. He
was often waspish, and on the set he was something of a benevolent dictator. He was loving and nurturing as long as actors
followed his orders, but he didn't welcome suggestions on the
interpretation of a scene, not even from his dear friend Katharine Hepburn.

Judy had enough sense to know she didn't know much
about film acting, so she followed Cukor's orders explicitly.
His idiosyncrasies appealed to her. One of the best things
about George, Holliday once said, was his roundabout way
of calling for a retake. "Wonderful, wonderful, wonderful!"
he'd cry, clapping his hands with enthusiasm. "Now let's try it
again!" Judy never protested; like Cukor, she was a perfectionist, and she delighted in arriving at a piece of business or a
line reading that would leave him nearly speechless, gasping
for the appropriate superlative, which, when found, would
always be repeated three times. Indeed, she welcomed multi-
ple takes; she was always to feel she needed at least four or five
run-throughs before she was ready to give her best to a scene.

But on the set of *Born Yesterday*, Judy was facing a different problem. She was playing a role she had already performed over a thousand times on stage. There was little in
the part of Billie Dawn she had as yet failed to explore. As
director, Cukor realized that his chief role would be to prevent her from routinely repeating what she had already over-
worked to the point of exhaustion; that he must help her
recapture the energy and spontaneity that had been the vital
ingredient of her original portrayal. He kept pushing her to

vary a piece of business, to reconsider the reading of a particular speech. The degree of success achieved was the result
of a great deal of ingenuity on both their parts, and it was no
small triumph.

The most valuable advice Cukor was to give, however, was
in another area. All during the shooting of Adam's Rib and
Born Yesterday, he had searched for ways of bolstering Holliday's ego. He kept telling her that she was a first-rate actress,
and that all this blather about being a writer or a director was
simply an evasion, a refusal to come to terms with her true
self. Some of what he said started to sink in, but Judy was still
not buying the entire lecture. She knew that she was good at
what she was doing, but what she was doing was still nothing
she had much respect for.

Kindness and consideration from Cukor was something she
had learned to expect. But consideration and kindness on the
part of Harry Cohn seemed about as remote a possibility as
Garbo returning to the screen role of Dorian Gray. Unexpectedly, however, she got a glimpse of the positive side of
Harry Cohn. She wasn't a major participant in this revelatory
scene, but even from the sidelines she had to agree that Cohn
had a heart—maybe not of gold, but it wasn't tin, either.

As was true of most studio bosses, Cohn rarely visited the
set of a Columbia production unless he was needed as a
troubleshooter. Holliday didn't miss him—after their first encounter, she would have preferred rolling over Niagara Falls
in a barrel to taking on Cohn a second time. Cukor kept telling her Cohn wasn't the bastard he seemed, but Judy's impression of him as a "thoroughbred son of a bitch" was
supported by Broderick Crawford, who reported for work one
morning screaming for blood. The day before, he had gone
to Cohn's office and asked for twenty-four hours' leave since
his son, who had just undergone surgery to correct a hearing

impairment, was returning from the hospital the following afternoon. Cohn said no—work was work. Crawford rose in fury and threatened to go AWOL. "Walk off that set," Cohn screamed, "and you're fired!"

On hearing his story, Holliday, Holden, and Cukor urged Crawford to return home. He thanked them, but said since he was there, he might as well stay put. Shooting went along halfheartedly until noon, when suddenly the motorized door at the rear of the sound stage opened and an ambulance drove onto the set. With perfect timing, Cohn appeared out of nowhere. "There's your son," he told Crawford. "Take him home. But don't you *ever again threaten* to walk off one of *my* pictures!"

It was, Judy reflected, a rather perverse way of playing the Good Samaritan, but, nonetheless, it did suggest that White Fang's bark was worse than his bite. As time went on, she found herself beginning to like Cohn—he had been more than decent to her since their initial set-to, and even that incident she could now view good-naturedly. His methods might be crude, but he got results: She *had* lost weight, and the advance reports on *Born Yesterday* were glowing.

Leaving New York, Judy said, was like "losing a leg," and returning was finding that, after all, "both legs were there and walking around." She loved the pace of the city, which was positively energizing after the semitropical languor of Los Angeles. She was invigorated by a cultural charge that was missing in Hollywood, which was then pretty much of an artistic wasteland, and she loved the city itself. It wasn't just the glamorous Fifth Avenue shops; she could wander for hours through Chinatown or the Village or in the seedy little shops hidden in the gloom under the Third Avenue El. New York was then at its most vital and stimulating, and Judy could imagine no better place to live.

Still, like most New Yorkers, she dreamed of having her own country hideaway, and Judy's homecoming was all the more joyous because David had a wonderful surprise for her. During her absence, he had discovered and purchased a nine-room Colonial-style house near Washingtonville, New York. It had come fairly cheap as it was badly in need of repairs, and the Oppenheims were soon spending most of their time and money on the restoration and furnishing of their country home. The Washingtonville place was intended for weekends and vacations; they planned to maintain their Greenwich Village apartment for workday purposes.

For Judy, it was bliss getting into slacks or denims and going off with David to scrounge through antique and secondhand shops in search of household objects they could refinish themselves. Judy had an eye for this kind of thing and found a lot of bargains along the way. It was a wonderful interlude filled with music, companionship, food, and David—lots of David.

But throughout this halcyon period, Judy had more than domesticity on her mind. After a couple of weeks, she was eager to get back to work—so eager, in fact, that as a promotion gimmick for the film *Born Yesterday*, she agreed to play Billie Dawn for a two-week stage engagement in Washington. This was, she quickly realized, a mistake. "It was fun for the first couple of days," she recalled. "But then I got bored. I guess I'd played the part too many times." It was time for her to move on. There was nothing left for her in Billie Dawn.

None of the stage scripts that came her way appealed to Judy, but there was an offer from another quarter that seemed attractive. The National Broadcasting Company had recently launched a lavish radio program called "The Big Show" as a last-ditch effort to lure Americans away from their latest national pastime, TV. The star and hostess of the show was the legendary Tallulah Bankhead. She would spend ninety minutes every Sunday evening exchanging quips and insults with a glittering and wide-ranging group of celebrities—Lauritz

Melchior, Jimmy Durante, Fred Allen, Ethel Merman, and Ethel Barrymore, among many others—before signing off with her inimitable and indescribable renditions of "I'll Be Seeing You" or "May the Good Lord Bless and Keep You." The program started its air life as a phenomenal success—and to keep it going and growing, the producers were on the look-out for celebrity guests who could act as comedy foils for Tallulah. Someone came up with the idea of pitting Holliday against Bankhead—two no-nonsense ladies who could share the pearls of wisdom they had acquired on their climb to success. Holliday was invited to appear as a semiregular cast member of "The Big Show" over a period of four months.

Judy's agent was all in favor of the project. "The Big Show" held top honors as the classiest and most talked-about show on radio, and national network exposure would be a definite boon for the *Born Yesterday* box office and for Judy's career in general. Ever since she had worked in radio as one of the Revuers, Holliday had maintained a high respect for the medium, and, like most Americans, she was a "Big Show" fan. From the outset, she had good feelings about the offer, and once she was granted approval over her material, she readily accepted NBC's invitation.

Despite the fact that Holliday was definitely expected to play second fiddle to Bankhead, the two women got along quite well, though they were never to become friends. Judy had seen Bankhead when she was still functioning as a serious actress in *The Little Foxes* and *The Skin of Our Teeth*, and she admired her greatly. Furthermore, even in her decline, Tallulah was thoroughly professional, something else that Judy always had tremendous respect for.

The staff of gag writers and comedy specialists who collaborated on the scripts for the show included a number of the most venerated names in the field. Chief writer was Goodman Ace, who was directly responsible for Holliday's material. He invented an alter ego for Judy who was, in his words, "fashioned in the mold of Billie Dawn." The Judy Holliday

who appeared on "The Big Show" was supposed to be "a little suspicious of the glamorous and intimidating Tallulah, but
always ready to stand up and fight for what she believed in."

The characterization was broad and farcical, but Judy insisted it must be consistent within this concept. "She read
every single line we wrote for her," Ace once wrote. "With
a keen and searching mind, she'd argue whether a line fit the
character she played, whether the comedic line was properly
motivated." Other performers just zipped through the dialogue and hoped the laughs were there, but not Judy. "She
gave us hours of rewrites," Ace remembered, "pushing us until
she was content with what she had to speak."

One of Ace's sketches for Holliday revolved around a discussion of career versus marriage as presented in the film *All
About Eve*, the heroine of which was supposedly based on
Tallulah. In the sketch, Holliday told Bankhead that she
didn't approve of women who were married to their careers.
"Better get a divorce," she said. "You can't warm your feet
on the back of a microphone."

If it is true, as Goodman Ace claimed, that Judy excised
any line she found offensive, it would appear that she approved
of this attitude. And if it caused her no second thoughts, it
was undoubtedly because she was experiencing no stress in
harmonizing her career with her marriage. As yet, the two
sides of her life were in perfect balance.

But even before Holliday spoke Ace's lines, her career had
started to move into a higher stratosphere, one that was eventually to disrupt that delicate balance. In December 1950, the
film version of *Born Yesterday* opened in New York to sensational reviews. There was some quibbling about "canned
theater," but the faults of the film were dismissed as the critics
raved on and on for paragraphs about Holliday's Billie Dawn.
A minority group objected to the high Hollywood gloss that
had vulgarized Holliday's original stage conception, but the
criticism was directed toward Columbia, Cohn, and "the
system," not at Judy. The triumph was virtually complete—

even the captious had to agree with *Life* that, at the very least, Holliday had given "the top comedy performance of the year."

Three months later, Judy received an Academy Award nomination. That citation had been anticipated by Cohn and the studio, but no one really expected her to walk off with the award—least of all Judy. This was the year of *All About Eve* and *Sunset Boulevard*, and the odds favored Bette Davis (*Eve*) or Gloria Swanson (*Boulevard*) as best actresses. Both of them had given powerful performances, and both had strong sentiment going for them. Swanson had a slight edge as Davis was also competing against one of her costars in *Eve*, Anne Baxter; in such situations there was often a split in votes between the two contestants. There was a second possibility for an upset: Swanson and Davis might cancel each other out, opening the way for a dark-horse victory. In that event, Holliday felt she had an edge over Baxter or Eleanor Parker (*Caged*), but the chances were too remote for her to give much thought to preparing an acceptance speech.

On the night of the awards ceremony, March 21, 1951, several of the more prominent nominees were in Manhattan. José Ferrer (nominated for *Cyrano de Bergerac* and a shoo-in for best actor) was appearing on Broadway with Miss Swanson in a stage revival of *Twentieth Century*. Judy was also in town, as were several other candidates—among them, Sam Jaffe (best supporting actor, *Asphalt Jungle*), Celeste Holm, and Thelma Ritter (both nominated as supporting actresses for *Eve*)—and Ferrer decided to host his own celebration at a West Side Spanish cabaret, La Zambra. Arrangements had been made for a coast-to-coast radio hookup (this was four years before the Academy Awards ceremony was televised) so that if one of the New Yorkers won the award, he or she would then be able to accept it verbally, if not in person.

Judy arrived at La Zambra wearing a full-skirted maroon taffeta dress with a matching velvet neckband and rhinestone buttons. Shortly after her arrival, Swanson swept in—just as though Cecil B. DeMille had whispered in her ear that the cameras were rolling and, yes, it was finally time for her close-up. She was wearing a black sheath; a white mink bolero jacket; a veiled pillbox with a feather cockade; long gloves; and two bracelets that looked as though they might have been lifted from the King Tut's tomb. On entering La Zambra, Judy had felt well turned out, but standing next to Swanson, her confidence crumbled. The photographers had flashbulbs only for Gloria. Once the tumult had subsided, Swanson settled down next to Judy and bared her heart. Never one to mince words, Swanson freely admitted that she was rooting for herself. This is probably my last chance, she confided. She felt she would never get another role like Norma Desmond, while Judy had so many years ahead of her.

Swanson, who had turned fifty-two just two days before, was correct in assuming that she'd never be offered another film like *Sunset Boulevard*, but of course it was to be Judy, not Swanson, who was pressed for time.

Holliday was not at all offended by Swanson's candor—she was touched and a bit shocked that this woman, after so many husbands and lovers and a fabulous career, should need an Oscar so urgently. Judy sat listening to her as her own inchoate hopes welled up in her, but she knew the odds were against her—it had been repeatedly explained to her that few actresses had won first honors in comedy roles: Marie Dressler (*Min and Bill*) and Claudette Colbert (*It Happened One Night*) were among the exceptions. But if she couldn't have it herself, she had no objections to Swanson winning. It seemed fair—after all, Bette Davis already owned two bronze statuettes.

The first real excitement at La Zambra occurred when José Ferrer won the Oscar as best actor. He went up to an impro-vised platform and gave a short speech that was broadcast to the West Coast and simultaneously sent out over the na-tional airwaves. The next award was for best actress. By this time, odds were high in favor of Davis: *All About Eve* was on a winning streak, far outdistancing *Sunset Boulevard*. But that could also work in Swanson's favor: She could take the best-actress award as compensation for all the minor awards her picture had lost during the evening. The atmosphere at La Zambra was taut while Olivia de Havilland, on the stage of the Pantages Theatre in Los Angeles, read off the list of nominees. After a dramatic pause, she unsealed the envelope, gasped, and then clearly enunciated, "JUDY HOLLIDAY."

Bedlam at La Zambra. Judy bolted out of her chair, hid her face in her hands, laughing and crying simultaneously. She had been prepared for defeat, but not for the emotions of victory. While Ferrer and Swanson cooed and hovered in the background, David was whooping with joy and George Cukor nearly strangled Judy with a bear hug. Meanwhile, in Hollywood, Ethel Barrymore (one of Cukor's dearest friends, who had agreed to accept the award in Holliday's stead) was approaching the Pantages podium. At the same time the crowd in New York was pushing Judy toward the microphone at La Zambra. But before she got there, Miss Barrymore had finished a brief and gracious speech in her behalf, and the network had unplugged its connection with the East Coast.

"Another case of Revuers' Luck," she told a friend the next day. "I don't even get a chance to say thanks before the ax falls."

But it had been a wonderful evening anyway. After the ceremony, Cukor—always the director—suggested they clear out of La Zambra and move on to a place that served decent food. Everyone was high on wine and exhilaration. It was also a night that marked a turning point in Judy's life. When she woke the next morning, she would be a national celebrity, but the complications, professional and private, that would grow out of this elevated status were nothing Judy thought about on this evening. This was a time for only celebration.

Chapter Nine
DREAM AND REALITY

Early in this century, during one of his stage appearances in New York, Sir Herbert Beerbohm Tree expressed astonishment at the freedom with which reporters invaded his hotel suite. "An American's home is an interviewer's castle," he quipped bemusedly.

The situation had not changed for the better over the ensuing years, as Judy learned early in 1951. She was besieged with requests for interviews, and soon there was a steady stream of journalists and photographers flowing through her Greenwich Village apartment. She was very liberal about granting interviews, but also extremely deft at fending off any question she didn't care to answer. As a result, the vast majority of magazine and newspaper stories about Holliday made for entertaining reading, but lacked depth and substance. The articles all insisted that Judy Holliday had nothing in common with Billie Dawn, but offered no distinct impression of who Judy Holliday really was.

It was easy, therefore, for the public to forget the press profiles and go on imagining that Judy really was Billie Dawn. Rarely a day passed without someone approaching her and pleading, "Come on, Billie, say it!" What they wanted to hear, of course, was Billie's withering put-down of Brock: "Do me a favor, Harry. Drop dead!" This *bon mot* had become something of a household phrase since the release of *Born Yesterday*—with, of course, innumerable names being substituted for the original "Harry"; but no one was ever able to duplicate that zing of malicious pleasure that Holliday brought to the line, making it momentarily seem the summit of vernacular wit.

Like many entertainment personalities, Holliday was of two minds about her newfound celebrity: It wasn't at all unpleasant to be recognized and greeted by strangers, when you were in the mood; when you weren't, it could be intrusive and exhausting. A New York stage star could stroll the aisles of a neighborhood supermarket without creating a commotion, but a Hollywood Oscar winner had no such luck. Naturally, Holliday wasn't the kind of star that fans mobbed or physically abused, but she did attract attention and, because of the warmth of her screen personality, people felt easy about approaching her for an autograph or a brief moment of conversation. On a few occasions, when David was with her, one of the primal celebrity scenes was enacted: Someone addressed Oppenheim as "Mr. Holliday." David sloughed it off with a laugh, but Judy was aware that it was a joke that could soon turn sour. So far, however, she had nothing to complain about in this area: David was a fine husband and their marriage was blissfully happy.

Fame had its benefits as well, one of them being the large number of offers Holliday started receiving from theater producers, all of them assuring her they had found exactly the right play for her return to Broadway. But her contractual commitment to Columbia made it unlikely that she would be able to appear on stage until the following year. She was due to return to Hollywood in the fall of 1951, and while Cohn had no project definitely set, he was determined to get a second Holliday picture into production before the tumult over

Born Yesterday had become a distant memory. There would be, he informed Holliday, no postponement of her next film.

There was no producer in New York who was prepared to build a show around Holliday only to have her withdraw two or three months after the opening. With one exception—the New York City Center Drama Company.

Along with the New York City Opera and Ballet (and, until 1948, the New York City Symphony, of which David had been a member), this organization was part of an adventuresome plan to present the best of the arts to the New York public at "popular prices." The City Center, a former Masonic temple, was roomy and acoustically sound, but ugly and inadequately designed for theater and opera productions. Still, it served its purpose and was to provide a blueprint for the grandiose and far more commercial Lincoln Center arts complex of the 1960s.

Each fall and spring, the City Center Drama Company presented a series of plays ranging from Shakespeare, Ibsen, and Shaw to revivals of popular successes of more recent vintage— Sherwood, Kaufman and Hart, Rodgers and Hammerstein. Each production ran for fifteen performances, and each featured at least a couple of Broadway or Hollywood stars who worked at the minimum Actors Equity scale—$50 a week. Despite the coolie wages, a fair share of stars did appear at City Center, some because they were given a chance at a role they had always wanted to play, others because they had no other offers: This was the beginning of the blacklist era, and City Center was a haven for those performers who were otherwise unemployable because of alleged left-wing political affiliation.

City Center had approached Holliday about appearing in one of its productions even before she took the Oscar for *Born Yesterday*, but Judy was then unavailable due to prior obligations—not, she emphasized, because she felt superior to City Center or because she did not sympathize with its goals. So, in the spring of 1951, when the company again in-

vited her to star in one of its productions for a two-week run,
Judy readily accepted, cautioning, however, that the arrangement was provisional until she and the City Center board of
directors had agreed on the choice of the play.

One of the first suggestions was *Peg o' My Heart*. Holliday
wanted no part of it. Written in 1911, it was charming, but
dated; it would require her to affect an Irish brogue, which
she wasn't at all sure she could manage; and worst of all, she
would be placing herself in direct comparison with the late
Laurette Taylor, who had created the role of Peg and was one
of Judy's idols (watching Taylor's Amanda in *The Glass
Menagerie*, Holliday later said, "was one of the greatest experiences of my life"). Other suggestions included *Dulcy*,
Rain, *They Knew What They Wanted*, and *The Late Chris-
topher Bean*. Judy rejected them all. "Each role was either a
prostitute or a scatterbrain," she told an interviewer. "I want
to do something different."

What she wanted to do was Elmer Rice's *Dream Girl*—the
play for which she had unsuccessfully auditioned five years
previously, during the difficult stretch between *Kiss Them for
Me* and *Born Yesterday*. As the play required a large cast and
an elaborate production, the City Center board of directors
was not thrilled by Judy's decision; but when she implied that
it would be *Dream Girl* or nothing, they decided to defer to
her choice.

There are several reasons why Holliday selected this sweet-
natured, moderately engaging, but distinctly minor comedy
for her return to the New York stage. The leading role was
showy without being overly demanding, and Judy was hesitant to take on a complex piece of characterization when the
City Center budget allowed for only a scant three weeks of
rehearsals. Most important of all, Rice's dream girl had nothing in common with Billie Dawn. Georgina Allerton is a
college-eduated, high-principled (almost priggish) young
woman, nearly overwhelmed by her sense of self-importance
and responsibility. To escape occasional moments of doubt

and feelings of inadequacy, Georgina takes refuge in a fantasy world where she sees herself as the Virgin Mother (of twins), a murderess, a scarlet lady, and a great Shakespearean actress. Eventually, a straight-shooting sportswriter makes her own up to the truth—she's an intelligent, loving, and lovable kid with no particular talent that would ever set her apart from the thousands of other girls riding the Manhattan subway in search of fame and identity. As compensation for abandoning her dreams of glory, Georgina weds the sportswriter and is just about to consummate the marriage as the final curtain descends. It's supposed to be a happy ending, but if the sports-writer is meant to be a prize, he's definitely of the booby variety.

Shortly before the City Center opening of *Dream Girl*, Holliday told a *New York Post* interviewer that she had always longed to play Georgina Allerton. But while it is possible— as the interviewer blithely assumed—that she wanted to show that she could handle a part she had formerly lost to another actress, it seems likely that she was drawn to the role for more personal reasons. Judy found something of herself in Georgina, and later she would be attracted to roles that were variations of Rice's dream heroine, most notably Gladys Glover in *It Should Happen to You* and Ella Peterson in *The Bells Are Ringing* (both parts created expressly for her by people who knew her well). She liked playing characters who wouldn't settle for being ordinary, who struggled to live their lives as responsibly and creatively as possible.

Holliday went into rehearsals with what was for her an un-usual amount of confidence. Playing the sportswriter, Don De Fore, a negligible Hollywood leading man, headed an otherwise first-class supporting cast, and the production was under the supervision of a talented and affable Broadway neo-phyte, Morton DaCosta (later to make his mark as director of *Auntie Mame* and *The Music Man*). Judy had very definite ideas about the part: There was not to be a single gesture or intonation suggesting Billie Dawn, and each of Georgina's fantasies was to be played in a contrasting theatrical style. (Holliday was determined to bring none of Billie Dawn's brassiness to the prostitute sequence; instead, she played it with bittersweet elegance, a tone suggested by the torch songs sung by Helen Morgan and Ruth Etting on old recordings.)

Judy had always been exceptionally quick at picking up blocking and stage business, a knack that proved to be particularly advantageous on this production, which was unusually complex in terms of movement and quick changes of costumes and wigs (many of which had to be executed during split-second blackouts). The technical side of the role presented no problems, but the rehearsal period was so brief that Judy, a slow study in this sphere of acting, was still working her way into the character of Georgina when the play opened on May 9, 1951.

The reviews the next day were generally favorable, but noticeably restrained in their appraisal of Holliday's performance. The only outright piece of adverse criticism came from Elliott Norton of the *Boston Post*, which then carried weekend summaries of important Broadway openings. Norton felt Holliday's performance was "broad" and lacked "mastery over the use of her body as a medium of dramatic expression." It was a peculiar remark as Holliday's movements were both flexible and expressive, although—and perhaps this was what Norton wanted to suggest in a gentlemanly way—she was twenty pounds over her ideal weight and far too hefty for Georgina, who was frequently described as slender to a fault.

Several reviewers advised readers they should not expect to hear Holliday speaking with Billie Dawn's voice, and many people were disappointed to discover that what the reviewers promised was true. Judy was justifiably annoyed. "I couldn't use the same voice even if I wanted to," she explained shortly after the premiere. "I'm not playing a dumb blonde in *Dream Girl*—Georgina's a girl who's had much more cultural and educational advantages than Billie Dawn. And I'm playing her in my own normal voice, presuming it is a normal voice...."

(The undertones of yearning and loneliness that were characteristic of Judy's professional voice were missing from her private conversation. Otherwise there wasn't much difference between her on- and off-stage voices.) Other than this, Judy took the lukewarm reception in stride; she recognized that she had a way to go before she was in control of the part.

On the strength of Holliday's name, the City Center run of *Dream Girl* was virtually sold out before it opened, and there were offers from several Broadway producers to move the show to Broadway for an extended engagement. Holliday's Columbia commitment made this impossible, which was regrettable since her performance became stronger with each appearance. Therefore, when a summer-stock entrepreneur asked Holliday if she'd like to take the show on the straw-hat circuit for a few weeks before returning to Hollywood, she said she might if the terms were attractive. She was then represented by Abe Lastfogel at William Morris, who passed along the deal to his brightest lieutenant, Hillard Elkins.

Elkins's conditions were to make summer-stock history. For a three-week tour, Holliday received $5,000 advance plus fifty percent of the gross, out of which she would contribute $4,000 for script rights and partial reimbursement to actors, director, and technical personnel hired for the tour. These terms raised violent protests from all the stock managers, but the tour, as Elkins had promised, was a bonanza for everyone: In three weeks, the show grossed over $55,000 and Holliday pocketed nearly $23,000. And as she went along, her performance got stronger and more polished.

There were several cast changes for the stock tour, including Marian Seldes, who took over the role of Georgina's girlfriend. Seldes was an acting student when she first saw Holliday in *Kiss Them for Me*, and instantly she became a fan. Now every night she stood backstage and watched Holliday at work. "*Studied* her, really," Seldes recalls, "because when you see what seems *real* on stage, it is so rare and so important you have to try to learn how it's done."

Seldes's description of what she learned backstage at *Dream Girl* is perhaps the most thoughtful analysis of Holliday's creative process as an actress:

"She knew her lines exactly. She never varied. What she did to keep her performance fresh was done within the limits of what she had rehearsed. Of course she used the reactions of the audience, but always intelligently. She included them in her work, but never misused their approval. This is, I feel, something she learned during the long run in *Born Yesterday*. By staying with the show and playing it so many times, she learned to repeat the *seemingly* improvised effects that were the hallmark of her acting—the swift changes of mood, that combination of vulnerability and strength that made the best of her characterizations so endearing."

Seldes and Holliday became friendly during the short tour. David joined her only for weekends, so for the most part Judy's only family companion was Helen. "Other cast members kind of giggled about that," Seldes remembers. "But Judy's relationship was strong and unsentimental. There was nothing of the stage mother about Helen. Judy was too sensible and Helen too unassuming for any of that." Judy was, Seldes says, very happy throughout the engagement. She seemed in total control of her life and content with the way it was going.

Just before the tour concluded, there were nibbles of interest from English producers about the possibility of Judy appearing in *Dream Girl* in London. Holliday rejected the offers peremptorily. Even if Columbia would allow her time off for a West End engagement, she couldn't face the prospect of a lengthy separation from David. The transcontinental partings were hardship enough, and another of them was looming on Judy's professional calendar.

Cohn and the Columbia experts had been thinking overtime about finding a new picture for Holliday, and the best they could come up with was a movie re-creation of the musical version of *Gentlemen Prefer Blondes*, then still running on Broadway with Carol Channing as Lorelei Lee, Anita Loos's diamond-happy flapper playgirl. It was all too easy to guess what was passing through the corporate Columbia mind: Here was another dumb blond who (as Carol Channing had amply demonstrated on stage) could be played successfully by an overweight comedienne without abundant sex appeal.

Much as she admired the show, Holliday was determined not to play Lorelei. But she never had to fight for her rights, since Columbia was outbid by Fox, who purchased the musical for its newest star, Marilyn Monroe.

In place of *Blondes*, Judy suggested to Cohn *Happy Birthday*, another Anita Loos play, which had enjoyed a lengthy Broadway run a few years earlier with Helen Hayes in the leading role of a spinsterish librarian (a kind of middle-aged version of Rice's Dream Girl) who goes on a binge one night and finds all her dreams coming true. As a film, the play presented censorship problems—it could be (and was) interpreted as an apology for alcoholism. Furthermore, Cohn's behind got a case of the premonitory itch every time he thought about a picture with a pickled old maid as its leading lady. But to keep Judy happy, Cohn announced that Columbia was negotiating for the rights to *Happy Birthday* as a future Holliday vehicle.

Though Cohn was now convinced that Holliday did have screen potential, he continued to refer to her as "that fat Jewish broad," and he wasn't at all sure how her potential should be developed. Judy's Slavic, peasant prettiness had no appeal for him and, since he regarded himself as the average filmgoer, he very much doubted that she would appeal to the general American public. For a time Columbia kept on trying to promote her as a glamour girl. She was given a high-fashion gloss for the photographers, bedecked in diamonds and furs and low-cut gowns, but the results were far from satisfactory: She merely looked uncomfortable and overdressed and vulgar.

Holliday didn't fit any of the conventional modes of Hollywood beauty: She wasn't the wholesome girl-next door like June Allyson or Jeanne Crain; she wasn't sleek and slinky like Lauren Bacall; she wasn't top-heavy like Jane Russell or a sexy come-on like Rita, Lana, and Ava; she wasn't an invitation to disaster like Crawford and Stanwyck. Her eyes and smile reminded some people of Turner; others caught a faint resemblance to Claire Trevor; and quite a few described her as the next Jean Arthur.

This last analogy made sense to Cohn—the talent and looks were similar, but there was one important difference: Arthur was average-pretty in a way that crossed state borders, while Holliday's average-prettiness was defined by a limited and very specific geographic locale—she was that nice girl from Queens, the Bronx, or Brooklyn who rode the subway to Manhattan each morning. The curse or distinction of the Revuers—call it what you will—still clung to Judy: She was thoroughly and unmistakably a New Yorker. And she was also unmistakably Jewish. It was not so much the way she looked or even the way she spoke—though in intonation she occasionally did sound like a third-generation Molly Goldberg—but some subtle quality made her heritage evident to anyone who, for whatever reason, concerned himself with such matters. And in the early Fifties many people *were* so concerned, and usually for the wrong reasons. The industry mentality that then ruled Hollywood therefore decreed that only comics and supporting players could be overtly Jewish, never the hero or heroine. Barbra Streisand would change all that—but in 1951, Streisand was nine years old.

What Columbia and Cohn resolved to do was to create a screen image for Holliday that would stress her averageness while removing the stigma of her ethnic origins: Never in any of her films did she play a character with a Jewish-sounding name. Subtly the public was urged to identify with her as one of themselves—a bit quirkier, perhaps; larger than life, certainly; but still, one of *us*.

The stratagem, however, was never executed precisely as

designed. Since Judy never bothered to play down her Jewishness, and since several of her screenwriters wrote dialogue that called for a Yiddish cadence to achieve the proper comic timing, her ethnic background is a subtle presence in all her characterizations. This worked both for and against Holliday: Often, it added tang to line readings; sometimes, however, in high dramatic moments, it made her sound like a budding yenta and reminded the audience of precisely what Columbia wanted them to forget.

There was an even more grievous drawback to this image: It was patently false and vaguely insulting to Holliday, who wasn't average either in intelligence or appearance. The tension between what she was and what she feigned to be gave a pleasing comic edge to her performances, but with time the joke became familiar and lost its point. There became something rather distasteful about watching Judy play women who were always so much cruder and less intelligent than herself.

It was Garson Kanin and Ruth Gordon who came up with the blueprint of Holliday's impersonation of Miss Average America, New York City Division. With Judy in mind, they were working on a screenplay called *The Marrying Kind*, which was an inversion of the plot of *Adam's Rib:* This time, the story centered on the unhappily married couple rather than their attorneys, and the couple—while unquestionably inspired by the Attingers of *Adam's Rib*—would be less caricatured and more sympathetically drawn. The story begins with Chet and Florence Keefer facing a woman judge, who asks them to reflect on their reasons for petitioning for a divorce. In a series of intricately structured flashbacks, the Keefers review the high and low spots of their marriage— this is the heart of the film—after which the judge again begs them to reconsider before she grants the final decree. It ends with Chet and Florence leaving the courtroom resolved to give it another try. Whether they will succeed is left to the audience to decide.

Judy liked the script, as did Cohn. It was funny and honest and a little off-center—the lower middle class had been ignored by the scriptwriters and producers of the postwar era. The Kanins had written Chet Keefer with Sid Caesar in mind —an idea that greatly appealed to Holliday—but Caesar's TV commitments made it impossible for him to accept the role. For both box-office and artistic reasons, Judy would have welcomed the support of a big-name leading man, but, once Caesar was out of the running, Cohn decided the part of Chet should go to Aldo Ray, a Columbia contract player who was then being groomed for stardom. Aldo DaRe had been a California constable before his screen debut in a Columbia football picture, *Saturday's Heroes*. The film had been designed to make John Derek a star, but it was DaRe, provisionally renamed Ray, who got all the fan mail. Cohn tried to force Fred Zinnemann to cast Ray as Prewitt in the Columbia production of *From Here to Eternity*, but Zinnemann insisted on Montgomery Clift. So as compensation, Cohn cast Ray as Chet Keefer, a role more suited to his abilities as an untrained actor.

For a while Cohn considered changing DaRe/Ray's name to John Harrison,* but Ray was so patently plebeian that it seemed pointless to straddle him with such an upper-crust name. He was a big strapping man with crew-cut blond hair and a raspy, blue-collar voice. His expression didn't suggest submerged depths of native intelligence; in fact, he was the perfect male complement of the dumb, Billie Dawn side of Holliday's screen personality. Casting them as man and wife made for a very clever visual joke.

George Cukor, who directed the film, recalls that Judy was impressed by the speed with which Ray picked up the basic techniques of comic acting, but friends say she had nothing

---

* Cohn's sons were named John and Harrison. Ray didn't much like the alias, but he was touched by Cohn's gesture in allowing him to assume his heirs' names.

very good to say about the actor. Ray and Paul Douglas headed her list of least favorite costars, and for much the same reason: Just as Douglas was too much like Harry Brock, Ray was too close to the beer-guzzling, thickheaded Chet Keefer to suit her taste. Even years later, the mere mention of Ray's name was enough to start the invective flying.

Like most of Holliday's films, *The Marrying Kind* was set in New York, and several scenes required location shooting. Starting at the end of August 1951, two weeks were spent filming around Manhattan in such locales as the Court of Domestic Relations on East 22nd Street, the Wollman Memorial in Central Park, Stuyvesant Town, and the Port Authority Bus Terminal. Then the *Marrying Kind* company, headed by George Cukor, moved to California. Since Judy was to be there for about ten weeks, her business manager encouraged her to buy a house, but she refused to make any long-term commitment to a place she could never call home. She insisted on retaining her transient status, and, from here on, managed to borrow houses belonging to friends for her West Coast visits.

The Marrying Kind had been designed as a showcase for the full range of Judy's talents. While essentially a comedy, it also contained dramatic scenes, a few of which required her to run the gamut of emotions from farce to despair. The most difficult—and most admired—segment of the film centered on the death of the Keefers' young son, Joey, during a summer outing. The boy and his sister run off to swim in a lake, and Holliday, feeling almost giddy from this momentary relaxation of parental pressure, picks up a ukelele and starts to strum and sing an old Frank Sinatra song, "Dolores." Just as she is finishing the refrain, strangers rush forward to tell her Joey has drowned. The scene as written pushes hard for an easy emotional response, and keeping it honest required a great deal of delicacy and tact from Holliday.

The relationship between Judy and George Cukor continued to build on the goodwill established during *Adam's Rib* and *Born Yesterday*. But Cukor was not so easy on Judy. Just as the sportswriter in *Dream Girl* kept telling Georgina she must stop fantasizing about what "might be" and start dealing with what "is," so Cukor continued telling Holliday she must stop dreaming about writing and directing and start accepting the fact that she was a gifted actress. More than accept it, she should take *joy* in her talent.

This time something clicked, and she realized that what he was saying was true. Less than a year before, she had told an interviewer that "acting isn't a proper career for a serious-minded person," but after *The Marrying Kind* she did an abrupt about-face. "Suddenly I realized that I really did want to be an actress," she told Gilbert Millstein of *The New York Times*. "I never admitted it before. . . . George Cukor had a lot to do with it." Some years later, while talking to Kenneth Tynan, Holliday elaborated. Tynan told her Katharine Hepburn had praised Cukor for his nurturing capabilities: " 'He makes you trust yourself. He maintains your illusion of yourself.' " Holliday laughed when Tynan read this to her. "He didn't *maintain* my illusion of myself—he *gave* me an illusion of myself."

After nearly every take, Cukor told her she was wonderful, but Judy would brush off the compliment with "You're a liar" or "Stop kidding me." Though Holliday worked hard at perfecting her performances, though she had won an Oscar and great acclaim, she still didn't see anything extraordinary about her talent; it was something she took for granted. Cukor had considerable experience in working with actresses who thought they were gifted and weren't, but never had he encountered the reverse phenomenon. He found it exasperating—he wanted to shake some sense into the girl. Instead, he resorted to less-violent measures. He talked about all the great actors he had seen or worked with, and as he chattered, he made it abundantly clear that Judy was a rightful member of this fraternity. In time, Holliday finally did see herself in this light—Cukor had succeeded in giving her an illusion of who she was, and of what she might be.

Working with him was such an exciting and creative process that Judy began to recognize the personal pleasure to be discovered in the technical process of acting. He was very demanding—that was one of the reasons Holliday came to believe him when he said she was wonderful—but his high expectations were one of the reasons he was such an invigorating collaborator. He wasn't an analytic or didactic director, but instead guided his actors through subtle suggestion. He'd give a helpful hint and expect the actor to pick up on it; and since the hints were often so inspired, the actor felt a sense of liberation in following them. Cukor also knew enough not to interfere when an actor was working brilliantly on his/her own inspiration: "Then all you do is stand back and edit," he said. He was the ideal director for Judy. He bolstered her morale, edited her whenever necessary ("Less, less," he'd comment), and stood back and admired most of the time. The films she made with him were the happiest professional experiences of her life.

Ironically, Holliday's acceptance of herself as an actress came at a time when her career was seriously jeopardized. This was the time when the Hollywood witch-hunts were reaching their peak, and for over two years Judy had been attacked by the conservative press for her left-wing activities. Near the end of 1951, she was subpoenaed to appear before a Senate committee investigating communist infiltration of American life. Judy was scared—the subpoena in itself was cause enough for Columbia to cancel her contract; and if that happened, she would certainly be blacklisted throughout Hollywood. With lightning clarity, she suddenly saw what acting really meant to her.

Chapter Ten
RED-BAITING

The House Un-American Activities Committee (familiarly known by the acronym HUAC) began investigating alleged communist infiltration of the film industry early in 1947. The movie colony's initial reaction was one of derisive amusement, but by the end of the year, when ten writers and directors were sentenced to prison for contempt of court, the snide remarks and laughter ceased. Goaded on by the Hearst papers, the conservative press turned on Hollywood, and their denunciations of the film industry as "a hotbed of communist propagandists" were taken seriously by a large segment of the general public.

To counteract the bad publicity, the studio moguls (or their deputies*) met at the Waldorf-Astoria in New York at the end of November 1947, and, after heated debate, issued the notorious Waldorf Statement in which they promised to rid themselves of any red devil lurking in their midst. "We will not," they promised, "knowingly employ a Communist or a member of any party or group which advocates the over-

* Harry Cohn was represented by his brother, Jack, who headed Columbia's New York operation.

throw of the Government of the United States by force or by any illegal or unconstitutional means."

By inserting the adverb "knowingly," the studios were trying to protect themselves against charges of collusion with alleged forces of communist infiltration, and at the same time they were also suggesting that they couldn't be blamed for what they didn't know. They promised to take action against any proven Communist, but they gave no indication that they were prepared to initiate investigations into their employees' political affiliations. And for a very good reason: Such investigation might well uncover incriminating evidence against a top moneymaking star, thereby forcing the studio to divest itself of a valuable asset.

There were, however, many organizations and individuals who were happy to do the work for the Hollywood studios. In June 1950, only a few days after President Truman turned the cold war warm by ordering armed intervention in Korea, three ex–FBI agents, egged on by the vigilantes in the American Federation of Radio Artists, issued an oversize pamphlet called *Red Channels*, a thick directory of entertainers and other radio and TV personnel whose political history suggested communist, progressive, or antifascist sympathies. (Being antifascist in the isolationist society of 1930s America was now viewed as an early form of subversive subterfuge, as was membership in early black-rights organizations, many of which were communist-backed.) *Red Channels* was distributed to every radio and television station in the industry and to all advertising agencies that handled network accounts. Within months of its publication, *Red Channels* became the basis for the most insidious blacklist in the history of the American entertainment industry. Anyone cited in its pages was virtually unemployable in the radio and TV field, and since many of the *Red Channels* personalities also worked in film, it followed that Hollywood would soon be forced to support the boycott.

Judy appeared in the *Red Channels* listings. So did Orson

Welles, Lena Horne, John Garfield, Garson Kanin, José
Ferrer, Charles Chaplin, Zero Mostel, Ben Grauer, and
Canada Lee. Many of the entertainers, as in this group, were
Jewish, black, or from some other ethnic minority. Jews, in
particular, were suspect, since so many of them were of
Russian or Middle-European stock, linked by heritage to
those countries that had been breeding grounds for twentieth-
century revolution. Behind the entertainment witch-hunts,
there were fears that went deeper than cold-war hysteria. The
angry core of it was American xenophobia, dormant during
the war years and now breaking out again with a vengeance.

At the time of initial distribution of *Red Channels*, Holliday was about to start work on the film version of *Born
Yesterday* and she felt relatively secure. But while in Hollywood, she was attacked by both Hedda Hopper and Louella
Parsons for her political past; and once the film had opened,
she was—as a newly arrived celebrity—a prime target for the
red-baiters. Shortly after Holliday won the best-actress nomination for *Yesterday*, Jimmy Tarantino, a lightweight, right-
wing columnist for the trade paper *Hollywood Life*, wrote an
exposé of several personalities, including Horne, Ferrer, Garfield, Chaplin, and Holliday. His dossier on Judy read as
follows:

JUDY HOLLIDAY, SINGER-ACTRESS . . . Holliday
is up for an "Oscar" for her work in "Born Yesterday."
. . . Judy only acts dumb. She's a smart cookie. . . . The
Commies got her a long time ago. . . . She was a singer
with the National Council of Arts and Sciences and
Professions, a Commie red front, which supported the
UN-Friendly Ten Hollywood writers who went to
jail. . . . Judy, in 1948, was a guest speaker during a rally
in the N.Y. Hotel Astor, for the STOP CENSORSHIP
COMMITTEE, a Communist front. . . . She was spon-
sor for the WORLD FEDERATION OF DEMO-
CRATIC YOUTH, a known Communist front. . . . In

1948, Holliday wired *greetings* of good luck and best wishes to the MOSCOW ART THEATRE. . . . She is a supporter of the CIVIL RIGHTS CONGRESS, a red outfit. . . . A few years ago, Judy performed free of charge at a dance and affair in the Hotel Capitol, N.Y.C., that was sponsored by the Commie Daily Worker. . . . Judy Holliday always knew what she was doing.

A few weeks later, Ferrer and Holliday were leading contenders in that year's Oscar contest, and when Ferrer got the award he made reference to the charges against him. "This means more to me than an honor as an actor," he said. "I consider it a vote of confidence and an act of faith and, believe me, I'll not let you down." Two months later he appeared before HUAC and swore that he was not then and never had been a Communist.

Holliday didn't have the opportunity to give her acceptance speech that night; but if she had, it's doubtful she would have taken the same tack. Though rumors were circulating, as yet she hadn't been subpoenaed, and it would have been foolish for her to call attention to what could still be passed off as right-wing gossip. Silence is sometimes the better part of valor; at the very least, it will pass for dignity—and to the world at large it did. "Of all of those who were harassed in the ugly days of *Red Channels* and blacklisting, no one was more steadfast or less craven than Judy," Garson Kanin recalls. "Her behavior under pressure was a poem of grace."

Judy maintained a veneer of calm, but when she was subpoenaed by Congress to discuss her political past, inside she was terrified. And with good reason. Holliday was to be investigated not by HUAC but by the Senate Internal Security Subcommittee, headed by the formidable Pat McCarran of Nevada. He was the author of the McCarran Internal Security Act—requiring the registration of all Communists and communist organizations, and establishing the Subversive

Activities Board to oversee "internal security emergencies" and the "detention of subversives."

McCarran's committee had made few excursions into what the senator considered the minor field of show business—he went after the big headlines by exposing communist infiltration of the military and the State Department. But in the spring of 1951 he lowered his sights and started looking toward Hollywood and Broadway. This was at approximately the same time McCarran was gathering support for a bill limiting the immigration of Eastern Europeans, and it was assumed that, by establishing that there was a susceptibility to communism among entertainers of Middle European background, McCarran was trying to prove and dramatize the necessity for passage of his pending legislation. Nearly everyone subpoenaed to testify before the McCarran Committee was Jewish. The best-known was Judy Holliday.

Holliday was in a vulnerable position. She had never been a member of the Communist party, but she was "guilty" of the actions mentioned by Tarantino (although "guilty" seems an inappropriate word for such an innocent act as wiring congratulations to the Moscow Art Theatre). There were many similar (and to the red-baiters equally incriminating) incidents in her past: Ever since her Revuers days, she had donated her time and name to many organizations, though since 1948 her schedule had precluded much participation in this area. Judy was not, however, a moving force behind any organization, nor was she much of a crusader. "She never mentioned politics to me," says Marian Seldes, "though I imagine we saw things pretty much from the same viewpoint." Other friends, who definitedly did not share her views, found her amenable to the policy of agreeing to disagree. She never pushed her beliefs on others.

Whether Holliday recognized that some of the organizations with which she had been associated were communist-backed or -infiltrated is not known. She was to plead innocence, but much of her testimony stretches the truth almost beyond the point of credibility. It had never been privileged information that many liberal organizations of the Thirties and Forties were communist-linked. At that time, however, there was no stigma attached to being a Communist or a Communist sympathizer—indeed, such allegiances carried an aura of intellectual chic. Certainly it was nothing that would have disturbed Holliday, who was in this regard a faithful granddaughter of Rachel Gollomb.

Judy's dilemma was this: She could truthfully answer that she was not and had never been a Communist, but, having said this, she could be forced to answer questions about the political faith of her friends, and if she refused to divulge this information, she could be cited for contempt of court. Moreover, since the McCarran group was primarily interested in the family history of the entertainers it was investigating, it seemed probable that Helen, Uncle Joe Gollomb, and many others would also come under discussion. How could she avoid implicating people she loved and respected and desperately wanted to protect?

The only way out was to refuse to answer any questions by pleading the Fifth Amendment at the outset. But "taking the Fifth" has generally been interpreted as a confession of guilt. If she went that route, her career in film, radio, and television would certainly be over. Even if she cooperated, the future looked bleak: The evidence against her, insubstantial though it was, could, with enough newsprint muscle behind it, convince the public that she was a red partisan. And that would be sufficient to keep her on the blacklist for years.

In an attempt to exonerate herself in the eyes of the press, Judy visited George Sokolsky, a columnist who was one of the more benign of the red-baiters. He listened to her story and then said he would consult with one of his colleagues— Westbrook Pegler, who was virulent, and obsessive in his exposés of the communist menace. Judy waited outside while Sokolsky talked to Pegler. An hour later, when Sokolsky emerged from the office, he shook his head. Pegler wasn't ready to buy Holliday's story of innocence.

Judy's friends rallied around her, offering advice, some good and some bad, but the pillar of strength she needed was found where she least expected to discover it—Harry Cohn and Columbia came to the rescue. The studio had been hard hit by the witch-hunts. Robert Rossen, writer/director of *All the King's Men*, and Larry Parks, star of *The Jolson Story*, had both appeared before HUAC as "friendly" witnesses, but their submissiveness had done little to redeem their reputations. Their professional lives were severely damaged by their testimony—Parks was virtually destroyed both as a man and as an actor.

"Crap!" had been Harry Cohn's initial comment about the blacklist. Though he had gone along with the Waldorf statement, Cohn had always believed his fellow moguls were cowardly dumkopfs. After what happened to Parks and Rossen, the mere mention of HUAC was enough to make him apoplectic. His outrage had more to do with business acumen than political conviction—valuable box-office properties were being led to slaughter just because they had been stupid enough to sign a petition or join a May Day parade some ten, fifteen years earlier. It was absurd. What, after all, did Larry Parks's performance as Al Jolson have to do with communism?

Cohn was determined Holliday wouldn't become another of the sacrificial lambs—she was too damned important to the studio. He had stayed out of the Parks affair—possibly because Parks's post-*Jolson* films had indicated that he didn't have the staying power of a real star—but Judy he was willing to support all the way. He put the Columbia legal team to work on Holliday's case, and his support—one of the few instances and possibly the *only* instance when a studio came to the support of a red-suspected star or player—was later to carry a lot of weight with the national press.

Columbia hired a distinguished attorney and former U.S.

district judge, Simon H. Rifkind, as Judy's legal representative. To prepare her for any questions the McCarran committee might ask, Rifkind and the Columbia attorneys decided to hire their own investigator to track down any piece of damaging evidence that could be used against her. The man chosen for this job was Kenneth Bierly, a former FBI agent who had done research work for *Counterattack*, an early publication unmasking communist influence in American corporations. Feeling that *Counterattack* and *Red Channels* had been misused to keep innocent people out of jobs, Bierly had a change of heart and began working to protect the people he had once helped to vilify. Bierly was a controversial figure; many people felt that he had switched sides only when he noticed that there was more money to be had on the other side of the fence. Still, he did his job well, and that was all that mattered to Cohn and Columbia. Unlike Parks, Judy was to be fully prepared for any curve the senators might throw in her direction.

Several of Holliday's friends urged her to be openly defiant before the committee, but Rifkind and the Columbia lawyers told her what she already knew—that anything less than a display of humble cooperation would amount to professional suicide. Cohn warned her (as he had Parks and other Columbia witnesses) to play it smart and, if necessary, to feign penitence. He stopped short of suggesting perjury, but it was clear that he couldn't fathom throwing away a career for anything as silly as a point of honor.

Judy was deeply troubled about the prospect of apologizing for acts that had been undertaken in good faith and from sincere conviction; but eventually she came to agree with Cohn, at least halfheartedly, that since the committee was a bad joke, the best way to handle the situation was to transform it into a good joke. The transformation, a crazy inversion of the truth, was brilliant. Judy had spent most of her career trying to extract herself from the image of the dumb blond, but now it could be put to use. The committee alleged that Judy had known exactly what she was doing when she got involved with various subversive groups. Jimmy Tarantino had called her "a smart cookie." Well, she would prove them wrong. She would give her final and maybe her best performance as Billie Dawn in a Washington, D.C., courtroom.

The Columbia attorneys informed the McCarran committee that Holliday would appear as a cooperative witness, and in return they requested two favors: first, that she not be asked to testify until after the opening of *The Marrying Kind*; and second, that the transcript of her testimony not be made public until a few months after that. The committee agreed to the first request, but they made no promises as to the second. The best they could guarantee was that Holliday's testimony would not be made public for several months.

When *The Marrying Kind* opened in New York in March 1952, the theater was picketed by members of the Catholic War Veterans, carrying placards that proclaimed JUDY HOLLIDAY IS THE DARLING OF THE DAILY WORKER and WHILE OUR BOYS ARE DYING IN KOREA, JUDY HOLLIDAY IS DEFAMING CONGRESS. The picture got nice reviews and grossed pretty well at the box office, but there were indications that it was not going to be a box-office bonanza like *Born Yesterday*.

Twelve days after the opening—March 26, 1952—accompanied by David, Helen, and her attorney, Judy entered a Washington courtroom to begin her testimony. She wore white gloves, a tastefully draped black dress, and a small, veiled hat—the kind of outfit Billie Dawn might have worn in a similar situation: provocative but ladylike. She looked composed, but was, she later admitted, scared to death. She had come prepared with a coverall refutation, which was read into the record as her closing remark: "I am not a member of the Communist party. I never was a member of the Communist party; I am not a subversive; and I have never associated with any movement known to me to be subversive. I am opposed to communism. I resent its threat to our existence."

Holliday was questioned mainly by Richard Arens, the committee's counsel, with occasional interjections by Arthur Watkins, a Republican senator from Utah. Arens led off by asking if the Revuers had entertained at parties given by the United American-Spanish Aid Committee.* Holliday said she couldn't remember, the group had played so many benefits. . . .

Arens next asked if she had ever been a sponsor for the Committee for the Negro in the Arts.** Judy smiled. "That is something I looked into last summer. As you can understand, my employers, Columbia Pictures, were very much disturbed about all the things that have been happening and coming up and they investigated me—"

With incredulity, Arens broke in to ask if he had heard correctly—did she say Columbia had *paid* someone to investigate her? Oh, yes, Judy replied, and with her agreement and cooperation. She had been eager to learn of any past indiscretion that could be held against her. Now, as for the Negro Arts Committee, she remembered nothing about it. One of Cohn's investigators had confronted her with a letterhead with her name listed as sponsor, and still she could recall nothing—maybe her name had been used without her consent.

Arens then asked if she had not participated, in 1946, in a strike action against the docking of a ship out of Franco's Spain. Judy looked vague. Arens, referring to a newspaper snapshot, tried to refresh her memory by asking her a leading question: "Were you wearing a bathing suit?"

Judy answered in a roundabout manner: "It was cold."

"Did you make any inquiry with respect to who was striking or why they were striking? . . . Did any of your friends ask you to have that picture taken?" Arens asked.

---

* This was one of many groups formed to support the Republicans against the falangists during the Spanish Civil War.

** This organization had been founded to stimulate job opportunities for blacks in the arts, particularly the theater, and to negotiate between them and managers who sought to hire them for substandard pay.

"Well, somebody asked me. . . . They must have, because I wouldn't wander off over to strikers and ask to have my picture taken," she responded.

At this point, Watkins entered the conversation. "It seems to me that a person in your profession has to have a trained memory."

Holliday, who was noted for her gift of almost total recall, now adjusted the facts to fit the present emergency. "Well, I'm getting one," she replied, "but I didn't know I needed one. Now I am so careful that I don't side on anything and I don't answer anything. I have answering services saying that I am not in. I didn't know I would have to have that kind of memory."

Behind the dumb-blond facade, Judy could occasionally be heard speaking her own mind, though always obliquely. Asked if she had sent a telegram to Thomas Dewey, then governor of New York, about the pistol-carrying mob who had disrupted an outdoor concert by Paul Robeson in Peekskill, New York, she said she had. But, she quickly added, she did not personally know Robeson, a self-proclaimed friend of the USSR. "I said that there should have been police protection for those who were not armed." Questioned about the picketing of the Catholic War Veterans against *The Marrying Kind*, Holliday upheld their right to express themselves: "It's better than their stewing around subterraneanly."

Predictably, Arens then moved on to the sphere of questioning that Judy had been dreading the most—the political activities of her friends. And it was here that Judy may have perjured herself. "Did you not have any friends who were Communists?" he asked.

"Never."

"Alvin Hammer, however, refused to testify before the House Un-American Activities Committee as to whether or not he was a Communist."

"That is correct," Judy admitted, but, she explained, he had never discussed his politics with her.

Did she know that Comden and Green had Communist-front records? She denied it. Are you sure? Arens insisted. "I am as sure of that as I am of anybody who isn't me," Judy responded. Tessa? Judy had been informed by her investigators that Tessa was a Communist, but she couldn't believe that her friend was anything but "the most blameless, the most patriotic and honest creature that I know." Her uncle Joe Gollomb? "True," she said, "but he had broken with the Communist party around 1941 and had been rabidly anti-Communist ever since."

Arens then switched gears. "Do you know the Communist-front record of Thomas Mann?" he asked. By introducing this topic, Arens may have been hoping to catch Holliday off guard and get her to admit that she was familiar with Mann, his works, and activities (which she was), and thereby prove she wasn't as dumb as she pretended.

But Judy remained cool. "How could I know about Mann's record?" she replied.

"And Mr. Albert Einstein," Arens shot back, "do you know the Communist-front record he has?"

Judy dismissed the whole issue with delicious, Billie Dawn-like illogic. "Then I am sure that Mann and Einstein [and the others], got into it the way I did, because I am sure none of them are Communists. I mean if you are a Communist, why go to a Communist front. Why not be a Communist? Whatever you are, be it!"

"Whatever you are, be it!" If this avowal was a genuine *cri de coeur*, a veiled and painful admission that on this particular day she had not been able to be what she really was —and certainly it reads that way—the message was far too subtle for her investigators. By the time the hearing was reaching its close, it became clear that Watkins had taken very kindly to Holliday. He said to her in a paternal voice, "Well, I guess you've learned to watch it now, haven't you?" In her best Billie Dawn delivery, Judy responded, "Ho, ho!

Have I ever! Now I don't say yes to anything except cancer, polio, and cerebral palsy!"

The pink haze that had hung over Judy's name lost some of its blush after her performance in Washington, but it did not entirely fade. For a year or so, the TV and radio broadcasting companies kept her on the blacklist, and she was to receive a considerable number of hate phone calls and letters. (Eventually, she was forced to remove her name and address from the New York telephone directory.) When, in September 1952, the McCarran committee released the transcript of her testimony, she was worked over by the right-wing press, a particularly vehement denunciation coming from Victor Riesel, a syndicated Hearst columnist. Riesel wrote:

> This is to let Hollywood's Oscar-winning blonde, Judy Holliday, know that we weren't born yesterday. . . . Had she gone to Screen Actors Guild sessions in Hollywood she would have learned from Ronnie Reagan and other officers just what Communist infiltration meant . . . she says, in effect, she was played for a sucker. . . . Now she's free to resume her career. There will be no demonstration against her. She has denounced the Stalinist world. But what will [she] do for the world besmirched by those [like her] who lent their name as they would to casual endorsements of toothpaste? They owe the world of decency a debt. . . . Let them speak out. Now!

After the publication of her testimony, Judy felt guilty about betraying those friends who had taken a belligerent stand before the congressional committees and who had urged her to do the same. Her apologies sounded lame even to herself, but she was able to find some consolation in her awareness that she had incriminated no one and had managed to protect everyone as best she could—she had named no names and survived the inquests without the penitent cries of "mea culpa" that pervaded the statements of such witnesses as Larry Park and Clifford Odets or Elia Kazan (judging from the small portion of Kazan's testimony that has been made public).

Most of Judy's friends told her to forget it, all was forgiven, she had made a joke out of the McCarran committee and the other witch-hunters, and maybe that was the best way to handle them. *Variety*, which has always been starchily conservative, appreciated the joke, as did the *New York Post* and other liberal publications that recognized Holliday's charade for what it was and gleefully pointed out that, by playing dumb, Holliday had outsmarted Arens, Watkins, and company.

Though Judy's political views were to remain liberal, she kept them very much to herself. She was never to campaign for any candidate, never to discuss world events in any of her interviews. She had promised the McCarran Committee that henceforth she wouldn't endorse anything except "cancer, polio, and cerebral palsy," but she was better than her promise: In the years ahead, about the only things she endorsed were beer and airplane companies. This might be condemned as cowardly or dishonorable, but American society in the 1950s was staunchly conservative, and if Judy wanted to survive professionally, she was obliged to remain silent. The one positive experience of her brush with the witch-hunters was that she survived it with a new perspective on her life: Her career, she now knew, was terribly important to her.

The Revuers around the time of their initial success (1939). Left to right: Adolph Green, Betty Comden, Alvin Hammer, Holliday, and John Frank. (Culver Pictures, Inc.)

The young Judith Tuvim (later known as Holliday), in 1940, doing one of the NBC Blue Network radio broadcasts of "Fun with the Revuers." This is one of the earliest professional portraits of Judy without her fellow Revuers. The press release says, " . . . at age nine her parents took her to Paris where she learned French from a governess . . . " The Revuers frequently provided fanciful biographies for the press. (Culver Pictures, Inc.)

Judy in 1945, at the time of her appearance in *Kiss Them for Me*. (Courtesy Museum of Modern Art Film/Stills Archive)

Paul Douglas (as Harry Brock) and Judy (as Billie Dawn) in the 1946 stage version of *Born Yesterday*. The stars seem to be having a quiet and pensive moment here, but actually Holliday disliked Douglas nearly as much as Billie disliked Harry. (Culver Pictures, Inc.)

Judy Holliday at her wedding to David Oppenheim on January 4, 1948. (Culver Pictures, Inc.)

Billie gets smart. Here, she is falling for William Holden's horn-rims in the film version of *Born Yesterday* (1950). (Courtesy Museum of Modern Art Film/Stills Archive)

Academy Award night at La Zambra. Judy with (from left to right) José Ferrer, Gloria Swanson, and Celeste Holm. (Courtesy Museum of Modern Art Film/Stills Archive)

Helen Tuvim and Judy in the early 1950s. One of their closest bonds was their mutual enjoyment of music. (United Press International)

On location for *The Marrying Kind* (1952). George Cukor (gesturing) directs Aldo Ray and Holliday in the scene leading to the death of the Keefers' son. (Courtesy Museum of Modern Art Film/Stills Archive)

Judy overhauled by the Columbia beauty experts. (Courtesy Museum of Modern Art Film/Stills Archive)

Judy and Jonathan in 1953.
(Courtesy Museum of Modern
Art Film/Stills Archive)

It Should Happen to You
(1954). Jack Lemmon and
Holliday are about to break into
a chorus of "Let's Fall in Love."
(Courtesy Museum of Modern
Art Film/Stills Archive)

Peter Lawford and Holliday at Ciro's in 1954. They were then, according to the gossip columnists, "Hollywood's newest duo." (Courtesy Museum of Modern Art Film/Stills Archive)

Sydney Chaplin and Holliday singing "Just in Time" in the stage version of *Bells Are Ringing* (1955). For a time, their off-stage relationship was nearly as exuberant as the gleeful shenanigans pictured here. (Courtesy New York Public Library)

Sydney Chaplin as he appeared in *Four Girls in Town* (1957). The film was being shot at the time Chaplin first met Holliday. (Courtesy Museum of Modern Art Film/Stills Archive)

Judy and Gerry Mulligan during the filming of *Bells Are Ringing* (1960). Gerry is holding sheet music for one of the songs they wrote together. (United Press International)

Chapter Eleven

A DELICATE BALANCE

Mercifully, Judy had one consolation to help her through the worst days preceding her appearance before the McCarran committee. Only a few weeks earlier, she had learned that she was pregnant. She and David were thrilled; both wanted children, and the timing was just about perfect. It meant, of course, that Judy wouldn't be available to make a film in 1952, and therefore would be off the screen until sometime in 1954, but even Harry Cohn had to agree that this wasn't such a bad idea: By then the public would have had time to absorb—and forget—Holliday's problems with the red-baiters. Judy's delicate condition was, indeed, a perfect excuse for lying low, refusing interviews, and just generally staying out of the spotlight.

Her condition was, in truth, not so very delicate. She felt fine for most of the pregnancy, and what complications she did encounter were to be of a strictly nonphysiological nature. Once it became known that she was expecting a child, she started receiving letters cursing her with the malevolent wish that her child be born dead or deformed. Most of the hate mail was inspired by her congressional appearance and written by women whose sons had died or been wounded in Korea. Naturally, it disturbed Judy deeply. Eventually, however, David or Helen would destroy such letters before Judy could read them.

Otherwise, Judy serenely passed the days doing the things she loved the most—staying close to David, reading, doing crosswords or Double-Crostics, and playing Scrabble, a new game in the 1950s and one to which she became immediately addicted. For a while she played at knitting and crocheting booties and other garments, but quickly gave it up. As she should have learned way back in junior high school when she had problems finishing an apron for her home economics class, she had no gift for any form of needlework. She left the crocheting to friends and bought the rest of the baby's layette at Best and Company. Judy loved to shop, usually for bargains, but she wanted only the finest for her child.

By nature Judy was a maternal person, though so far this trait had remained latent, expressed only in her devotion to Helen, whom she often protected as though their roles had been reversed: she the mother, Helen the child. In dealing with Helen in this way, Judy was possibly satisfying unconscious urges within herself. With the birth of her child, when her maternal instincts were unleashed, this trait began to color all her relationships: It crept into her romantic involvements and was to be a major factor in her support of and generosity to many young actors and singers, who were nearly overwhelmed by her encouragement and enthusiasm.

Judy had no trouble during her pregnancy—no morning sickness, just an exceptionally hearty appetite. Her doctor kept cautioning her about taking on excessive weight; but by the ninth month, Judy had ballooned to 190 pounds.

On November 11, 1952, Judy gave birth to a son, Jonathan Lewis Oppenheim, at Doctors Hospital, one of the most prestigious New York hospitals. The patients, by a considerable majority, belonged to the worlds of show business or big money. The private rooms were larger than most single-occupancy rooms at a luxury hotel, and the staff conveniently ignored the amount of champagne and caviar that was carried in as get-well gifts. Judy's postnatal convalescence would have been a lovely vacation except—as her doctor had warned might happen—she now had to face up to the fact that she hadn't shed a lot of weight following Jonathan's birth. Tipping the scales at 172, she was forced to leave the hospital dressed in the same maternity clothes she had worn when she had checked in.

But this indignity was swiftly forgotten in the pleasure of taking Jonathan home and taking care of him. Helen seemed absolutely thrilled by her grandson, and her reaction was glad tidings to Holliday, since her mother had shown signs of distress when she learned of the pregnancy. She had reacted almost as though the unborn child could be a sibling rival— indeed, according to one unverified report, Helen came close to a nervous collapse at this time.

One of the methods psychiatrists suggest for handling sibling rivalry is to give the older child a sense of responsibility toward the younger—and, on her own, this is precisely what Judy did. Involving Helen made her feel important, and she quickly responded to the therapy. It was good for Judy, too; it gave her time to be alone and plan for the future.

The Greenwich Village apartment was too cramped for the three Oppenheims, plus Helen, who often stayed over in the spare bedroom, sometimes for weeks at a time. And now that they would have to cope with baby carriages and strollers, they started to feel the inconvenience of living in a walk-up apartment. They needed a bigger place in an elevator building.

Judy and David searched for several weeks before they heard of a vacancy at the historic Dakota Apartments at 72nd Street and Central Park West. New York City's first luxury apartment building, the Dakota had been a haven for artists and theater people since its construction in 1884, and among the tenants in the Fifties and early Sixties—roughly the period of Holliday's occupancy—were José Ferrer and his wife, Rosemary Clooney; Zachary Scott and Ruth Ford; Boris Karloff; set designer Jo Mielziner; playwright Sidney Kingsley; fashion columnist Eugenia Sheppard; Lauren Bacall and Jason Robards. Chief among the Dakota's many virtues were its security system* and its large apartments with spacious rooms, high ceilings, and elegant detail: wood paneling, etched glass, imposing entrance halls. Best of all, perhaps, were the rents. When the building had opened, a seven-room apartment rented for $500, and there had been only minimal increases since then. Nowhere, in the 1950s, were so many rooms to be had for so little. Price was important to Judy. While not exactly tight, neither did she approve of indulgent expenditures.

The Oppenheims' apartment was on the seventh floor of the Dakota and consisted of seven rooms plus baths. The entrance hall had a checkerboard marble floor and two oak-and-smoked-glass doors with polished brass trim. The living room was paneled in mahogany and contained a marble fireplace, as did the dining room. The latter was so large that it amply held a couch and two easy chairs as well as all their dining furniture. Judy took care with the decoration, choosing Early American and Victorian pieces, including—this was one of her rare impracticalities—a very fine horsehair and bentwood sofa that was meant to be admired, not sat on, though occasionally Judy would perch on its edge for photographers.

Judy decided she'd have a real holiday while recovering from Jonathan's birth—not that there was much to recover from; she felt absolutely splendid. The Oppenheims hired a nurse to attend Jonathan along with Helen, so they were free

* This may seem a strange statement considering that John Lennon was killed at the Dakota in 1981. However, in the 1950s, before adulation was expressed through violence, the Dakota was noted for the protection it offered its celebrity tenants.

most evenings to do as they pleased. They went to the theater many times, seeing, among other shows, *The Seven Year Itch* (written by one of their friends, George Axelrod) and Katharine Hepburn in Shaw's *The Millionairess*, a London success that had fared less happily on Broadway. Judy visited Hepburn backstage and told her how shabbily she felt the New York critics had treated the play and Kate's performance. A month or so later she attended Rosalind Russell's opening in *Wonderful Town*, a musical version of *My Sister Eileen* with a score by Leonard Bernstein, Adolph Green, and Betty Comden. Judy adored it; in fact, she was somewhat envious that it was Russell, not she, in the leading role.

There were also concert evenings, including one in which David was a featured soloist. The performance was fine, but the evening left Judy apprehensive. At a reception afterward, the guests clustered about, congratulating her for David's contribution. "Please tell *him*," she said softly. "Don't tell me." David took this in stride, but Judy was certain that there must be a simmering and possibly growing resentment beneath the facade of indifference.

Judy's theatergoing revived her interest in returning to the stage. Not that her interest had ever really flagged, but no play had come along that seemed appropriate. Now, however, she did come across a script that had possibilities. It was called *My Aunt Daisy* and had been sent to her by John S. Wilson, an elegant playboy who had been Noel Coward's lover, the husband of a princess, and a Broadway entrepreneur who presented plays written by or starring Coward, Terence Rattigan, Cole Porter, Jean Cocteau, Tallulah Bankhead, Gertrude Lawrence, and the Lunts. *Vogue* once described him as "Shubert Alley's only resident mandarin," and while Holliday was duly impressed by his invitation (Cukor had told her she belonged to the great stage aristocracy, and this seemed verification of his avowal), she wasn't so dazzled that she lost her critical abilities. She liked the script, but felt it needed revision—and anyway, she wasn't free to commit herself at this time; Harry Cohn wanted her back in Hollywood as soon as possible.

As in the past, there was much indecision as to what she was going to do once she got there. *Happy Birthday*, which had briefly been scheduled as her third Columbia picture, had been postponed due to "script problems." For a time there was talk of remaking *My Sister Eileen*, the film rights of the original play being owned by Columbia, but that was shelved while Cohn debated about bidding for the rights to *Wonderful Town*. He couldn't decide whether to spend a tidy fortune for the score by Bernstein, Green, and Comden, or to start from scratch and create his own musical version of *Eileen*.

On one point, however, Cohn was not to waver: Holliday's next film had to be a lot stronger than *The Marrying Kind*, which, as the early returns had indicated, wasn't to wind up as a box-office champion. It wasn't, however, a financial or popular flop: People went to see it, most of them enjoyed it, and a few found it very special. Its reputation has, if anything, grown over the years. Feminists admire it because it is Florence Keefer, not Chet, who walks out the door and demands breathing space to think things out—*A Doll's House* revisited perhaps, but nonetheless real progress in terms of movie history. Social-conscious commentators also have good words for *The Marrying Kind*, singling it out as one of the few 1950s movies that dealt intelligently with lower-middle-class American life. But for the typical moviegoer of the time, the characters and settings seemed terribly drab for all the pungency of Kanin and Gordon's dialogue and the sympathy with which they drew the Keefers.

For her next vehicle, Cohn and his Columbia assistants wanted a story that would present Judy in a more entertaining, enhancing way. There was nothing wrong with her staying Miss Average New York—but not *too* average. There was very little glamour in being average. And no romance. That was one of the problems with *The Marrying Kind;* there had been too few romantic interludes.

Still, they had no idea where they would find the right kind of picture until Garson Kanin came along with another script. It had started out as a vehicle for Danny Kaye, but, on reading an outline, Ruth Gordon said, "Sounds like a Holliday property to me." Kanin ignored the comment, but after plotting out a few scenes, he, too, realized that his central character should be female and that the script was ideal for Holliday.

A Name for Herself—or *It Should Happen to You,* as it was later titled—was the story of Gladys Glover, a young woman whose ambition exceeds her talent. Unable to make any headway in the entertainment world, she spends all her savings on leasing a Columbus Circle billboard and covers it with gigantic letters spelling out GLADYS GLOVER. Like Rula Lenska in the 1970s, Gladys becomes an instant celebrity because everyone passing through Columbus Circle asks, "Who the hell is Gladys Glover?"

The film was a flash forward to an era when Andy Warhol could say "Everybody has a right to be a celebrity for at least five minutes" and pass as an astute social commentator. Kanin was there before Warhol, but after some perfunctory overbroad comment on how Gladys is manipulated by the mass media, the picture begins to concentrate on Glover's inability to choose between two suitors. One is a documentary-film maker who keeps telling Gladys she's making a fool of herself, the other a suave, slick, sweet-talking media executive who sees Gladys as a profitable short-term client and playmate. At the end, Gladys predictably gives up the billboards, commercials, and TV appearances for marital bliss with the cameraman.

Like so many of Garson Kanin's scripts, including *Born Yesterday,* this one has its roots in the screwball comedies of the 1930s, which featured a larkish, often batty heroine (usually played by Claudette Colbert, Irene Dunne, or Carole

Lombard) who carried on outlandishly and often unscrupu-
lously before being semidomesticated by the likes of Fredric
March, Joel McCrea, or Fred MacMurray. *It Should Happen
to You* is particularly indebted to *True Confession* and *Nothing Sacred*, in each of which the heroine attains overnight
celebrity because of a singularly unattractive trait: In *True
Confession*, she's a pathological liar; in *Nothing Sacred*, she
publicizes a false diagnosis that she's dying of radium poison-
ing. Both roles were played by Carole Lombard, and it took
all her considerable beauty and talent to make them appealing.

Gladys Glover is pretty much the same sort of character;
she's loveable, but oh, so bizarre. To make her genuinely lika-
ble and sympathetic was not going to be an easy task. To make
it seem original would be even more difficult, since Gladys was
only a slight variation of Billie Dawn, a dumb blond who gets
wised up before the final reel, although Gladys, unlike Billie,
seems to be settling for less rather than more. Billie is awak-
ened to political responsibility; Gladys seems to settle for
domesticity as a woman's ultimate reward.

Though Kanin provided stereotyped answers to all the
questions he asked, Judy liked his script. Besides, Garson was
a faithful friend and anyway, she was happy playing wife and
mother at this time. Cohn was also pleased with the script—
as was George Cukor, who again agreed to direct what was to
be his fifth and final Holliday film. Once again a newcomer
whom Cohn was grooming as a star was cast in the romantic
lead—Jack Lemmon. And as Lemmon's rival, Cukor and
Columbia chose Peter Lawford.

For Judy, the roughest part of any picture was getting
herself in shape for the cameras. Shooting for *It Should
Happen* was scheduled to begin in May 1953, and in February, three months after Jonathan's birth, Judy was still
weighing in at about 160—thirty pounds over what her
camera weight should have been. Once again Judy began one
of her difficult diets, and the pounds started coming off,

cherry tomato by cherry tomato. But by the time she arrived in California, there was still a long way to go.

Judging from her interviews, Holliday enjoyed making fun of her weight problems. Shortly after she arrived in Los Angeles for *It Should Happen to You*, she was asked, as she had been in the past, to pose for some glamour shots for the Columbia still photographer. Look sexy, the photographer said. She tried to oblige, but he kept demanding "Sexy! Sexier!" In desperation, she asked him what he had been eating recently. He mentioned a thick, sizzling steak, an onion soup with croutons and lots of cheese, a cold pasta salad, strawberry shortcake. Judy's mouth began to water and her eyes became liquid. "That's the look I want!" the photographer shouted.

Probably the anecdote was cut from whole cloth. Fabrications of this kind made good copy and prevented interviewers from digging too deeply into private, sensitive areas. But it went deeper than that, perhaps. Behind her jolly pose as the fat lady at the Columbia circus, there was an obstinate, ingrained disbelief that she was or could be physically alluring. Columbia's attempts to make her glamorous only intensified her self-deprecation: She wasn't ever going to be a bouncy cheerleader like Debbie Reynolds or an obvious turn-on like Monroe or a cool sophisticate like Grace Kelly who could ask a beau (in *To Catch a Thief*) whether he wanted a breast or a leg and make it sound as though all she had on her mind was the chicken in her picnic basket.

Judy was out of place in 1950s movies and felt very much the outsider living in the California film colony of the period, though by 1953 she had many friends who were living there and who were anxious to make her feel at home. Adolph Green and Betty Comden were contract writers at M-G-M, and recently had completed work on what was to be their shining hour, the script for *Singin' in the Rain*. One of the roles in that now classic musical—the dumb blond 1920 screen star whose career is destroyed when sound comes in and she starts to squeak like Billie Dawn—was clearly inspired by Holliday (and was to win an Oscar nomination for Jean Hagen, one of Holliday's *Born Yesterday* replacements). Betty and Adolph kept talking about writing something for Judy, and she certainly would not have discouraged them, but as they were under contract to different studios, their future as a team looked unpromising.

Betty and Adolph were always asking Judy to drop by, but they lived in a lavish Beverly Hills style that didn't appeal to her. The parties at their houses were showcases for the right food, the right wine, and the right people. Judy liked her parties small so that the conversation wasn't limited to superficialities—shoptalk and gossip—the kind of chatter at which she was ungifted. And she didn't much care for conspicuous consumption, particularly on the part of friends who had once built a career on poking fun at ostentation and pompousness. As often as possible, Judy refused their invitations, pleading a headache or an early camera call the next morning.

She preferred the intimate and conversationally stimulating dinner parties at George Cukor's elegant home on Cordell Drive, high up in one of the many canyons that surround Los Angeles. Or the relaxed get-togethers hosted by Gene Kelly, featuring good music and party games. On the whole, however, she stayed at home in the rented house she shared with Helen and her baby son. As in the past, David was detained in New York and would be able to join them for only a few days sometime during their stay. Judy missed him terribly: For the first time, she was seriously concerned about the separations and the effect they were having on their marriage.

Once or twice she had dinner with her new costar, Jack Lemmon—another transplanted New Yorker. He, too, had left a spouse back in New York and was looking for some platonic companionship. Though a veteran of over 400 TV shows, Lemmon was making his screen debut in *It Should Happen to You,* and he was very apprehensive about working with pros like Holliday and Cukor. He found Judy very intimidating when they met at a wardrobe test. "She weighed about a hundred and fifty pounds. I'm about five-ten, and in heels she was about five-ten. So it was decided I should wear lifts in my shoes."

Realizing he was nervous, Judy tried to put him at ease; and when Lemmon mustered up the courage to ask her to dinner, she accepted without hesitation. Lemmon picked her up in a rented car and, at her suggestion, they started off for an Italian restaurant near the San Fernando Valley. Neither of them knew exactly where they were going. They got lost, and then the car broke down in the middle of a deserted stretch of roadway. Lemmon started off in search of help, but after walking a mile and finding no assistance, he headed back to the car.

"It's okay now," Judy said. "I fixed it." Growing bored during his absence, she had left the car and lifted the hood, played around with some wires, and finally got the motor running. Lemmon was astonished, as indeed was Holliday: She didn't have any mechanical knowledge, but through trial and error she had somehow managed to set things right.

Whatever fears Lemmon still harbored about working with Holliday vanished at this point: She was obviously a resourceful lady who did what had to be done without fuss and without worrying about glamour or her star image. Holliday would always head his list of favorite leading ladies. "Working with [her], you never, ever got a feeling she gave one goddamn about how the lighting is on her face or where the camera is. It was into the eyeballs and you did the scene and you acted *with* the person and not *at* her." Like everyone else, Lemmon was also amazed at Judy's ability to give an impromptu air to scenes that had been worked out with great care and deliberation.

One of the reasons Judy was so generous toward Lemmon was that she immediately spotted his talent and was eager to encourage him. She had an eye for up-and-coming beginners and was extraordinarily supportive, urging them to nurture their gift and work arduously to perfect it. Also, she genuinely liked Lemmon—he was in fact one of the few of her Hollywood leading men whom she did respect. One of her frequent beefs was that Cohn kept dropping the dregs of the lot into her pictures, making her work twice as hard to make comic points. But she couldn't complain about Lemmon—he always met her more than halfway.

David spent a few days on the Coast during the filming of *It Should Happen to You,* and then returned to New York. His visit wasn't much of a success. For the past few months there had been an undercurrent of tension in the Oppenheim marriage, and it came to the surface at this time. It was not just a matter of long separations, though they were beginning to take their toll; it went deeper than that. The source of the trouble was the disparity in their rank. Marriage between professionals is always a difficult business, whether they work in the same field (which can breed competitive feelings) or, as in Judy and David's case, separate ones that offered widely disparate rewards.

Judy was in awe of David's musical ability and knowledge —he was, she felt, more talented than she. Once or twice she implied that David agreed with her assessment, but this was probably only a fantasy nurtured by her own wavering sense of self-esteem as David was never heard to belittle her ability or profession. Judy could see no reason why he should feel overshadowed; the training and skill required of a first-rate musician was, in her opinion, much greater than anything demanded of an actress. Within his own circle, David was well known and respected; he was also financially successful, since, besides performing, he had recently taken on an executive position at Columbia Records.

Still, the recognition given him was nothing compared to what was showered on Judy, and as he settled down at the Columbia job, his career as a performer gradually diminished: He was never really to make a lasting name for himself as a musician or a composer. Judy's success as an actress—particularly since it was won so easily and had been neither desired nor particularly valued by her until only recently—served to heighten the irony of his own lack of progress as an artist. Judy recognized his anxiety and disappointment; indeed, she had recognized the threat as early as 1950 when she won her Oscar, but for a long time her fears had proved groundless. Now, however, she knew why she had experienced a shiver of premonition whenever in the past anyone had treated David as though he were Mr. Holliday.

The tensions underlying the marriage increased in Hollywood where, naturally, everything revolved around Judy—Miss Holliday's schedule, Miss Holliday's makeup call, Miss Holliday's limousine. . . . Even if they went out to dinner, the waiters toadied to Miss Holliday, not Mrs. Oppenheim. Judy was at a loss as to how to handle the situation—there really was no way to manage it, except to be affectionate, understanding, and reassuring, but that made David all the more irritable.

After he returned to New York, Judy felt gloomy and terribly lonely. Still, when Peter Lawford, her second leading man in *It Should Happen to You*, invited her to a party, she flatly refused. Lawford ran around with a hard-drinking, fast-living crowd that she found distasteful. She had taken an instant dislike to Humphrey Bogart when, at a Sunday brunch, she had noticed him acting abusively toward Lauren Bacall; and Frank Sinatra (one of Lawford's closest friends in this pre-Camelot period) was obnoxious, she decided, except when he was singing. One day when Sinatra visited the set of *It Should Happen to You*, Judy pointedly withdrew to her dressing room whenever she was not needed before the camera.

As filming went on, however, she found Lawford to be courteous and considerate, always very pleasant (though he was cast in a very ungratifying role). He wasn't exactly a ball of fire intellectually, but he was still as good-looking as when he had been one of M-G-M's leading juveniles. Judy was flattered by his attention—there was something intoxicating, almost dangerous, about playing a game of adulterous flirtation with this smooth and sweet-natured Lothario. There was also a strong element of guilt—maybe that was part of the attraction—but Judy overcame it. Soon she and Lawford were (in the words of a gossip columnist) "Hollywood's newest duo." They spent a weekend at Palm Springs and frequently were seen dining at Ciro's or one of the other fashionable supper clubs frequented by the film colony.

The movie reporters began predicting marriage, but they had jumped to false conclusions. Lawford wasn't as yet to abandon his playboy image and he dropped Holliday almost as soon as the picture was completed. Judy later admitted that she was "terribly hurt"—the abruptness with which the affair ended was a blow to her vanity—but in a way she was also relieved. In time she would clearly see that Lawford wasn't the man for her, and even while the romance was at its height, a strong part of her was determined not to give up so easily on her marriage to David.

Chapter Twelve

PHFFT!

When Judy returned to New York, she was greeted by a phalanx of reporters who wanted to know the truth about the status of the Oppenheims' marriage: Were they breaking up? "There is nothing to the rumors that have been circulating," she answered quietly. "They are untrue, but since there is no way that I can stop them, I wish to ignore them."

She had come home determined to salvage the marriage. Despite the fling with Lawford, she was not by nature promiscuous. She believed in long-term, committed relationships and was willing to fight to see them succeed. She still loved David and she felt that he still loved her, so it would be senseless to call it quits without struggling to make their relationship work. She also wanted Jonathan to have a father: She knew all too well what it meant to grow up in a broken home. If there was to be a separation, she would be more generous to David than Helen had been to Abe, but Jonathan would still grow up with divided and conflicting loyalties to his parents, as indeed she had. The problems in her own marriage had unleashed a reassessment of her own childhood

—an area of recollection she had previously done her best to avoid.

David and Judy thrashed things out. Though David was as uncertain as Judy was about their chances for success, he too wanted to try to salvage their marriage. This was good news, but Judy remained despondent. Ever since childhood she had suffered periodic spells of depression—passed off by some of her earlier friends as "a quiet withdrawal" (Sylvia Regan) or "dreaminess" (John Houseman)—which had become more pronounced during the McCarran investigation. These fits of moodiness subsided during her pregnancy and Jonathan's infancy, only to return dramatically on her return to New York after *It Should Happen to You.*

Now when the black moods occurred, Judy was quick to lose her temper, and much of her anger was directed, with or without motivation (usually the latter), toward her mother. Helen was a convenient scapegoat. She was *always* around and was ever ready to forgive, though only after exacting a brief period of penance. It became almost a ritual. Following one of Judy's outbursts, Helen would flee the Dakota and take refuge with one of her old Socialist cronies (who would be sworn to secrecy about her whereabouts) for three or four days. While she was in hiding, Judy would be filled with remorse and anxiety about her mother's well-being. When Helen eventually returned, the two women would fall into each other's arms, the daughter begging forgiveness, the mother insisting that there was nothing, really, to forgive.

Judy hated herself after these outbursts, but she didn't know how to handle them. A couple of drinks never helped—she had no appetite for alcohol—and tranquilizers weren't effective. The only release came through games. She spent hours absorbed in Double-Crostics, and the drive to complete them became so ferocious that she was known to make transcontinental calls in search of a proper definition, an unusual extravagance for a woman who was careful about her pennies. She also set up Scrabble matches that often went on all night. Abe Burrows, Tessa, and other friends were commandeered for these tournaments, but none of them really enjoyed them. Judy was destined to win—her top score a whopping 825.

But Scrabble and the occasional poker evening with Maureen Stapleton brought only temporary uplift. The depression returned, and Judy realized it was affecting her marriage. There seemed to be no way out of a vicious circle. Her marital problems had intensified her tendency toward depression, and her depression only served to intensify the problems in her marriage.

Eventually Judy decided to seek psychiatric help. She wanted to talk about the present, but her therapist pushed her back further, demanding that she confront the entire spectrum of her past, a process that was to be more painful and time-consuming than she had ever anticipated: Her analysis stretched over a period of five years. One of the first areas of distant memory she was asked to explore was her relationship with her father, about whom she continued to harbor highly ambivalent feelings.

Judy had never severed relations with her father. She made a point of inviting him to all the important events of her life—her wedding, the Oscar party at La Zambra, Jonathan's *bris*—even though she knew Helen would have preferred never to see him again. Their meetings were always cordial, but she rarely spoke about Abe to friends, and few of them had ever met him. And yet, Marian Seldes, among others, sensed that Abe had always meant something very special to Judy, if only because of the extraordinary glow she brought, as an actress, to any scene touching on father-daughter relationships.

Seldes mentions two examples. The first is a scene from the second act of *Born Yesterday* in which, after studying the often quoted "happy peasant" passage from Robert Ingersoll's biography of Napoleon, Billie Dawn begins to reminisce affectionately about her father (who once denounced her as

"a concubine"). The second concerned the warm rapport
between Georgina Allerton and her father in *Dream Girl*.

Unquestionably, there were some real-life parallels for Judy
to draw on in creating her characterizations for these plays.
The dominant parent in Georgina's family is the mother
who is *always* there; whereas Mr. Allerton, a lawyer, is usually absent, spending most of his time in Washington fighting a losing battle for the poor and downtrodden. Georgina
loves but is frequently exasperated by her mother; her father
she adores without reservation. And Billie's dawning in *Born
Yesterday* begins when she realizes that her father, who once
hurt her by withdrawing his love, only wanted to do the best
by her and suffered more than she from their separation.

Abe had never meant to hurt or desert Judy, and, as much
as she and Helen would allow, he had tried to keep a place
for his daughter in his life. His love for his daughter had
increased over the years as other emotional attachments diminished or proved unfulfilling. In his chosen field, he could
count himself a reasonably successful man, but in private life
he had not been so fortunate. His main source of joy in later
years was the satisfaction he took from watching the progress
of Judy's career. Sylvia Regan remembers encountering him
at a Catskills resort in the mid-Fifties and noting how "gray
and sad" he appeared. "He only seemed to come alive when
he started talking about Judy."

Holliday's analysis allowed her to see how her ambivalence
toward Abe had colored her relationships with other men.
Her sense of having been rejected as a child had not only
left her shy and diffident in her dealings with the opposite
sex, but also pushed her sexually toward men who bore a
close resemblance to Abe—who, in his middle years, had cut
a dazzling figure, at least in his daughter's eyes: He was lean,
vital, filled with fun, and, for Judy, every inch as glamorous
as the matinee idols she saw at the movies or in the pages
of the theater magazines. There were to be several Abes in

Judy's life. She had to learn, as Helen had learned before her, that it took more than cleverness, charm, and a handsome face to make a dependable husband or lover.

Through her analysis, Judy was to come to terms with her feelings about Abe, and eventually a rapprochement was effected between father and daughter. The psychiatric sessions were, however, less than successful in stemming the estrangement between husband and wife. Judy had heard rumors that David was seeing other women, and she had little doubt that they were true. One day, as she was entertaining a lady friend, the phone rang and Judy picked it up. "Yes," she said. "Fine . . . See you later." She hung up and then confided to her companion, "That was David. He says he'll be late because he's having martinis with a friend. The friend's got to be a woman—he drinks whiskey or beer with the boys." She passed it off as a joke, but she wasn't particularly amused.

Outwardly, at least for the press, Judy continued to present herself as the devoted wife and mother, often playing with Jonathan, now a chubby and good-natured toddler, while she chatted with reporters. As far as her feelings for Jonathan were concerned, there was no artifice—she adored her son, and wanted to be with him whenever she could. Remembering her own bleak youth—when she had been left to her own devices most of the day with only Grandma Rachel as companion—she couldn't agree with the new theory that quality of time is more important than quantity in establishing a healthy parent-child relationship.

Nonetheless, in the next few years, Jonathan would start spending more and more hours under Helen's supervision as Judy began picking up the pace of her professional life. One reason for this spurt of activity was her eagerness to finish out her Columbia contract as quickly as possible. (She was to make three pictures in the next two years.) Another factor was that working seemed to stave off her depression, at least temporarily. In addition to moviemaking, she began making frequent TV appearances during the mid-1950s, a period when film stars of the first rank regarded the small screen as beneath their dignity.

Judy's first TV appearance was in a half-hour drama, *The Huntress*, telecast by NBC's "Goodyear Playhouse" in February 1954, with Tony Randall playing the male lead. John Crosby of *The New York Times* found Holliday's character "uncomfortably similar to Billie Dawn and her role in *It Should Happen to You* [which had been released a month earlier]," and the other critics agreed that *The Huntress* was pretty much a total fiasco. But it did have its significance as a historic event. Only two years before, following her appearance before the McCarran committee, she had been told she would never work in radio or TV, and yet now she had broken the boycott, one of the first of the *Red Channels* performers to do so. That the networks had decided to take a chance on her was a testament to her status and her exemplary behavior during the past years. NBC had been very apprehensive about the reaction to her appearance, but when there were no repercussions, the network approved a deal whereby Holliday would appear in three ninety-minute "spectaculars" staged by Max Liebman, the producer of the famous "Show of Shows" series starring Sid Caesar and Imogene Coca.

When Liebman first approached Holliday about his new project, Judy was certain he'd never be allowed to hire her. Liebman promised to make a fight of it, but Judy told him not to stick his neck out: She didn't want to get involved in any more battles of that kind. Liebman went ahead anyway, and Judy was eventually to take pride in helping to crack the red barricade.

She was unfortunately to find less satisfaction in working on the Liebman productions. Each of these three variety shows was to be lavishly mounted and telecast in color (still something of a novelty at the time), and the entertainers who would share top billing with Holliday included Steve Allen, newcomer Dick Shawn, the Three Stooges, and members of the New York City Ballet. It was a motley mix of talent, and none of the headliners came off well, not even Judy, who was saddled with second-rate material. The critics, however, were exceptionally generous in sparing her from their otherwise scathing commentaries on the Liebman series. Such reviews, combining personal praise with general dissatisfaction, were to become a commonplace in Judy's life during the next two years.

There was, in fact, a slight but still noticeable slump in Holliday's professional standing at this time, a period when she desperately needed the support of a flourishing and ful-filling career. About the only bright spot was *It Should Hap-pen to You*, which opened in January 1954 to enthusiastic reviews. Though there was some quibbling about Kanin's failure to maintain the satiric tone his script established in its opening scenes, nearly everyone agreed that this was an exceptionally pleasing comedy, and Holliday's Gladys Glover received nothing but mash notes. Anything freaky or un-pleasant about Gladys's character had been eliminated by the purity, innocence, and gaiety of Holliday's performance. Something about Gladys Glover captured and enchanted the public imagination. People fell in love with her just as earlier they had fallen in love with Billie Dawn, perhaps because they weren't such awfully different types: Both were all-American dreamers, both were determined to get ahead, though Gladys chose a billboard instead of a boudoir as the fastest route to success. Whatever the reason, Gladys and Billie were to be two of the three roles for which Holliday is most affectionately remembered.

Her next picture was one that most everyone would like to forget, but unfortunately it sticks in the mind, if only because of its title: *Phfft!*—possibly the worst-named picture in American film history. "Don't say it! See it!" a Columbia publicity campaign urged viewers. But how many people want to see a picture with a name they can't pronounce and don't understand? Columbia eventually had to send out press releases explaining that, according to Walter Winchell (the columnist who had coined the word), "phfft" was a sound that occurred when a marriage collapsed. Columbia got a lot of copy out of this, but none of it encouraged people to say or see *Phfft!*

Initially Judy had good feelings about the script, which was written by George Axelrod as a sort of companion piece to his hit comedy *The Seven Year Itch*, which was then still running on Broadway. *Phfft!* was also a sort of upper-crust, more suggestive version of *The Marrying Kind*. Axelrod's plot concerned a couple who separate, fool around a bit, only to realize they were much happier when they were married. Possibly the story appealed to Holliday because it bore some resemblance to her own personal situation, and possibly she liked the character of Nina Tracy, a Park Avenue denizen and former debutante who had absolutely nothing in common with Billie Dawn and Gladys Glover—hence no one could accuse her of repeating herself by playing Nina. It is also possible that the script read better than it played: It was stodgily staged by Mark Robson, a Hollywood veteran with a few first-class credits behind him, but never a director noted for his light touch.

George Cukor wasn't free to direct, as he was then in the midst of nursing Judy Garland through *A Star Is Born*. But this disappointment was offset by Judy's pleasure in working again with Jack Lemmon, who had scored a big hit in *It Should Happen to You*. About the picture's second leading lady, Kim Novak, she had no particular feelings. They were not to meet until the first week of shooting.

By then, Judy had learned that Harry Cohn referred to Novak as "that fucking Polack broad." Ironically, in light of her own difficulties with Cohn, only now did she begin to realize that he put on his "White Fang" act for newcomers in whom he took a special professional interest. Showering them with foul epithets was his way of grooming them for

the rigors of stardom. There could be no doubt about it—
Novak was being prepped for the big time.

Judy swiftly realized that no matter what the screen credits
or press releases said, *Phfft!* wasn't intended as a Holliday
picture; it wasn't even intended as a Holliday-Lemmon picture; it was designed to be the picture that established Kim
Novak as a full-fledged star. Everything was being arranged
for Novak to steal *Phfft!* from its two stars.

This wasn't going to be much of a feat. Judy's part, while
offering a change of pace, was on the bland side and afforded
few opportunities for her to display her individuality; at
least twenty other actresses could have played Nina Tracy as
effectively. Novak's role was small but flashy, a series of
vignettes that allowed her to parade around in revealing
gowns. Robson wasn't much good at comedy, but he had a
gift for making sultry starlets look like actresses—witness
what he had done for Ruth Roman, Marilyn Maxwell, and
Lola Albright in *The Champion,* made five years before.
Recognizing that Novak was frightened and confused by the
hullabaloo Columbia was creating around her, Judy wanted
to be cooperative and helpful, but it wasn't always easy to
stifle her resentment.

At the request of the Columbia publicity department,
Holliday, Lemmon, and Novak agreed to attend an automobile show at the Pan-Pacific auditorium in Santa Monica.
All three posed with some of the automobile people, and
then the photographers started shouting for some solo shots
of Novak, who was nearly bursting out of a low-cut black
taffeta dress. She was also carrying a small black purse, which,
without a murmur of apology, she thrust into Judy's hands as
she walked off to join the photographers. Holliday was flab-
bergasted. A Columbia producer standing next to her chuck-
led and then whispered, "They sure learn fast in this town!"
Judy forced a smile, but she wasn't amused by being up-
staged by another blond doxy: Novak had the looks and

insensitivity to make a perfect Billie Dawn, but not—as far
as Holliday could see—the talent. After a pause, Judy snapped
back: "They grow them on the back lot—where the cabbage
patch used to be."

Returning to New York in August 1954, Holliday was in
very low spirits. This was one occasion when work had failed
to take her out of herself. Partly because of Novak's inexperi-
ence, *Phfft!* had gone way over its shooting schedule, forcing
Judy to cancel a summer-stock engagement in *My Aunt
Daisy*, the play John Wilson had brought her a year earlier.
Phfft!, she felt sure, was going to be a bomb, and she was not
very pleasantly disposed toward Columbia or Harry Cohn.
She had a sinking feeling that the studio was starting to lose
interest in her, which wasn't so surprising since neither of
her post-*Yesterday* films had been box-office smashes. They
had done pretty well, but she was really a prestige star—the
rewards came mainly from the critics and connoisseurs, not
from cash-register accounts. Money, however, meant more
than prestige in Hollywood, and no matter what the New
York reviewers and intellectuals felt, one Kim Novak was
(in black-ink terms) worth five Judy Hollidays.

To make matters worse, Judy had been in physical pain
for several days. Shortly before leaving California, she had
twisted her ankle, and she was still in pain when she arrived
in New York. As soon as she got home, she saw a doctor,
who told her surgery would be needed to correct the problem,
a torn ligament that hadn't healed properly.

After the operation had been performed at Harkness Pavilion, Judy convalesced at her apartment in the Dakota.
Most of the time was passed brooding about her life and
career. She was scheduled to start work on another film
before May 1, 1955, but before leaving Hollywood she had
talked informally to Cohn about the possibility of a postponement, just in case she decided to return to the stage.

Cohn had said he thought something could be worked out. This was what Judy wanted to hear, but the good tidings, delivered so casually, tended only to deepen her depression. That Cohn hadn't cursed her out suggested that he really didn't care whether she returned to Columbia immediately or not.

So she began to think seriously about picking up her stage career. It seemed a wise move. She was disenchanted with moviemaking; she was fed up with Hollywood and with separations; she wanted to stay in New York with David. Not that her presence at the Dakota changed anything—the situation remained very much the same; there were still those martini phone calls. But spending three to four months out of the year away from home was no way to save a faltering marriage.

On the other hand, to stay in New York and return to the stage was a frightening move, since she would be placing her reputation on the line. She would be a Hollywood star returning to the stage, and the New York critics have never been noted for their charity toward actors who desert Broadway for the screen. She also knew she would have to prove herself with those theater people who claimed she had debased her talent and sold out her promise by appearing in a lot of Hollywood ephemera. And she could not help but remember that her last New York stage performance, in *Dream Girl*, had hardly set the town on fire. If she were to return, it would have to be in a really solid, failproof property—though, as she was well aware, nothing is ever foolproof in the theater.

Judy began to discard one script after another. A revised version of *My Aunt Daisy* went first—she still was not happy with the script. Next to go was *The Sleeping Prince* by Terence Rattigan, a current London success starring Vivien Leigh and Laurence Olivier (who would later appear with Marilyn Monroe in a blowsy film adaptation, *The Prince and the Showgirl*). Initially, Judy was so pleased with Rattigan's comedy that the producers announced that she had agreed to appear in it, only to issue a withdrawal of the statement a week later. Charming though it was, Holliday had decided *The Sleeping Prince* was flimsy and too English for American taste. (She was right. When the play reached New York in 1956, it was a quick flop, despite a generally satisfactory production with Michael Redgrave and Barbara Bel Geddes in the leading roles.)

Then came prolonged discussions about the possibility of Holliday replacing Rosalind Russell in Bernstein and Comden and Green's *Wonderful Town*, the reigning musical hit of the period. Everyone involved agreed that it was a great idea—the part was a natural for Judy—but eventually it was Carol Channing (who had been searching for a good role since *Gentlemen Prefer Blondes* in 1949) who went on as Russell's replacement. Judy backed out of the show, it was announced, because she felt she couldn't cope vocally with Bernstein's score. This was a patent fabrication, since Bernstein had written his songs for Russell, whose voice could take honors only in a three-way sing-off with Lauren Bacall and Katharine Hepburn. The real problem was that Holliday would be *replacing* Russell. "Replacement" was a word that carried déclassé connotations in the 1950s American theater: A star who took over a role someone else had created was a star on the skids—and that was definitely not the impression Holliday wanted to convey.

While these negotiations were going on, Judy rehearsed and taped two of the Max Liebman TV specials. The reviews for the specials were bad; the reviews for *Phfft!* (which opened in December 1954) weren't measurably better, and on every newsstand there were cover pictures of Kim Novak showing lots of décolletage and a sensuous mouth that suggested an appetite for something less fattening than pasta.

Everything was pressing in on Judy—David's after-hours martinis, the bad reviews, even Kim Novak. She felt out of control. Sometimes she'd start to cry for no real reason and she'd call Helen to take Jonathan out of the room. Helen would return to ask, "What's wrong?" What isn't wrong? Judy wanted to scream. Phfft! Everything's Phfft!

As the weeks passed and the ideal stage script continued to elude her, Holliday decided it would be foolish to postpone her return to Hollywood. Much to her surprise—maybe the studio *hadn't* written her off, she thought—Columbia had purchased for her the hit Broadway comedy *The Solid Gold Cadillac*, written by George S. Kaufman in collaboration with her old and dear friend Howard Teichmann. Judy had seen the play shortly after its opening and loved it, though she never imagined it as a vehicle for herself. The play centered on Laura Partridge, a little old lady who, with ten shares of stock in a huge, General Motors-esque corporation, succeeds in wresting control from a selfish and underhanded board of directors.

The part of Laura Partridge had been tailor-made for Josephine Hull (best remembered for her performances on stage and screen in *Arsenic and Old Lace* and *Harvey*), who was in her mid-seventies when the play opened. Without Hull, the critics said, the satire and jokes of Kaufman and Teichmann's script would look pretty thin; it probably wouldn't work with another actress in the lead. Several film producers disagreed, and the bidding for the film rights was very lively. Paramount wanted it for Shirley Booth, Fox saw it as a Marilyn Monroe vehicle, and Cohn was determined to get it for Holliday.

When he succeeded, Judy was thrilled. This was a property about which Judy felt truly enthusiastic. While hardly a devastating comment on capitalism, *The Solid Gold Cadillac* was a lighthearted portrait of the American underdog, which struck a deep chord in Judy. Many of her great roles ran along similar lines: She was nearly always the representative and/or champion of the little folk of America, a girl who thwarted big business and came down solidly on the side of "the happy peasant," as in *Born Yesterday*. Certainly she wouldn't be breaking new ground with *Cadillac*, but she had always favored and responded best to scripts with an edge of social criticism. Perhaps she could have lobbied for a sharper edge in the script, but for her to have pushed more openly into the arena of social criticism would undoubtedly have allowed the red-baiters (who were still very vocal in 1955) to raise the ghost of her pink past. Anyway, since her days as a Revuer, Judy was satisfied that the best way to treat a topical subject was with good-natured tongue-in-cheek.

Abe Burrows was hired to fashion the screenplay for *Cadillac*. Like Holliday, he had been a victim of the congressional witch-hunts; and perhaps because of this experience, he played safe and watered down the already adulterated satire of the playscript. Laura comes off funnier—many of Burrows's gags are cleverer than the ones they replace—but also kookier: She loses much of the dignity she possesses in Teichmann and Kaufman's original. This is partly because Burrows's attempt to rejuvenate Laura is less than satisfactory: There is often a sense of dislocation when Laura's speech and actions seem distinctly those of an older woman. Even the name Partridge seems wrong—appropriate for a biddy, but not for a woman in her early thirties.

The picture also suffered from the casting of Paul Douglas as the automobile executive who falls in love with Laura. Always a heavyweight as a leading man, Douglas had grown stouter since *Born Yesterday*, and his comedy timing was now almost as broad as his figure. Judy felt no greater affection for him than she had during the stage run of *Yesterday*, and on screen they make a singularly unattractive couple— perhaps the least exciting pair of movie lovers since Beulah Bondi and Victor Moore in *Make Way for Tomorrow* or Katharine Hepburn and John Wayne in *Rooster Cogburn*. When they gaze at each other, they seem to be envisioning a golden retirement in Saint Petersburg, not an explosive sexual congress. Holliday looks truly dreadful in this film: She might be an overweight Bronx matron sporting a new Peck and Peck wardrobe for a Miami Beach vacation.

Nonetheless, Judy took pride in her performance as Laura Partridge; otherwise she certainly would not have told an interviewer of the preparation she lavished on the role, precisely the sort of analysis she had scrupulously avoided in the past. "There was, for instance, this one line," she volunteered: "Now there were nine ways it could have been read and gotten a laugh, but only one way to get the laugh and still be true to the character; I found it through trial and error."

The Solid Gold Cadillac was to be another personal triumph for Holliday, and the film as a whole was generally well received by both the critics and the public: It was to be one of the top-grossing films of all time in England. For all that, there's something very wrong about Holliday's performance, and the problem goes way beyond the way she looks. Technically she's as good as ever, but the performance is all technique, and whatever it may have been about Partridge that drew Holliday to the role is missing. She mugs her way through the film.

There are all kinds of mugging, including a variety that passes as great acting when it is executed so subtly that it looks like "real life." Spencer Tracy in his Hepburn years was the undisputed champ in this area, but Holliday was definitely the heir apparent. Tracy's mugging, however, is aggressively smug, almost contemptuously so, while Judy's seems motivated by an overeagerness to please. As Teichmann explains, she went "straight for the laughs," but, as any actor knows, to play for laughs is to lose them.

There are any number of more plausible reasons as to why she fell into this trap, which had been one of her weaknesses since the start of her career. Sometimes she mugs because the role, as written, demands what Tracy once described as "a little extra dressing"; on other occasions, it seems as though,

like many actors, she slips into it to compensate for contrived and poorly conceived characters. But coming to the
fore just at the time it does, this overplay for audience affection seems a touching expression of Judy's personal need for
love and approval. In *Cadillac*, she comes on like a lady who
settles for playing the clown because there is no other way
she can attract attention.

This clownishness was also indicative of Judy's ambivalent
feelings about her skills as an actress. Over the last five years,
she had gained confidence—she could now speak authoritatively about the technical side of stage and screen acting—but
this self-assurance was a security blanket, comforting Holliday for her lack of courage in pushing onward. At the time
of her stage appearances in *Kiss Them for Me* and *Born
Yesterday*, many authorities were confident that Holliday
would someday become a great actress—a new Laurette
Taylor, several predicted. There was a widespread belief that
(in Marian Seldes's words) "as Judy continued to live and
develop as an actress and a person, she would play roles
written for her by our best writers and that we would have
the joy of watching her progress." But Holliday's develop-
ment and progress as an actress had been limited. There had
been few risks, no roles by Tennessee Williams or Arthur
Miller, and by the time of *Phfft!*, *Cadillac*, and the Liebman
TV appearances, Holliday was being regretfully dismissed by
many of her former supporters. Even interviewers began
asking embarrassing questions.

"Wouldn't you like to do a dramatic film or play?" a
reporter asked Holliday at about the time of *Cadillac*. Well,
yes, she replied, "but I don't think the public would accept
me. As soon as they see me, they start to laugh. They see me
as a clown. I doubt they could accept me in a serious role."

This was an evasion, of course. The public's acceptance of
Holliday as a serious actress had never been tested; it was she
who saw herself as a "clown," a role that she was reluctant to
throw away as long as it supported and protected her career.

But as easy and comfortable as it was to go on playing the clown, it also got to be boring and uninspiring after a while. It became a matter of technique. Technique is vital, but an actor who's got nothing else going for him, particularly an actor with a touch of genius, starts to go stale when he has to go over the same patch of road again and again. It happened to Tracy in the 1950s and it was happening to Holliday after only five years in Hollywood.

Her sixth film for Columbia, *Full of Life*, made directly after *Cadillac*, is the most inconsequential of all her films and the most negligible of her screen performances. There are, however, two saving notes of grace. First, since she is (as the title suggests) playing a pregnant woman, living in the Napa Valley with her husband and despotic Italian father-in-law, she is liberated from those frizzy blond hairdos and Jean-Louis gowns that Columbia inflicted on her and which always made her look like a transvestite Harpo Marx. Second, her Mussolini-like papa-in-law is played by Salvatore Baccaloni, an operatic basso buffo who scene-steals his way through the film as though he's still at the Met playing Rossini for Rudolph Bing. Next to him, Holliday comes across as a model of simplicity and understatement.

All during shooting, Judy was terribly upset about *Full of Life*, which she recognized was nothing more than an extended TV situation comedy. She was also seriously concerned about what her future could be in the new Hollywood. The studio system was crumbling, and most companies were divesting themselves of overhead, particularly of contracts with actors whose box-office value was minimal in the current screen era of glossy, wide-screen, technicolor super-entertainments like Columbia's *Picnic*, starring Kim Novak. Judy wasn't sure that she could fit into the new scene; nor was she at all certain that she wanted to be a part of it.

To make matters worse, while she was mulling all this over, she received a terrible blow. David informed her that he wanted a separation. Judy was deeply depressed, but it seemed futile to argue: Their marriage hadn't improved in the past two years, and, though she wasn't sure, she suspected that David was now seriously involved with another woman. Maybe at a different time she would have fought for another chance, but now she was emotionally too low to wage what appeared to be a losing battle.

Judy stayed down for a good while, but, in a strange way, David's decision ultimately provided the catalyst she needed to get her life moving again, to pull herself out of the quagmire she had been wading through these past months. Despite her frequent fits of depression, she had always possessed an inner core of resilience, which was there waiting for her to call on. The hour had arrived. Ever since she could remember, she had allowed other people to orchestrate her life—"Someone's always been pushing me onto a stage," she once remarked ruefully. Now, as she was approaching her thirty-fifth birthday, it seemed high time for her to start managing herself.

In the early summer of 1956, Judy returned to New York. In the few weeks before her departure, a number of possibilities, on a number of fronts, had presented themselves. Her prospects, instead of closing, were opening wider than ever. It was the beginning of a new period of her life that was to be more challenging, more exciting than ever.

PART THREE

Beginnings and
Endings

Chapter Thirteen

NEW BEGINNINGS

Judy spent the plane trip back to New York studying the pages of a bound script of a yet-to-be-produced Broadway musical. The title page read *"The Bells Are Ringing* by Adolph Green and Betty Comden." The script had some rough patches, she felt, but on the whole it looked like a winner.

Comden and Green had come to her just as she was about to start filming *Full of Life* and told her they had an idea for a musical that they wanted to develop around her talents. It was to be based loosely on the experience of Betty Printz, a friend of Comden and Green's and a woman who operated a telephone-answering service (mainly for celebrities) and was notorious for involving herself in her clients' lives. As Judy had done a stint as a telephone operator at the Mercury, she seemed a natural for the part. Judy laughed and said the idea sounded terrific, but that she couldn't make a decision until they had something on paper.

In short order Betty and Adolph were back with a detailed outline and two brief scenes. Judy read what they had written and made a provisional commitment. There was still one obstacle to be hurdled! Judy owed Columbia one more film on her 1950 contract, and she would have to ask Cohn's approval for an extended leave of absence. As Columbia had nothing lined up for Holliday in the near future, Cohn sent her off to New York and *The Bells Are Ringing* with his good wishes.

Judy had boarded the plane at the Los Angeles Airport with a sigh of relief—her stretch of California commuting looked like it was coming to an end. But when she finally reached her apartment at the Dakota, she was momentarily engulfed by a wave of sadness. David had cleared out, and there was no one to greet her except Helen and Jonathan. She loved both of them, but they were not what she most needed right now. Though she had resigned herself to the wisdom of David's decision to separate, the loss of the man she had spent some ten years with left a terrible gap in her life. And in a certain way, no one could fill it. But on another, perhaps more superficial level, Judy was already shifting gears. In fact, California, despite all the bitter blows it had dealt her, had also offered her a man who might one day begin to fill the place David had now abandoned.

But that could wait for the time being. Now she had to concentrate on *Bells*, and there was one side of this assignment that terrified her. Singing. "Nonsense," Comden and Green told her, "you've been singing all your life." Yes, Holliday admitted, but with a difference. As a Revuer, she had faked her way along as a comic vocalist, and in several of her films she had been required to sing only a few bars of a popular song: "Delores" in *The Marrying Kind*; "Let's Fall in Love" in *It Should Happen to You*; a scat version of "I Can't Give You Anything but Love, Baby" in *Born Yesterday*. "But that was acting, not singing," she explained. "I sang the way the character would, which was pretty rotten. I don't have a real voice." She made Comden and Green promise that she wouldn't have to sing any ballads in the show—"I'll do the patter stuff; leave the love songs for the male lead."

Reluctantly they agreed, but still Judy expressed anxiety. To build up her confidence, Adolph Green suggested she study with Herbert Greene, a well-known vocal coach and arranger who had helped several nonsinging stars prepare for their Broadway debuts.

Judy threw herself into these lessons with a ferocity that Greene found unsettling. She was not a born singer, but her voice was true, she was instinctively musical, and from the start she was able to use her vocal capabilities with great effectiveness. Her phrasing was impeccable, "but she was violently and destructively self-critical," Greene recalls. "Her strongest feelings were negative—she was driven by unfounded fears about her talent, her femininity, and her appeal to men." When she failed to measure up to her own standards, "she had nasty periods of depression," during which all her insecurities would come pouring out in an angry jumble.

Obviously Judy was both excited and terrified by the direction her life was taking. Coming back to Broadway after an absence of nearly a decade (excluding the brief, not-so-successful *Dream Girl* engagement) and in a big, brassy musical that would succeed or fail according to her performance— this was an enormous risk. And it was one for which she had to take total responsibility—no one but herself was pushing her on stage this time around. She had days and nights of dreadful insecurity, fed by the memories of David's desertion and the virtual collapse of her Hollywood career, but she drove herself ahead, seeking perfection. If she was going to do it, it wasn't enough that it be good, it wasn't even enough that it knock them dead—it had to be *perfect*. Undoubtedly, one of the reasons for Judy's low self-esteem was that she continually set such inordinately high goals for herself.

There were moments when Herbert Greene found Judy's intensity unbearable. Several times he considered suggesting another teacher, but he came to understand and sympathize with her inner drives. She worked harder than anyone he had ever known and she was, in her best moods, "kind and generous and intensely loyal."

At Holliday's request, Greene was hired to work on the

vocal arrangements for the show, which was now officially
titled *The Bells Are Ringing*. By mid-August most of the
other important members of the production team had been
assembled and were working on the show. Jule Styne had
nearly completed the score; Jerome Robbins had agreed to
direct; Bob Fosse was signed as choreographer. Judy had
warned Fosse that she wasn't much of a dancer. Can you do
the cha-cha? he asked. She said she could probably manage
that, as long as he remembered she wasn't another Gwen
Verdon. "Good," he said with a smile. He had in mind for
Bells a cha-cha number that would, he hoped, top the showstopping mambo routine he had created for Verdon in *Damn
Yankees* two years before.

That left only one piece of business: the selection of a leading man.

Judy knew exactly who she wanted, and she wasn't going to
take no for an answer. A few weeks before leaving California,
she had been a guest at one of Gene Kelly's Sunday brunches,
and though she had planned to spend no more than an hour,
she had found herself staying on until early evening. She
couldn't pull herself away from an exceptionally lively bout
of charades ("The Game," as it was then called) or from
the attentions of a glib yet attractive and very agreeable young
man who, relaxed by a few drinks, was quite obviously flirting
with her. She felt she should be annoyed or maybe amused;
instead, she was blushing with pleasure and excitement.

Her admirer was Sydney Chaplin, the son of Charles Chaplin and his second wife, Lita Grey. He was then thirty (five
years younger than Judy) but as yet had done little to suggest
he would bring new glory to the family name. After making
his screen debut in his father's production of *Limelight*
(1952), he had appeared without distinction in a few West
Coast stage productions and a handful of second-rank films.
But while he was outclassed by his father as an actor, he
equaled the old boy's reputation as a vigorous lover. Prior to
Holliday, his name was linked with Joan Collins (the leading

lady in his most memorable Hollywood film, Howard Hawks's *Land of the Pharaohs*) and prior to her marriage to Rex Harrison, witty and bewitching Kay Kendall.

Judy's friends were somewhat uneasy about her overnight romance with Chaplin. As an antidote for postmarital depression, Chaplin was the ideal prescription—handsome, charming, and according to Beverly Hills scuttlebutt, absolutely fantastic in bed. He was the kind of a man who was wonderful for a fling, but a dubious prospect for enduring romance. Judy, on the other hand, was not a woman inclined toward frivolous or casual commitments.

Later it was to be rumored along Shubert Alley that Chaplin had used all his sexual wiles on Judy solely to win the role in *Bells Are Ringing*. Similar stories persist to this day, but they are not entirely fair to Chaplin. Judy wanted him to play the part of Jeff Moses at least as much as he wanted it himself: Having him on stage with her eight times a week seemed a foolproof way of building a solid relationship—after David, she was through with long-distance romance. There is no proof that Chaplin ever suggested to Judy that he was growing weary of bachelorhood, though friends feel that he did lead her to believe that he might be corralled into some kind of a permanent arrangement. Judy definitely believed so—she was always to insist, even long after the affair had reached its conclusion, that Chaplin was as crazy for her as she was for him. But the consensus is that she may have willfully misinterpreted the tenor and intensity of his affection. She was, after all, on the rebound from David, and Sydney (in appearance) was a more glamorous version of Oppenheim.

One thing is certain: Chaplin would never have won the role in *Bells* without Holliday behind him. Adolph Green liked Sydney and supported Judy's choice, but nearly everyone else was aghast. After hearing Chaplin sing, Jule Styne was at a loss for words. Chaplin sang so consistently off key that on those rare occasions when he did hit a note square on, he sounded as though he had suddenly strayed from pitch. Since

Judy refused to sing love songs, Styne had written all the big
ballads for the male lead, and now he was faced with the
prospect of a Jeff Moss who couldn't carry a tune. Of course,
he could write new songs to fit Chaplin's very limited vocal
range, but, as he told Comden and Green, he doubted whether
any musical could be a smash when the two leads couldn't—
or wouldn't—sing. One, maybe—but *two?*

Jerome Robbins was even more staunchly opposed to Chaplin, who, in his view, had the looks but not the talent or the
experience needed for the role. At his insistence, other singer-
actors (with an emphasis on the former) were discussed and
auditioned, including Johnny Johnston and Bill Johnson, a
handsome baritone who had scored a personal hit in a Rodgers and Hammerstein fiasco, *Pipe Dream,* a season earlier.
Everyone agreed that either would be ideal, but Judy wanted
no part of them or anyone else except Chaplin. If necessary,
she could be just an autocratic as Robbins, and she wasn't
going to give an inch. She had known Jerry for years; she
loved him; but she knew talent when she saw it, and Sydney,
she was convinced, had the makings of a first-rate musical-
comedy lead. Maybe he didn't sing as well as John Raitt or
Johnson and Johnston, but he had something the others
lacked: sex appeal. Since Alfred Drake in *Kiss Me, Kate,* there
hadn't been a magnetic leading man in musicals, just wooden
dummies who hit the right notes and paraded around the
stage like wind-up toy soldiers.

Robbins, however, thought she was besotted with love, and
while he was fond of Judy and a great admirer of her talents,
he wasn't going to let her pull a Sarah Bernhardt and foist off
one of her bedmates as a Broadway leading man.

After prolonged and frequently acrimonious discussion, a
compromise was worked out. Robbins would take on Chaplin
with the understanding that if he didn't come across with a
reasonably professional performance by the first week of the
out-of-town engagements, he would be dismissed without fuss
from Miss Holliday. She agreed, and, with only a touch of

lingering animosity, the two principal leads started rehearsing with Robbins at the beginning of September 1956.

Those rehearsals necessitated little exploration of character or plot motivation—both of which were virtually nonexistent in the script. *The Bells Are Ringing* was the story of Ella Peterson, a young woman working for a New York answering service; owned and operated by her cousin Sue, the business is called "Susanswerphone." To offset the tedium of her job, Ella takes a personal interest in the lives of the Susanswerphone subscribers, and for each customer she adopts a different personality as she doles out advice and optimism over the phone. For Plaza O-double-four-double-three, known to the world at large as playwright Jeff Moss, she's "Mom," a little old lady who urges him to leave off the doxies and the booze and the ponies and get down to writing his next Pulitzer Prize winner. When Jeff fails to answer a wake-up call, Ella/Mom rushes over to his apartment, pulls him out of bed, and introduces herself as Melisande Scott—the first name to come to mind. Then Ella/Mella/Mom gets him to the typewriter and pronto, he finishes Act I.

Jeff, of course, immediately falls in love, which pleases and yet upsets Ella, who believes he's in love with Melisande Scott, not Ella Peterson. Just like a Pirandello character, poor Ella starts to crumble under the weight of an identity crisis. "I've spent half my life tuning in on other people's lives, playing all kinds of imaginary characters—even with some I fell in love with," she tells cousin Sue. "And when the make-believe love became *real*, it had no place to go—because *I* wasn't *real*."

Naturally, just before the final curtain, Jeff arrives to show Ella who she really is: the girl he loves and wants to marry.

Even in 1956, the book for *Bells* seemed contrived and clumsily constructed, defects that were to become increasingly noticeable in Comden and Green's subsequent work. Still, the script had its positive sides: It was unpretentious and lively and raffish in its subplotting, and there were any number of colorful characters to hold the stage while Judy was changing costumes. Another plus was Jule Styne's score, definitely not as strong as his music for *Gypsy* (1959) but certainly on a par with his work for *Funny Girl* (1964). There was never, however, any question that the success of the show would depend entirely on Holliday—*Bells* wasn't to be the last musical built around a specific star, but it was one of the last song-and-dance vehicles to make it to the winner's circle virtually on star power alone.

The very best that can be said of Comden and Green's script is that it worked not only as a star vehicle but as a vehicle that liberated its star from an overly confining image. Ella Peterson owed a small debt to some of Holliday's earlier roles, particularly Georgina Allerton, Elmer Rice's *Dream Girl*, but there is nothing freaky or kooky about her, nothing that suggests the stereotypical dumb blond. Described in the script as "pretty, warm, sympathetic . . . with a quick mind and a vivid imagination," Ella Peterson was really Comden and Green's tribute to the Judy they knew and loved: The librettists had created a character that reflected their friend's positive traits and ignored what was dark or negative. It was a deeply affectionate portrait, and was to provide Holliday with her most satisfying and appealing role.

Since she had gone almost directly from *Full of Life* to rehearsals of *Bells*, Judy hadn't had the opportunity to eat her way beyond her professional weight of 125 pounds. During rehearsals she managed to lose more weight, so that by the first out-of-town engagement she was positively svelte. Because of the demanding nature of the role and the energy used up performing it eight times a week, she was to keep the weight off for the entire Broadway run.

Never again would she look as lovely or as relaxed as in *Bells*. Indeed, this was to be one of the happiest times in her life. She was in love and surrounded by friends, her former differences with Comden and Green having been totally forgotten. Once, during a work session with Betty and Adolph, she put down her script and exclaimed, "Let's stop for a second. This is such a wonderful moment. Whatever happens afterward, we must always remember it."

After all the years of uneasy friendship, it was wonderful for all of them to get back to the camaraderie of the Revuers days. But a big, expensive musical is a tricky thing to put together, and eventually Comden and Green were forced to pull an underhanded, yet necessary, trick on Judy. There was a spot late in the second act that demanded a love ballad for Ella—there was no way of skirting it; the situation could only be resolved by having Ella sing of her decision to disappear from Jeff's life. A ballad called "The Party's Over" had already been written—the problem was to get Judy to sing it.

Remembering that Judy loved to sing harmony, Comden and Green told her that Styne's score included a song requiring her to sing counterpoint to a melody carried by the chorus. For several days, Judy worked diligently with Styne on mastering the "harmony"; then, out of curiosity, she asked, "What's the major melody like?" Styne smiled. "You should know, you've been singing it for the last week." Judy started to protest, but realized she had been outfoxed. She agreed to go on singing "The Party's Over," but that was it—the other ballads were to be left to Chaplin.

And, as even Jerry Robbins had to agree, Chaplin was coming along very nicely. He never did conquer his pitch problem, but, on key or not, he sang stylishly and with gusto. In the nonmusical moments of the show, he exhibited a quality that twenty years later would be described as "laid back." He was casual, narcissistic in an appealing, boyish way, so cocky and self-confident about his charms that he made up in presence what he lacked in ability. All in all, he was, as Judy had predicted, an agreeable change from the booming-voiced tenors and baritones who stolidly marched their way through most Broadway musicals.

Much of Chaplin's progress was due to Holliday's tutoring:

She drilled him on his line readings, his songs, his characterization. Later she would put on his makeup before the show
and help him remove it afterward. There was a maternal flavor
to her fussing over him, and people responded to it in different ways. Some thought they were "adorable" together; others
found them ridiculous: "He acted like a spoiled child and
she was as giggly as a teen-ager." Foolish or not, their feeling
for each other had its advantages, at least professionally: It
spilled over to their onstage relationship as Ella and Jeff,
giving *The Bells Are Ringing* a tenderness that is not to be
found in Comden and Green's script.

Rehearsals passed smoothly and spirits were high as the
company moved to New Haven for the first out-of-town engagement. Then came a minor setback. During a final run-
through, Judy stumbled and smashed her hand against a piece
of scenery. No bones were broken, but a doctor advised her
to support her arm with a sling for the next two days. Scheduled for the following evening was a preview performance of
Bells, and management suggested it be canceled. Judy
wouldn't hear of it—she would go on wearing a silk scarf as a
sling. Her performance was a little shaky that night—as it was,
even without the sling, the following evening, which marked
the official world premiere of *Bells*. An hour before the curtain, Holliday came down with a particularly virulent case of
stage fright, a professional ailment that had recurred with
varying degrees of intensity throughout her career.

The reviews the next morning were guarded. There were
good words for Styne's score, strong reservations about the
book, tempered praise for Holliday, and unqualified enthusiasm for Chaplin, who was hailed as "the real surprise of the
show." Judy was noticeably cool when she dropped by the
suite Chaplin was sharing with Styne at the Taft Hotel, and
later that day she remarked bitterly: "Of course I wanted
Sydney to make a hit, but not at my expense." Backstage gossips predicted the romance had seen its best days, but Judy

was too much in love to start a feud. By the end of the New Haven run, she and Chaplin were as cozy as ever before.

When the show moved on to Boston, the reviews were much the same as in New Haven, only more positive for Holliday. She still wasn't getting raves, however, and there was now a general consensus that the fault was not in Judy's performance but in the positioning of her material in the show. She had two strong comedy numbers early in the first act ("A Perfect Relationship" and "Is It a Crime?"), and two equally bright routines in the second ("Drop That Name" and Fosse's cha-cha routine). Then, as what had been intended as the crowning moment, she sat down alone on the stage and sang "The Party's Over."

The moment was indeed memorable. With her piping, vulnerable little girl's voice, Holliday transcended the easy sentiment of the ballad and made it both honest and heartrending. But as a sign-off, "The Party's Over" just didn't work. It was a downer, not the kind of song that elicits a standing ovation, and it was placed almost fifteen minutes before the final curtain. What was needed was a showstopping number during that quarter-hour, one that would leave the audience stomping and screaming for Holliday. The difficulty lay in creating a rousing song that would also be in keeping with Ella's character. It had to be upbeat and funny, but also expressive of Ella's despair at renouncing Jeff.

Comden and Green came up with the idea that Ella leave Susanswerphone and return to her former job at a lingerie factory, where there had been no chance of her getting involved with the customers. They would write a song lampooning all those Al Jolson–type numbers about goin' back (to Swanee or Carolina or Alabamy), but where exactly was Ella going back to? They needed a catchy or funny name for Ella's professional alma mater. Betty Comden happened to be reading Françoise Sagan's *Bonjour Tristesse*, then a top bestseller, and the title now came back to her as an amusing idea. "I'm going back," she ad-libbed, "to the Bonjour Tristesse Brassiere Factory (a little modeling on the side)." Green smiled gleefully. "You've got it!"

The song went into the show just after the Philadelphia opening, and when Judy finished singing it for the first time, the audience made such a joyful commotion that she had to sing it all over again from the top. With the introduction of "I'm Going Back," nearly all the pieces had fallen into place, and while it was clear that *Bells* wasn't going to be one of the landmark American musicals, it was equally clear that it was going to work triumphantly for Judy.

Which is precisely the way things turned out. When the show opened in New York at the Shubert Theatre on November 29, 1956, most of the critics lambasted Comden and Green's script and raved on and on about Holliday. Walter Kerr was about the only reviewer who liked both the story and the star. The others agreed with Brooks Atkinson, who wrote in *The New York Times*: "Miss Holliday sings, dances and also carries on her shoulders one of the most antiquated plots of the season." There were kind words for Styne's songs, Robbins and Fosse's contributions, and the performances of the supporting cast (which included Jean Stapleton, Bernie West, and Jack Weston). Sydney Chaplin was proclaimed the discovery of the season. But there was no doubt in anyone's mind that *Bells Are Ringing* would have had only a brief tenancy at the Shubert without Holliday's name in lights on the marquee.

As long as it stayed there, a period of over two years, *Bells* was a box-office smash. Ticket sales were boosted enormously by word of mouth: Audiences liked the show much more than the critics had, and they responded to Judy with an intensity that went far beyond the adulation typically paid a wonderful performance. People came away from the theater feeling that they actually knew Judy, that she was their friend. In the 1950s there were few stage actresses who elicited this intimacy of response— Helen Hayes, perhaps; Mary Martin in *Peter Pan;* Shirley Booth in practically anything: These are about the only names the spring immediately to mind.

Every night for the next two years, a huge crowd would gather outside the stage door in Shubert Alley. It wasn't the usual throng of rapacious autograph seekers who lurk in front of Sardi's or around the side entrances of nearly any theater in the Broadway area. This group was quiet, well mannered, and conspicuously suburban-middle-class. Around midnight, the stage door would open and Judy would emerge, usually accompanied by Chaplin, occasionally with her mother bringing up the rear. A long Cadillac limousine would be waiting to take her to dinner or drive her uptown to the Dakota. No one asked for her autograph, no one pushed toward her or tried to touch her. Occasionally someone would shout "Hi, Judy" or "We love you, Judy" and she'd smile and wave before driving off. Then the crowd would slowly, happily disperse.

This nightly ritual was quickly to become something of a legend along Shubert Alley. No star has ever received so gentle and civilized a display of heartfelt affection. Judy was deeply moved by it. Later she would recall it as one of the nicest things about one of the best years of her life.

Chapter Fourteen

THE PARTY'S OVER

The good days were ultimately to add up to something less than a year. But the good days were very good indeed— though they were based on very slender underpinnings. Judy counted her blessings on two intertwined fingers: *The Bells Are Ringing* and Sydney Chaplin. When the romance went sour, the show no longer seemed so sweet. But at the start of 1957, everything seemed to be in perfect balance.

At least that's the way it looked to Judy. Her friends were less sanguine. Chaplin had repeatedly told her, in so many words, "I like you, I like us, but I don't *love* you." Judy, however, was deaf to the downbeat note at the close of the refrain. She chose to hear what she wanted to hear. Everyone knew she and Chaplin were in love. The gossip columnists had started linking their names even before the first rehearsals for *Bells*, and by March 1957 they were predicting marriage. Judy never bothered to deny the predictions as she secretly hoped they would soon be fulfilled.

In March of 1957, with Holliday's approval, David Oppenheim had flown to Juarez, Mexico, and since the suit was not contested, within minutes of his court appearance he had been granted a divorce. Judy was represented by a lawyer who requested neither alimony nor child support. His client, the attorney stated, wanted nothing more than freedom. The reason that she demanded only release from the burden of being Mrs. Oppenheim—or so the press speculated—was that she was in a great rush to become Mrs. Sydney Chaplin.

As it turned out, David acted more precipitously than she. Only two months after the divorce, he remarried. His new wife was Ellen Adler, the daughter of Stella Adler, the celebrated actress and "method" acting teacher. Like her mother, Ellen was admired for her beauty and intelligence; if she had been a frumpish nonentity, Judy might not have minded as much. She claimed that she was upset only because David had remarried with indecent haste, but friends suspected that what really bothered her was David's choice: a bright, pretty, clever girl with a distinguished theatrical heritage—in other words, a girl who had everything Judy thought she lacked. No one dared suggest she would have remarried just as quickly had Chaplin asked her; no one dared suggest that her resentment of Ellen was a classic case of dog-in-the-manger behavior: She didn't really want David back, but she wasn't prepared to hand him over to somebody else, certainly not someone as pedigreed as Ellen Adler.

Had anyone dared say this to Judy, she would have dismissed him as a traitor. She demanded absolute, unconditional loyalty from her friends. Loyalty was one of Judy's most cherished values, one she practiced herself almost to a fault, and she expected everyone to follow suit. People who wanted to be friends with David and his new wife could not be her friends as well. Judy was cool, sometimes quite rude, toward people who went on seeing Oppenheim after the divorce. She would even cut acquaintances who had happened to run into David only accidentally or in the line of business. Many years after Holliday's death, a hostess asked Howard Teichmann if he would object to having David Oppenheim as a dinner partner. "Why should I object?" Teichmann asked. "Well, he

was Judy Holliday's husband," she said, "and you were one of
Judy's friends. . . ."

One of the most upsetting aftermaths of the divorce was
that Jonathan reacted precisely as Judy had when Abe left
Helen: He felt abandoned and resentful. This was a situation
Judy should have understood, but, because of her own attitude toward David and her involvement with Chaplin, she
handled the situation poorly. She said the right things, but
her manner belied her words, and Jonathan was to go through
a very difficult period of adjustment.

Holliday's other source of distress during the first months
of *Bells* was her health. She had a throbbing pain in her
shoulder and arm, which her doctor diagnosed as bursitis. She
was advised to take it easy, but she never missed a performance. "When she came to the theater with slings matching
the colors of her costumes, I knew I'd never go on," said
Marge Redmond, Holliday's understudy at the beginning of
the run of *Bells*.

While Judy did go on with her sling on a few occasions,
Redmond should have stayed on a bit longer than she did.
Judy, who until now had been exceedingly conscientious about
going on, had, by the spring of 1957, missed several performances—often on the same nights that Chaplin was indisposed.
Years before, a reporter had asked Holliday what she thought
about when she kissed her leading man. "Germs," she answered. Certainly that wasn't what she thought about when
she puckered up for Chaplin, but that's what she got. "Holliday's out of *Bells* with influenza," reported Leonard Lyons.
"Sydney Chaplin tried to kiss it away and now he's indisposed,
too."

That spring, Holliday and Chaplin both won Tony Awards
as best musical actress and supporting actor against such rough
competition as Julie Andrews and Stanley Holloway for *My
Fair Lady*. A month later, Judy rented a house in Connecticut
for the summer. Though she retained ownership of the farm
David had bought for her in upstate New York, she needed a

weekend hideaway closer to Manhattan, and chose the Connecticut place mainly for Jonathan, she said. Under Helen's supervision, he could play at the beach while his mother slaved away at the Shubert Theatre. Every weekend she'd be there for a day or so. Usually with Mr. Chaplin.

The rumors that Holliday and Chaplin would soon marry intensified when, at the end of September, it was announced that they were traveling together to Europe for a brief vacation and would be stopping off in France and Switzerland. There was a chance they would also be going to London, where there was interest in a West End production of *Bells*, with Holliday (a great popular favorite in England) and Chaplin re-creating their Broadway roles. All the gossips, from Dorothy Kilgallen to Hedda Hopper, predicted that on their return to the States they would be husband and wife. Apparently Judy believed it, too.

Despite the fact that their romance was common knowledge, they chose to play at discretion during their European travels. The *Herald-Tribune*, with tongue in cheek, reported: "[Holliday and Chaplin] arrived on the same plane, but pretended hardly to know each other. They booked rooms in the same Right Bank hotel [George V] . . . on separate floors . . . and have deliberately avoided the tourist circuit." Chaplin had formerly lived in Paris, and now he took Holliday on a tour of his favorite haunts, introducing her to such old cronies as the music-hall entertainer Moustache, who would later team up with Chaplin as co-proprietor of a Left Bank cabaret, Chez Mous'.

After three days in Paris, Judy and Sydney moved on to Switzerland where they planned to visit Chaplin's father and stepmother at their villa, Manoir de Ban, near Vevey. Judy was both excited and apprehensive about the visit: Like nearly everyone, she was in awe of the elder Chaplin's reputation and talent. As it turned out, she was right to be nervous—the trip was the prelude to disaster. Precisely what happened in Vevey no one except the participants will ever know, except that the visit ended abruptly, and shortly after their return to France, Holliday and Chaplin parted company. Bitterly, it seems. Judy left almost immediately for the States, while Sydney lingered on in Paris for a week or so.

Back in New York, Judy made it clear that Chaplin was a taboo subject even for her closest friends, none of whom were ever to learn the cause of the dramatic upheaval. For a couple of days, she took to her bed with a fifth of Scotch, but liquor neither loosened her tongue nor deadened the hurt; it just left her with a devastating hangover. As another Lillian Roth, she was a flop—she could laugh about that—but as for the reasons that led her to the booze, they were to remain bottled inside her.

Chaplin was equally reticent. Only once was he known to speak about his affair with Holliday, and then only obliquely. In her autobiography, Lauren Bacall recalls that when Chaplin was appearing with her in *Goodbye, Charlie* (1959), he warned her at the outset that, though he liked and admired her, there wasn't going to be any romance; he had gone that route once before and was resolved to bypass it in the future. Ordinary lovers could walk away from each other once the romance was over, but Broadway lovers had to go on facing each other, feigning emotions they once sincerely felt, eight times a week. And that could be painful, very nasty, as he had learned from experience. (Apparently, however, the flesh is stronger than the will, since according to rumors, Chaplin was to go through the whole ordeal again when he co-starred with Barbra Streisand in the 1964 Broadway production of *Funny Girl.*)

By the fall of 1957, when Holliday and Chaplin had returned to *Bells Are Ringing,* rumors were already flying about their feud. The animosity wasn't evident on stage, but now when Holliday left after the show, she got into the big black Cadillac by herself. The gossips of Shubert Alley had several explanations for the estrangement. One was that the senior Chaplin had disapproved of Holliday, though no one was able to suggest why he should, except that he was reputed to be an anti-Semitic Jew. Whatever the reason, he *did* disapprove, and Sydney, who knew that his father had left him a tidy fortune in a trust fund that was about to mature, wasn't about to force a showdown with the old man. Once they got back to Paris, he dropped Holliday as though she were a carrier of the plague.

Judy, too, may have come to some stark realizations. It is very likely that sometime during the trip she suddenly recognized that Chaplin wasn't playing hard-to-get when he said I don't love you and I don't want to marry you. Perhaps the truth finally struck home during the visit to Manoir de Ban: This would have been the ideal opportunity for Sydney to introduce Holliday as his fiancée, and when, most likely, he didn't, she must have had to face facts.

As had been the case when she broke up with David, Judy once again demanded total loyalty on the part of her friends: Anyone who went on socializing with Chaplin was sure to feel the full force of her wrath. When Adolph Green visited her dressing room one evening, Judy slammed the door in his face: She knew he had lunched with Sydney that afternoon. Green told her she was acting irrationally, that there was no reason why he couldn't go on being friends with both her and Chaplin. But Judy couldn't see it that way: Chaplin was the enemy, and consorting with him was an act of betrayal.

The atmosphere backstage at the Shubert was tense and demoralizing for the other actors, who found themselves unwittingly caught up in the feud between the star and her leading man. Communication between Holliday and Chaplin was limited to notes carried back and forth by an assistant stage manager, and the messages were exclusively concerned with matters of stage deportment. Judy had taken to bickering about Chaplin's performances, accusing him of sloughing off, of stepping on her laughs, of various forms of flagrant unprofessionalism. Sometimes he was guilty; more often not.

When Chaplin's contract expired in the early months of

1958, he neither requested nor was offered an extension. The role of Jeff Moss was taken over by his understudy, Hal Linden, later to gain fame as TV's "Barney Miller." Holliday liked Linden; but after the Chaplin upheaval, much of the fun had gone out of *The Bells Are Ringing*, and, with it, some of the exuberance she had originally brought to her portrayal of Ella Peterson.

Soon after Chaplin's departure from *Bells*, Judy suffered another emotional setback. In January 1958, at age sixty-four, Abe Tuvim died of cancer. Though he had looked sickly for some time, no one had realized how ill he really was, and Abe, if he knew, had never told his daughter or former wife. Judy had learned to forgive Abe for all the real and imaginary neglect of her childhood, and she had wanted to grow closer to him, but she sensed that she would be hurting Helen, who still harbored a great deal of resentment toward her former husband. After Abe's death, Judy was guilt-stricken; she couldn't help but feel that she had failed to bridge the gulf between them as solidly as she should have. About the only tribute she could give him was to miss a couple of performances of *Bells* and that seemed so trivial. All the personal strands of her life seemed to unravel and fall apart in her hands, no matter how hard or how lovingly she struggled to weave them together.

Judy remained down in the depths for the better part of 1958. She continued giving expert, though increasingly mechanical, performances in *Bells*, which was still doing nearly SRO business. To make a little extra cash—not that she needed it; she got a percentage of the *Bells* receipts—she made a few guest appearances on TV shows and plugged Rheingold beer. Maybe it wasn't dignified, but it kept her busy, and staying occupied had always been the best medicine for her spells of depression.

Her one labor of love during this period was a record album she cut for Columbia Records in February 1958. Initially she had to be nearly browbeaten into doing it, but Goddard Lieberson, who was head of artists and repertoire at Columbia and had personally supervised the best-selling original-cast recording of *Bells*, eventually convinced her that she had the vocal ability to carry a solo album. Judy spent weeks deciding on precisely the right songs—she chose a mixture of the familiar and the esoteric, ranging from Berlin and Bernstein to Ralph Blaine and Alec Wilder—and her drive for perfection made the taping sessions something of a trial for everyone concerned. Judy's performance was favorably received, but the album (called *Trouble Is a Man*, after an Alec Wilder ballad that Holliday sang as the opening number) sold modestly and was swiftly deleted from the Columbia catalog. (Today, it is a collector's item, even a battered copy going for over $80.)

All through this period Judy tried to find as much time as possible for Jonathan. He still had not entirely adjusted to David's absence, and while Judy wanted to compensate for the lack of a father, there was not much she could do except shower him with attention. Although she was a stern disciplinarian, she worried about Jonathan becoming spoiled. There were too many women around him: Tessa and Helen were always hovering about, worrying whether he was eating the right foods, pampering and smothering him. He needed a man to take him in hand. That wasn't, Judy thought, such a bad prescription for herself, either.

After the breakup with Chaplin, Judy was occasionally seen around town with various men. One of her escorts was Morton Gottlieb, a young theatrical producer, who took her to Broadway openings and the screenings of movies, both new and old—Gottlieb was a FOOF (Friend of Old Films) and adored Griffith and the Gish sisters, Swanson and De-Mille. But her evenings with Gottlieb were pure companionship—there was no idea of romance at the back of either's mind. She saw a few other men, but none was a serious candidate for a lasting relationship.

It was not until spring 1958 that Judy met the man who would be possibly the most important love of her life. His name was Gerry Mulligan, and he was a bass saxophonist jazz composer and arranger who was acclaimed as one of the great innovators in his field. Judy had admired his music and now she found herself being drawn to him in a more personal manner.

He was, she would later discover, six years younger than she—a vital statistic that was never to bother either of them. Born in New York, he grew up in Philadelphia, and it was there that he became involved with jazz. From early childhood, his one consuming passion had been music. In the late Forties, he had started playing with Gene Krupa and Miles Davis, also arranging and composing for them. In 1952 he moved to California and, with Chet Baker and Chico Hamilton, started experimenting with a pianoless quartet, a novel concept that produced a new and provocative tone color and, according to connoisseurs, "enriched the modern jazz palette." Along the way he had married and then separated from his first wife, but continued to see their son. Details were vague— he didn't care to dwell on his past.

Mulligan was, in fact, a very private person, quite reticent and inclined to be moody—"a true black Irishman," as Anita Loos once called him. But when he did have something to say, it was often wildly funny. "He had that crazy musician's knack of giving the obvious a delicious, almost surreal slant." Tall, redheaded, and lanky, he was good-looking in an oversize Tom Sawyerish way. Women generally found him very attractive, and Judy was no exception. Almost immediately she and Mulligan were engaged in an intense and richly satisfying romance that would endure for the better part of five years. One of their first public appearances together was at Birdland, where they listened to Billie Holiday, the great jazz singer who was to die a year later. (Holiday was Judy's favorite vocalist; she had all her records and played them incessantly at the Dakota.) In April 1958, Mulligan formed a new combo that played lengthy engagements at the Village Vanguard, the Revuers first home. "Judy was there every evening," recalls proprietor Max Gordon. "She was Gerry's number one fan."

Usually, she arrived right after her performance in *Bells*, and would stay until Gerry was finished, at about three. She'd sit at a back table, where she was rarely noticed, nursing a drink and chatting with Max and the members of the combo between sets. Once or twice, according to Gordon, she went out to the kitchen and rustled up a Scrabble game with some of the help. After the club closed, she and Gerry would go out for a bite to eat, often for corned beef sandwiches and cheesecake at Reuben's on 58th Street.

Unquestionably, one of Gerry's strongest attractions for Judy was his talent—she had always had an almost exaggerated respect for musicians. Gerry's first love had always been arranging, but recently he had decided he wanted to concentrate on performing. Judy encouraged him. Songwriting was an endeavor that had always fascinated her, and one that she had fooled around with when she was much younger. Maybe they could form a team: He'd write the melodies; she'd provide the words. Gerry was all for it, but right now neither of their schedules allowed them the opportunity to do more than discuss the project.

By the fall of 1958, business for *Bells* had started to fall off, and it seemed doubtful that the show would survive much past the early months of the new year. Judy was indifferent; if the run extended beyond February 1959, she would have to leave the cast anyway, because she was scheduled to be in Hollywood by then to begin work on the film version of the play at M-G-M.

Bells finally closed in mid-February, after 924 performances, but Holliday asked M-G-M to postpone the start of production so that she could appear with the road company in Wash-

ington, Los Angeles, and San Francisco. The idea of a brief
tour appealed to her, and at the same time it would be a boon
for her producers. The studio readily agreed to her request,
partly because Comden and Green were yet to turn in an ac-
ceptable film script, partly because they wanted to accommo-
date Holliday in any way possible.

Judy was in fine fettle when she opened at the Philharmonic
in Los Angeles on April 20, 1959. She looked lovely, and the
change of locale brought a renewed luster to her performance
(all actors work a little harder in Los Angeles where they know
a major portion of the audience will be made up of their
peers). Adding to her sense of well-being was the presence of
Mulligan, who, in an attempt to expand the perimeters of his
career, had been doing a lot of work for the movies: A year
earlier he had performed the score for *I Want to Live!* and
now he was working as an actor in *The Rat Race* at Warners,
to be followed by a role in *The Subterraneans* for M-G-M.
Later, when the show moved to San Francisco, he would fly
up to spend every weekend with Judy.

Holliday returned to Los Angeles for preproduction meetings on *Bells* in mid-August—actual shooting wasn't scheduled
to begin until October. Most of her preliminary duties revolved around costume fittings and conferences with director
Vincente Minnelli and producer Arthur Freed, the master-
minds behind many of the great M-G-M musicals of the Forties and Fifties. Judy told Freed she thought the script for the
film was pedestrian, and though he didn't say so, Freed
tended to agree: Comden and Green had cut a couple of
scenes and added a few others, but they hadn't corrected the
weaknesses of the original, they had only prolonged the story
without making it cinematic. Judy also told Comden and
Green what she thought, and they definitely did not agree.
The three friends had been on the outs ever since the Chaplin
incident, and this argument was to put yet another dent in
their relationship. But Judy didn't care: She knew she was
right about the script—it was seriously flawed.

Since she had little work to do for almost two months, Judy fell once again into the pattern of brooding and eating. By the time filming started, she was so overweight that all her costumes had to be refitted or redesigned and she had lost confidence about the outcome of the film—her first in four years. She was so afraid it would be a failure, she distrusted everyone and everything connected with the picture. Freed, who was affable but inarticulate and unimaginative in the area of personal relations, tried to establish a rapport with Holliday, but he found her progressively less communicative. Hoping it would bolster her morale, he hired Mulligan for a small role in *Bells*, but Judy barely acknowledged the gesture.

Vincente Minnelli was also surprised to find he couldn't gain Holliday's confidence. He had been one of her fans since the Revuers days, and had expected no difficulties in working with her. As onetime director and former husband of Judy Garland, he was not unaccustomed nor unsympathetic to temperamental actresses, but he was unable to get to first base with Holliday. Why, he wondered, should she be so apprehensive about filming a role she had played nearly a thousand times on stage? It was really not such a mystery: Holliday needed to rethink the part for the screen, but, getting no incentive from Minnelli or from Comden and Green's script, she was at a loss as to where to turn.

After the first week of shooting, she became so distraught that she begged to be released from the picture: She would even contribute her entire salary if they would only start all over again with another actress—maybe Shirley MacLaine. The offer was politely refused. Judy resigned herself to finishing the film, but her anxiety broke out in a new form: Suddenly she was afflicted with a scourge of diseases. Her bursitis returned; then she came down with laryngitis; then a bladder ailment; finally a kidney infection. Later there was to be a series of freak accidents. First a heavy suitcase fell on her foot, causing her to limp for a few days; then, in a scene requiring her to walk across a room with the back of her dress

on fire, the igniting apparatus became overheated and she
was badly burned.

At the time, most of Judy's ailments were generally considered to be psychosomatic in origin; but in light of what was
to happen a year later, this seems a false assumption. Holliday was truly ill, otherwise she would never have acted as
she did; she had never been difficult or temperamental in the
past. The cast and crew were extremely considerate, almost
compassionate in their deference toward her. Minnelli did
his best to reassure her, but he failed to win Judy's confidence
simply because she was convinced that the entire concept of
the film was hopelessly, irredeemably wrong. The production
was a nightmare from start to finish. Judy had frequent crying
jags, and when she wasn't in front of the camera, she was
sequestered in her dressing room with Mulligan, rarely speaking to anyone else, not even her costar, Dean Martin, who
remained good-natured though he let it be known that he
thought the role of Jeff Moss was a waste of his time and
talent.

Judy's only other trusted companion on the set was Ralph
Roberts, who was cast in a small role in the picture. Known
as "Big Ralph," this muscular actor with a soft southern
drawl had for years been moonlighting as a masseur, and,
much to his consternation, his therapeutic fingers were in
greater demand than his acting abilities. Marilyn Monroe
was his most fervent fan—she was always calling for him at
ungodly hours.

Now Judy began to sing Roberts's praises. His mere presence was nearly as soothing as his invigorating massages. He
had this effect on everyone, an ability to restore harmony to
the most tension-filled room. He and Holliday became good
friends, and in the future she would call on his services whenever she was passing through a period of distress.

Following the wrap-up of the film in December 1959, Judy
rushed back to New York, angry at nearly everyone, convinced
that the picture wasn't worth the celluloid it was printed on.

And, as it turned out, she wasn't entirely wrong. Her performance is amazingly good, but the script is even weaker than the original, and the production is lethargic and synthetic, a mediocre example of canned theater.

The picture opened six months later to favorable, if less than enthusiastic, reviews, and the public reaction ranged from good to tepid. Ultimately the picture failed to recoup M-G-M's investment, because, it was claimed, musicals were temporarily out of favor with American filmgoers. The explanation, however, rests on shaky ground since the top-grossing films for the next five years include *West Side Story, Mary Poppins, My Fair Lady,* and *The Sound of Music.* Filmgoers had rejected not musicals in general but specifically *The Bells Are Ringing.* It was Judy's first out-and-out box-office bomb. It was also to be her last picture.

Chapter Fifteen

UNRAVELINGS

For most of 1960, Holliday stayed out of the public eye. Her professional visibility was limited to a few TV appearances and, of course, the film version of *Bells*. A few stage offers came her way, but nothing terribly intriguing; and anyway, after over two years of steady work, she felt she deserved a prolonged vacation. She desperately needed an extended period of relaxation after the trauma of filming *Bells Are Ringing*.

She now began spending a lot of time at her country home in Washingtonville. She had worked hard to give the house the ambience she wanted: It had never been intended as a showcase, but rather was meant to radiate warmth and hospitality. Downstairs there was a large L-shaped living room with big mullioned windows and plank floors covered with hooked rugs. Books were scattered everywhere. Off the main room was a bright and airy kitchen. Upstairs there were four bedrooms off a central hallway. The front of the house was surrounded by gardens, and in the back there was a swimming pool.

One of the first gifts Mulligan bought her was a bumper-pool table. Judy was an aficionada of any form of billiards and was a regular at the neighborhood taverns where the game was played. The clientele at these dives was scruffy, if not dangerous, and Gerry tried to persuade Judy to steer clear of them. When she refused, he bought her a table of her own. She was enchanted by his present, though later she secretly confided to a friend that, for her, pool's major attraction was the shady establishments where it was played.

Jonathan was now a student at the Ethical Culture School in Manhattan, but he spent nearly every weekend with his mother and Gerry. Judy was thrilled at the rapport developing between them—they had become very close and Jonathan was starting to accept Gerry as a surrogate father. She in turn had taken in hand Gerry's son (an occasional overnight visitor): He was a rambunctious, highly active child who tried nearly everyone's patience, but Judy handled him beautifully. There was a family feeling about the Washingtonville house, and Judy and Gerry were as comfortable together as an old, happily married couple. Marriage, however, was not a step either one contemplated taking at this time; blissfully content just as they were, they saw no reason to risk an idyllic relationship for the sake of a ring and a slip of paper.

Judy spent her days at the country hideaway gardening and cooking and writing songs with Gerry. Their proposed collaboration had finally gotten under way in California some months earlier, and now they were really forging ahead. Gerry had a small electric piano, which he brought to Washingtonville, and a good part of every day was spent working on their music.

Judy's lyrics dealt with simple human emotions expressed in intricate, often unorthodox patterns of rhythm and rhyme. She was bubbling over with ideas, and Mulligan kept asking for more. In the past, he had been known to spend a year on a song, but now he worked with lightning speed, and often in a more melodic and popular form than his previous jazz-oriented compositions. Judy was thrilled when Dinah Shore introduced one of their songs, "Blue Christmas," on her TV program. "It meant as much to me as winning the Oscar," she told a reporter.

But as yet their songs weren't bringing in much money, and, with a mother and a son to support, Judy soon became concerned at the amount of money flowing out with nothing coming in. She decided that, for the time being, she should concentrate on acting and leave songwriting for her spare time. She had found a play that was challenging, and also a little terrifying, since it was unlike anything she had ever done before. Called *Laurette*, it was based on the life of the legendary American actress Laurette Taylor, who in middle age had declined into alcoholism but eventually returned in triumph to the stage as Amanda Wingfield in Tennessee Williams's *Glass Menagerie*.

Alan Pakula, a young producer with a few Hollywood and Broadway credits (later to achieve celebrity as the director of the films *Klute* and *The Sterile Cuckoo*), had been assembling the pieces of the production for over four years, and several times asked Judy to take on the leading role. She was intrigued—she had, after all, railed against the "fluff" she had been forced to make in Hollywood—but still she kept putting him off with the old excuses: She was a comedienne; people wouldn't accept her in a dramatic role. She also came up with some new ones: She didn't drink and she wasn't Irish, and so wasn't the right type to play Laurette. Pakula, however, wanted Holliday—and by offering her extremely lucrative terms, he finally got her. She was to receive fifteen percent of the gross plus fifteen percent of the net profits, with a salary guarantee of $3,000 a week.

When she signed, it was still with very mixed emotions: She was excited by the opportunity, but also filled with doubts about how competently she could carry out the assignment. The idea of impersonating Taylor terrified her. She had seen the actress in *Menagerie* and agreed with George Cukor and Spencer Tracy and nearly everybody else that Laurette was the first and greatest of them all. Two years earlier, when *Life* had photographed several Broadway stars in the costumes of the character they most wanted to play, Holliday had chosen Amanda in *The Glass Menagerie*. She had done so as a tribute to Taylor, not because it was a part she expected or really wanted to play. How could she after seeing Taylor? And how dare she portray Taylor herself? There were still many people around who had seen and known Laurette and would undoubtedly scoff at her presumptuous impersonation. Or so she believed. Actually, George Cukor, among others, thought she was a superb choice.

There were other reasons for Judy's initial apprehension. Adapted from Marguerite Courtney's harrowing biography, the script by Stanley Young (a British dramatist whose major Broadway credit was a middling Dickens adaptation, *Mr. Pickwick*) was pretty poor. Pakula assured her that revisions were underway, but Holliday, who had a very astute story mind, wondered whether there wasn't a fundamental problem with the original material: Reduced to a conventional dramatic narrative, Courtney's biography seemed destined to become another *I'll Cry Tomorrow*; and while that might be ideal for Hollywood and Susan Hayward, it wasn't what people paid $7.50 to see on Broadway.

She knew that the success or failure of the show was going to depend mainly on her own performance. And the weight of responsibility was all the heavier because there were such high hopes for her first appearance in a dramatic show. She had always been wrong about her fans' expectations, at least about those fans who took time to consider such matters: They, like many of Judy's peers, longed to see her extend herself, wanted her to push beyond *Born Yesterday* and *Bells Are Ringing* and all her other Broadway and Hollywood ephemera. Now it looked as though she were going to take the step. And how appropriate it was that she was taking it by playing Laurette Taylor, a woman who had squandered her talent on roles that never really challenged her until she got to *Menagerie*.

By the time of its first out-of-town engagement, *Laurette*

had built up a hefty advance on Broadway, entirely on the strength of Holliday's name. Holliday as Laurette was a shoo-in as the theatrical event of the season. But on the Sunday before the New Haven opening, September 26, 1960, the *New York Herald-Tribune* carried an article saying the show was in serious trouble. Several members of the company read the *Tribune* piece as they were about to set off for New Haven. They shrugged it off stoically—it only told them what they already knew.

Though there were many contributing factors, the source of the trouble lay with the director and his inability to relate to Holliday. José Quintero, a Panamanian by birth, had first achieved prominence in the early 1950s through his work at the Circle in the Square in Greenwich Village. In 1956 he staged two of the most memorable productions of the decade —a revival of Eugene O'Neill's *The Iceman Cometh* and, six months later, the American premiere of O'Neill's *Long Day's Journey into Night*. Afterward there were a few Broadway flops and a number of off-Broadway successes, notably an intensely erotic, if somewhat muddled, staging of Jean Genet's *The Balcony*.

For all the esteem and critical praise, there was a coterie of theater people who held that Quintero's work had started to fall off, that there had been a shoddy, half-baked finish to several of his recent productions. Rumors circulated that drink had started to interfere with his work.

"I was very much puzzled by the way he operated," said one of his stage managers. "He'd come in at ten, rehearse for about forty-five minutes, then call a twenty-minute break. Then he'd wander off by himself. The same pattern went on all day, day after day: An hour or so of work, followed by a generous period of time off. One morning I decided to tail him—I was curious as to what he was up to. Well, he left the theater and went straight across the street to a bar."

Quintero was eventually to conquer his drinking problem, but in 1960 it had yet to reach its peak.

Rehearsals began in the middle of August 1960. Jack Gwillim had been brought from London to play Laurette's husband, English playwright J. Hartley Manners. Other members of the cast included Joan Hackett and Clinton Kimbrough (as Laurette's children); Patrick O'Neal (as Laurette's lover, silent-screen star John Gilbert); Nancy Marchand; Bibi Osterwald; and James Olson. Many of these actors—including Betty Miller, Holliday's standby—had worked with Quintero previously and were extremely loyal; nearly all of them had been trained either at the Actors Studio or in Stella Adler's version of the Stanislavski "method," giving them a common language that Judy didn't speak. Intuitively she approached a role in a similar fashion, but she was largely a self-taught actress and didn't understand their jargon. Already prone to feelings of inadequacy, Judy quickly lost whatever assurance she had managed to muster.

Judy arrived for the first rehearsal at the Forty-sixth Street Theatre surrounded by her own small band of adherents, including her mother; Gerry Mulligan; Elizabeth White, her backstage maid and dresser; and Paul Davis, who was to work as her secretary and general factotum on this production (Davis was the husband of Judy's close friend, comedienne Alice Pearce). They stayed in the background, but at least one of them was always close at hand in case Judy needed tea or sympathy. Throughout rehearsals, Holliday was remote: She was never less than polite, and never exhibited any symptoms of star temperament, but she kept very much to herself, rarely fraternizing with the other actors. And they gave her lots of latitude; it was clear that she was extremely nervous and unsure of herself.

For the first two days, Quintero had the actors read through the script. Then he got them on their feet and began to block the action. For the next week that's all he did. He spent all morning—with several fifteen-minute breaks—blocking a scene; and then he'd break for lunch, return, and start again from scratch. The constant revisions bewildered the other actors, but Judy took it in stride. "Once I picked up her script and leafed through it," recalls Gwyda Kean who was understudying Joan Hackett and also playing the small role of Laurette's French maid. "There was not one mark anywhere. She kept everything in her mind, all those senseless changes, and she *never* made a mistake. It was amazing."

Though Quintero was notorious for the excessive amount of energy he spent on blocking, in this instance he was justifiably stalling for time. Like Holliday, he had been disturbed by the flimsiness of Stanley Young's script, and, without Young's approval, he had asked critic and novelist Gavin Lambert to overhaul the play scene by scene. Lambert was working around the clock in a hotel suite at the Algonquin, and some of his material was actually being rehearsed— blocked—when Young stopped by the theater and realized what was going on. He threatened legal action if Quintero did not return to the original script. Later Young made his own alterations, but his rewrites failed to clarify the play's episodic and confused narrative.

During the second week of rehearsals, Quintero worked on interpretation, but by then he had lost faith in the script and in his ability to surmount its shortcomings. He guided Judy gingerly, but what she needed most was reassurance, and this he couldn't give because he was in search of it himself. "It was an insane situation," remembers production assistant Norman Kean (who was married to Gwyda Kean). "José wanted Holliday to tell him how great he was, and she wanted him to tell her how wonderful she was going to be, and neither was ready to meet the other halfway."

Judy's rehearsal performances were very small, very delicate, almost birdlike in quality. She never spoke above a whisper, and, following her lead, the entire cast began murmuring their lines. It was clear that if they didn't turn up the volume, they wouldn't be heard beyond the proscenium arch. But no one was unduly disturbed by the fact that Judy was holding back. She had always been extremely tentative in rehearsals, as were many actors, including (it is reported) Laurette Taylor, who never gave any indication of what she was going to do on stage until she faced her first audience. "We were all confident that on opening night Judy'd pull it all together and give a really great performance," says Norman Kean.

But at the New Haven premiere, Holliday was still giving her rehearsal performance. Though effective at moments, she was noticeably unsure of herself and frequently inaudible; patrons at the back of the theater complained that they missed over half of her lines. The reviews the next morning were lukewarm but not unencouraging. *Variety* would report later that week: "*Laurette* must probe deeper into its subject. . . . as of now, it varies from pedestrian to engrossing. . . . Holliday hasn't yet found the heart of the character, but her initial performance presents optimistic possibilities."

Judy took the reviews in stride: They were better than she had expected, better than she deserved, and they gave her the incentive to go on to sharpen the definition of the character she had begun to build. And for the first time Quintero really began to direct. "I really think it'll come out all right," Judy told Norman Kean, with whom she had become friendly. Each of her subsequent performances gained a little in strength and focus, and she was now clearly audible throughout the theater, though the effort of projecting her voice left her with a nagging and persistent sore throat. Nonetheless, she was now confident that she could create a performance of which she could be proud.

To do that, however, she needed the support of the entire company, and on one disastrous evening she discovered, in the worst of all possible ways, that such support was not to be had. After the performance on the penultimate night of the New Haven run, she returned to the Taft Hotel to study some dialogue revisions for the next day's performance. It was difficult for her to concentrate as there was a party going on in an adjacent suite, which, she knew, was occupied by Quintero. The walls of the Taft were thin and an air vent between the rooms had been left open, so she could hear practically every word that was being said, could even identify several of the speakers, especially Quintero whose heavy Spanish accent was easily recognizable. It was even more pronounced than usual, as he had had too much to drink.

For a while she tried to block out the conversation, but then Quintero began speaking about her, and there was no way not to listen. He called her performance incompetent. He predicted that she'd never improve. He wondered why she didn't face facts and quit the show. Other voices piped in, and Judy caught the phrases "ruined by Hollywood," "totally inept," "rank amateur."

She was devastated. And very, very angry. She had always been her own harshest critic, and if she thought she could pull off this performance, she wasn't going to accept a cheap put-down from another quarter. She spent most of the night alternating between anger and hurt—and pondering what she should do the following day. Constructively, there were only two courses of action open to her: She could confront Quintero with what she had heard and try to resolve the dilemma; or she could go to the producer and request Quintero's dismissal. There was no earthly reason why she shouldn't have him removed—what loyalty did she owe someone who held her so cheaply?

She chose neither of these alternatives, however. In the morning she phoned Norman Kean and asked him to stop by her suite. Over a cup of coffee, she told him what had happened. Kean was shocked—he had worked with Quintero in the past and couldn't believe Quintero, even drunk, could be capable of shooting off his mouth so indiscreetly. Was it possible she was mistaken? Impossible, Judy insisted. Then briefly she lost control of herself. "What am I doing?" she sobbed. "Why am I here?"

Regaining her composure, she went on to explain that though once she had planned to give everything to the play, now she wasn't sure she should bother. "This is just too demoralizing," she said. "I can't cope with this kind of betrayal."

Kean left her room with the definite impression that she was going to withdraw from the show. But not wishing to be the bearer of bad tidings, he decided to keep the information to himself.

Judy's performance at the matinee that afternoon was listless and perfunctory. She seemed lost in her own thoughts rather than in her character's. During the second act, as she was making an onstage costume change, she began muttering to Gwyda Kean, who was helping her arrange her dress. Referring to the audience, she whispered, "They hate me. I can feel it. I know they hate me...."

Gwyda Kean was aghast. "I finally managed to whisper, 'Oh, Miss Holliday, I'm sure that's not true.' And, of course, it wasn't true, it was all in her mind. But that only made it more upsetting."

Before that evening's performance—the final one in New Haven—Judy's spirit came back and anger replaced the former despondency. "She gave a *real* performance that night," recalls Norman Kean. "One with gumption and energy and volume—every word came through clear as a bell. It was as if she were saying to Quintero, 'Well, this is what I could do, but you blew it.' "

After the performance, Mulligan picked her up at the theater to drive her back to New York. Gerry had stayed very much in the background throughout the production. When he had taken a small role in *Bells*, there had been some snide comments about how he was taking a free ride on Judy's coattails. It was all ludicrous nonsense, since in his own field he was as celebrated as she, and made just as much money; and if he had wanted to get ahead in the movies, he could have done so very well without her help. He adored Judy and would do anything in his power to protect her, but he was determined not to be mistaken as the man behind the throne. Whenever she needed his advice, he'd be around to give it—but discreetly, very far from center stage.

Judy planned to spend Sunday resting at the Dakota before joining the other actors in Philadelphia, where *Laurette* was to continue its tryout tour. But many people besides the Keans wondered whether she would show up for the opening on Monday. She had been complaining of throat and chest pains, and it seemed likely that she was planning to pull a Jean Arthur and leave the play on grounds of poor health.

Judy fooled them. That Monday she checked in at the Bellevue-Stratford Hotel in Philadelphia and was in her dressing room at the Forrest Theatre an hour and a half before curtain time. The performance that night was a preview before the official premiere the following evening. Judy looked pale and jittery before going on stage, which was not unusual, but on this occasion, fifteen minutes into the first act, she was still floundering. Once again she had started whispering, and past the first five rows she couldn't be heard. Soon there were shouts from the auditorium, "Speak up!" and "We can't hear you!" Judy tried, but her voice remained constricted; no matter how hard she pushed, she couldn't project to the back of the theater or to the balcony. At the curtain calls, there was nearly as much hissing and booing as perfunctory applause.

The performance left Judy emotionally and physically depleted. She had used every ounce of strength and energy she possessed, but to no purpose. "It was a nightmare," she later recalled. The sensation of audience hostility that had been no more than a fantasy in New Haven was now a reality— no doubt about it: The Philadelphia crowd really did hate her. This rejection, combined with Quintero's insult and her physical condition, was more than she could handle.

The next morning Holliday informed the producers that she was leaving the show for reasons of ill health. Later that day Richard Maney, press agent for *Laurette*, announced that Judy was suffering from "a bronchial infection." Before Maney's statement had been released to the press, Judy was on her way back to New York. Just as she was about to get into her car, parked in front of the Bellevue-Stratford, she spotted Norman Kean and stopped to thank him for everything he had done. Then, after a moment's pause, she said, "I've spent a lot of time in this corner of the world." Down the block was the Shubert Theatre, where *The Bells Are Ringing* had played, and on an adjacent street was the Locust, where she had appeared in *Kiss Them for Me* and *Born Yesterday*. "Those were the good times," she said with a wan smile. Then she abruptly got into the car, and Gerry Mulligan, seated behind the wheel, pulled away from the curb.

Chapter Sixteen

RUNNING OUT OF LUCK

Just before rehearsals of *Laurette* had started, Alan Pakula had insured the production with Lloyd's of London against possible cancellation due to the indisposition of the star. Insurance of this sort was common in film production, but was still something of a rarity in the theater. The policy had been taken out for publicity purposes, not because anyone anticipated that Holliday might become ill during the run of *Laurette*—or so members of the production team claim, not too convincingly. After all, how much press coverage is Lloyd's of London insurance worth? (In the case of Holliday and *Laurette*, the answer is none, not even a squib in the daily gossip columns.) Whether the producers had anticipated problems with Holliday or not, the fact was that now she was incapacitated. Lloyd's would have to turn over almost $250,000 (the production cost of *Laurette*), provided there was medical verification that Holliday had been too ill to continue. It was doubtful, however, that such proof would be forthcoming; nearly everyone connected with the show, indeed nearly the entire theatrical community, was convinced that her vocal problems were no more than a convenient alibi.

Even Judy had no idea of how ill she really was. Since the filming of *Bells Are Ringing*, she had been plagued by a series of minor ailments, all of which had run their course and eventually disappeared. But on her return from Philadelphia, her doctor ordered her into the hospital for a thorough examination. She entered the Harkness Pavilion of the Columbia Presbyterian Medical Center on October 6, and three days later she reportedly underwent an operation to remove a tumor in her throat. Later that day, it was announced that the growth was nonmalignant and that she would spend two weeks recovering in the hospital, during which period she would be forbidden to speak. In other words, she was unavailable to the press.

What the initial report failed to mention was that the doctors had also found a lump in one of Judy's breasts, and that the prognosis was unfavorable. On October 12, a biopsy was performed, then a mastectomy. Judy was told that the cancer appeared not to have spread, and that the chances it would occur elsewhere were slim. On November 3, precisely a month after the closing of *Laurette* in Philadelphia, she was released from the hospital to begin the long and painful process of rehabilitation.

Judy was deeply depressed and terribly frightened. Despite her doctor's reassurance, cancer was a dread disease, one that her father had recently died from. Furthermore, breast cancer in particular—especially at this time—was a subject never discussed in polite circles. There was a strange aura of shame and revulsion that surrounded it, which made it all the more terrifying to Judy.

As many women did, Judy felt disfigured; she saw herself as grotesque. Throughout her life she had been self-conscious about her appearance, but now the problem was aggravated ten times over. All actresses depend heavily on physical allure, and Judy, who now felt she had absolutely none to offer, refused to consider returning to acting. Every attractive woman she met now seemed a threat, a rival she couldn't hope to match, so she stopped going out to parties and clubs. Trying on clothes in front of a salesgirl was an embarrassment, so she gave up shopping, an activity that in recent years she had begun to enjoy.

The trauma was so severe that Judy rarely discussed the operation, even with her closest friends, and then only fleetingly and almost impersonally. It was something she never chose to reveal to the public—this was long before the era when celebrities shared such information with their fans. Some years later, Jerry Tallmer, a hip and sympathetic entertainment reporter for the *New York Post*, broached the subject, but Judy cut him off immediately. "I don't want to talk about it," she said. "It'll just make me feel bad all over again. . . . The one thing I can tell you is—it's trite to say, but it's absolutely true—that adversity strengthens. I could go into a tizzy much easier before than now, though it's too bad I had to learn it the hard way. But then it wouldn't be adversity if you didn't have to learn it the hard way."

As soon as she had learned that she might have cancer, Judy's first concern was Jonathan and Helen—she forbade any mention of cancer in their presence. But after the operation, the truth couldn't be hidden for very long from Helen, and, as Judy had feared, her mother became distraught when she learned what had happened. Irrationally, Helen blamed Abe for transmitting the disease to their daughter: "That's just about the only thing he ever gave Judy," she commented bitterly, conveniently forgetting that there was a history of cancer on both sides of the family—Judy's grandmother, Rachel, had also died of the disease.

Mulligan helped Judy cope with Helen: His was the one unwavering voice of sanity during this long ordeal. Their affair was at its most intense just before the operation, and of course Judy was initially terrified that his physical attraction to her would swiftly deteriorate, or—worse yet—that he would feign desire out of pity. Mulligan, however, remained steadfast, and in the months ahead, Judy, convinced of his love and devotion, came to depend on him even more heavily than in the past.

Holliday's doctors lectured about the importance of getting back to work quickly—a productive and positive existence being, in their opinion, the best treatment for post-mastectomy depression. Judy could see the wisdom of this advice and she tried to follow it. Less than three months after her surgery, she made a guest appearance on Perry Como's TV show, and a few weeks later she told the press that she was looking forward to returning to the screen in an adaptation of the then-popular English novel *Swans at My Window*, with Jack Hawkins as her costar. But the Hollywood studios expressed no interest in the project—with the failure of *The Bells Are Ringing* Holliday's ranking as a box-office star had declined dramatically—and Judy herself wasn't all that enthusiastic about the project, or, for that matter, about appearing in any production, whether for screen, stage, or TV.

The problem was that she was reluctant to pick up her career until she felt at ease about her disfigurement, and she had not as yet reached that point of self-acceptance. It didn't matter that "nobody knew"; it was enough that she knew and was uncomfortable. And, anyway, people *did* know—not the general public, perhaps, but in show-business circles her secret was common knowledge. "But, Judy, darling," said one well-meaning friend, "the people who are aware will admire you all the more." Judy couldn't see it that way; she didn't want to collect notices for her bravery.

Judy was not entirely guilty of malingering when she cited her mastectomy as the source of her reluctance to perform, but she wasn't entirely truthful, either. The problem cut deeper—or wider—than that. She was, in fact, recovering from two wounds. The ordeal of *Laurette* had left her doubtful as to whether she ever wanted to perform again, no matter what her physical condition. Finding an alternative career to acting had been an insistent preoccupation since the filming of *The Bells Are Ringing*, and now the search for an

alternative intensified. To explain her position, she revived
some of her adolescent reasons for disparaging a life on the
stage: It was childish, exhibitionist, socially insignificant, emotionally and physically debilitating, unfulfilling except in
terms of financial and vainglorious rewards.

By the late spring of 1961, Holliday's mood was so black it
began to spill over, untypically, into the few interviews she
gave at this time. "I don't know," she told a reporter from the
Tribune. "Everything's lousy . . . maybe my luck's run out."

Adding to her depression was an accident that befell her
mother. One day that May, as Helen was waiting with Jonathan for a taxi to take him to school, an unattended car
parked in the Dakota's driveway suddenly started to roll
backward, struck her, and pinned her beneath its chassis. A
doorman immediately phoned the police and summoned Judy,
who dashed downstairs, a cloth coat hurriedly thrown over her
nightgown. The police used a jack to free Helen, and then
rushed the unconscious woman to the hospital. Judy, sobbing
and in a state of near-hysteria, rode in the ambulance. Mrs.
Tuvim's injuries were dismissed as slight—a minor concussion
and a few abrasions and contusions, nothing more—and she
was swiftly released from the hospital, with the advice that
she spend the next few days in bed. But Judy was deeply
shaken, and couldn't seem to accept it for the fortunately
minor accident it was.

Then, during her recovery, Helen began to attract newspaper attention because of a legal suit against Arthur Murray.
According to Helen, a representative of the dance school had
promised her a convertible model of a "low-price car" (a
Ford) in exchange for persuading her daughter to appear as
a guest on Murray's TV show. The program, featuring skits,
dancing lessons, and contests, had a camp appeal and attracted top name entertainers, but it was never exactly a
class act. Judy didn't want anything to do with it, but Helen
was so taken with the image of herself behind the wheel of a

convertible that eventually Judy gave in and said, okay, she'd make a fool of herself so mama could have her car.

But the producers reneged on the deal—no car, collapsible-topped or otherwise, was forthcoming. Eventually, they offered $1,650 as a settlement. Helen demanded the car or its market value—$2,999. Before the suit was resolved out of court, the Murray lawyers tried to subpoena Holliday as a witness, and reporters hung out at the Dakota, watching as a process server waited for an opportunity to deliver the writ. The story was back-page news, of course, but the coverage was nonetheless considerable and it was all unflattering for Judy: Why, the reporters asked between the lines, was a top-flight actress like Holliday haggling over the price of a not exactly topflight automobile?

This tempest over a Ford served to dull yet a little more the Holliday luster; and after the financial disaster of her last movie and the fiasco of *Laurette*, her reputation couldn't withstand further devaluation. That Judy was a penniless has-been reduced to using her mother as a business manager, as these stories implied, was a gross exaggeration. But she *was* feeling pinched. Her last substantial income had been earned for the film version of *Bells*, the aborted run of *Laurette* bringing in virtually nothing. And what was going out was tremendous—doctor and hospital bills on top of the usual household expenses.

Aggravating Judy's growing concern over money matters was yet another problem. The status of her apartment was becoming increasingly uncertain. The Dakota had been losing money for many years, and the proprietors were threatening to either raze it and use the space for a parking lot or, preferably, turn it into a cooperative, with the apartments selling at very aristocratic prices. Judy, who usually kept her distance from the other tenants—except at Christmas, when she would join other residents for the annual Carolfest in the courtyard —turned up and was unusually vocal at the many meetings held to protest the board of directors' proposal. Nothing as yet had been decided, but it seemed likely that if Judy wanted to stay on at the Dakota, she might have to pay as much as $500,000 to buy her apartment.

A quarter of that was more than she could easily afford. Between 1961 and the first months of 1963, a period when she was, except for an occasional TV appearance, inactive as an actress, she had pushed ahead with her songwriting. But as yet she and Mulligan had found few outlets for their work; their songs were in the jazz or theatrical idiom, and by the early 1960s the trend was already toward rock 'n' roll and rhythm and blues. Many times they had casually discussed the feasibility of writing the score for a stage musical, and in the spring of 1962 Judy became convinced that they should forge ahead. Broadway was just about the only showcase for the kind of sophisticated material they were turning out, and she needed, now more than ever, to sell something.

As the basis for their musical, Holliday—and there is no doubt that she was the moving force behind the project— had chosen Anita Loos's *Happy Birthday*, a play she had wanted to film during her years with Harry Cohn. The plot concerns a mousy and teetotal librarian who sneaks into a neighborhood tavern one night, gets pleasantly crocked, loses her inhibitions, and wins the man she has loved from afar for many months. The heroine, Miss Addie Bemis, was one of those dream girls who held such a strong attraction for Holliday, though at this point she had no intention of playing the role herself.

Judy called Anita Loos and asked if she would like to collaborate on the musical: Loos would write the book; Mulligan and Holliday, the score. Judy went on to say she had taken the liberty of mentioning the project to a couple of producers and had received encouraging responses.

"I was pleased that someone thought there was still some life in *Happy Birthday*," remembered Miss Loos shortly before her death in 1981. "But I was hesitant." A staunch conservative, Loos had avoided Judy over the years because of her reputation as a "hatchet thrower; a girl who was always messing up her life with politics." This was a peculiar opinion, since Holliday had been politically inactive since her brush with the McCarran committee a decade earlier. It was also an opinion Loos changed once she got to know Judy.

The three met at Loos's apartment across the street from Carnegie Hall. Loos recalled that Judy "talked about how she went there as a young girl with her father, and reminisced briefly about some of the famous artists she had seen—she fell into a brief and really wonderfully exact impression of Kirsten Flagstad." Holliday did most of the talking that evening; as Gerry was extremely laconic, she had taken on the role of conversationalist whenever they were with outsiders. "But I like people who have enough sense to keep their mouths closed unless they have something to say," Loos commented. "I liked him enormously, and Judy was adorable."

After an hour of small talk, Judy came to the point and proposed a *modus operandi* for their collaboration: Gerry was planning to rent a beach house at West Hampton for the summer, and she, her mother, and son would be staying there as houseguests; they would be delighted if Anita joined them for a working vacation—typewriters in the morning, the beach after lunch. Loos agreed to spend a week or so with them "to see how things went." As it turned out, things went extremely well, and Loos stayed for most of June and all of July and August.

There were some adjustments to be made. Gerry and Judy were, by nature and inclination, night people; while Loos preferred to rise at 4:00 A.M. and go to bed no later than 9:00. Every morning she pursued a rigorous physical-fitness plan (she was then in her early seventies, under five feet in height, and had never in her life weighed more than ninety pounds); while Judy and Gerry were prone to let nature take its course.

Every morning Helen would take Jonathan to the beach

while the collaborators pursued their course of creative think-ing. Later in the day, when the lyrics had been set to a melody, Judy would run through the song; and when she was pleased by what she heard, she'd comment, "You know, I don't think I want anybody to sing that but me!" Through her work as a lyricist, she was beginning to recapture her incen-tive to perform, was in fact getting back the excitement of those days when the Revuers were caught up in the exhilara-tion of creating and performing their own material.

The doctors had been right—work was the best therapy for Holliday's depression. But then something occurred that brought a halt to the work on *Happy Birthday.*

"I came down for breakfast one morning," Loos recalled, "and ran into a wall of gloom." Gerry and Judy were barely speaking to each other, and when the overcast atmosphere failed to lift after four days, Loos decided to clear out.

"I never knew exactly what happened," Loos said. "But from things Judy said later, I gathered that he had a girl on the side and she had got on to the situation." It is also possible that Judy wanted a final commitment from Gerry, and, for all his love and devotion, this was not something he could give at this time; the failure of his first marriage, it has been suggested, had left him reluctant to repeat the experience. Possibly it was nothing more than a lovers' quarrel over nothing terribly important. Only Judy and Gerry knew for sure, and neither of them cared to share this information.

What is known is that the animosity did pass. Returning to New York after their Hampton vacation, the couple seemed as blissfully happy as ever. Gerry had recently formed a thirteen-piece band—Mulligan's Concert Jazz Band—and they were soon performing at the Village Vanguard to great acclaim. Judy was there every evening, often alone, occa-sionally with two new friends, Herb and Rita Gardner. Herb's play *A Thousand Clowns* was a recent Broadway smash hit, and Rita was enjoying great success for her performance in

The Fantasticks, in which she introduced the song "Soon It's Gonna Rain."

The Gardners were frequently invited to Holliday's apartment, invitations that Rita initially found somewhat intimidating because of the awe in which she held Judy. But then, after an hour or so, Holliday would ask Rita to sing, and when Rita did so, accompanied by Gerry, Judy was always enthusiastic. "That was one of the best things that ever happened to me," Rita Gardner remembers, "having Judy Holliday as a fan."

Occasionally, either at the Dakota or at the Gardners' apartment on East End Avenue, Judy would get up and perform some of the songs she and Gerry had written. Often she would ask Rita to sight-read the material so that she could get a listener's perspective on how it sounded. She wanted and welcomed criticism. Much of the material Mulligan and Holliday performed at this time had been written for *Happy Birthday.* They had continued to work on the score, since there continued to be Broadway interest in the project. "Mulligan's music was brilliant, but Judy's lyrics snowed them under," said Anita Loos. "Those lyrics will stand up with the best of Cole Porter's or Oscar Hammerstein's or Larry Hart's." But the Broadway producers who had first refusal on the script turned it down politely and with regrets. They liked it, but . . . they all felt it needed revision. Even with Judy starring as Addie Bemis—which was becoming a definite possibility—there was still a series of rejections.

The refusals are easy to understand once one has read the script, as that's where the problem lies. Instead of rethinking her script as a musical, Loos had merely lifted chunks out of the dialogue so that songs could be inserted, often arbitrarily, in their place. Judy's lyrics are often touching and witty, Mulligan's music is clever, but there's no fusion between the musical and dramatic elements. Possibly the problems could have been resolved if the collaborators had stuck to it, but each had other things on his mind. "I had to write another project," Loos explained, "and while we took it up again and again, nothing was ever to come of it. It never seemed to be the right time for *Happy Birthday*."

Chapter Seventeen

THE LAST SHOW

As the chances for an immediate production of *Happy Birthday* grew progressively more remote, Judy became increasingly disturbed about her financial status. Nothing had changed in this area—money kept going out with little, if anything, coming in. The situation became even more precarious when, late in 1962, Holliday learned that the Internal Revenue Service had been reviewing her back returns and had uncovered certain irregularities. She was warned by her attorney that she might be liable for as much as $100,000 in unpaid taxes.

Holliday was stunned. Every year she had signed and promptly paid her taxes, which of course had been professionally calculated. As far as she was aware, there had been no fraud. But during the Fifties and Sixties, many show-business personalities found themselves in a similar fix: Reputedly responsible accountants had whittled away at their returns, taking an illegal thousand off here, another thousand off there, always confident that they would never be checked or caught. But the thousands often added up to a considerable sum, and eventually the IRS grew suspicious and began

to investigate—and penalize. Holliday was to be one of the
first victims of this inquisition.

There were only two ways of freeing herself from this
dilemma: Either she would be forced to declare bankruptcy,
or she must get back to work as swiftly and as lucratively as
possible. Of the two alternatives, the second was the more
attractive, so she decided to return to acting, either in Hollywood (where the big money was) or maybe in a Broadway
show if the producers were willing to offer a percentage deal.

There were no signs of interest from Hollywood. Judy was
now in her early forties, an age when most film actresses face
the prospect of diminishing offers, and the financial returns
of her last few pictures reduced her stature as a bankable
star. On Broadway, her name still carried considerable weight,
but this was a dull period for the New York stage in terms
of both quantity and quality. Since Judy couldn't afford to
bide her time while looking for the perfect project, she had
to settle for the best of what was available.

With a good deal of fanfare, she signed for a musical
called *Hot Spot*, which had a talented group of craftsmen
behind it. The book was by Jack Weinstock and Willie Gilbert, who were responsible for *How to Succeed in Business
Without Really Trying*. Music was by Mary Rodgers (daughter of Richard Rodgers), who had supplied the score for
Once Upon a Mattress, which had catapulted Carol Burnett
to Broadway stardom in 1959. Lyrics were by Martin Charnin
(later known for his work on *Annie*). The producers were
Robert Fryer and Lawrence Carr, who had presented *Redhead*, *Wonderful Town*, and *Auntie Mame*.

On this occasion, unfortunately, none of the collaborators
were in top form—certainly not Weinstock and Gilbert, the
librettists. *Hot Spot* was intended as a spoof of the Peace
Corps, an organization whose satiric possibilities had already
been explored on TV and by journalists to the point of
exhaustion. Sallie, the heroine, has done duty for Sargent
Shriver in many backward lands, creating havoc in each,

until finally she is stationed in a postage-stamp-sized third-world country called D'hum (and pronounced—this is a cue for a running gag—Doom). Everybody in D'hum is unemployed, happily so. They shake their hips, fornicate, and smash coconuts to prove how happy they are. But Sallie's heart bleeds for their poverty and, egged on by D'hum's ruler, Nadir (another running joke), she decides that the only way to help the natives is to inform the Pentagon that the Russians are planning a take-over. Immediately D'hum is engulfed by American diplomats, one of whom uncovers Sallie's subterfuge but also finds himself fatally attracted by her pert naïveté.

Several people who were later to work on salvaging *Hot Spot* insist that it was a good idea that never panned out. "That often happens," remarked one reviser. "A perfectly viable project just fails to jell." But *Hot Spot* could never have looked all that promising: A spoof of the Peace Corps, while suitable material for a ten- or fifteen-minute sketch, was destined to seem awfully flimsy as the basis of a full-length musical. Perhaps the show would have worked had Charnin and Rodgers's score been witty and tuneful, but it was in fact far inferior to the songs Holliday and Mulligan had written for *Happy Birthday*, a comparison that made *Hot Spot* all the more disagreeable to Judy.

From the outset, she was fully aware of the show's shortcomings, but she reasoned that perhaps they could be overcome during the rehearsal and preview period. As she had learned from *Laurette*, however, shows that enter production in an unhealthy state have a way of declining rather than improving, no matter how much tender care is lavished on them. Some days she was able to convince herself that it would come out all right in the end, and she felt cheerful; other days she resigned herself to failure.

Most of the time, she felt resigned. She really didn't want to go back to performing, except perhaps to perform her own material. *Laurette* had convinced her that she would never again enjoy the experience of acting; she had reaped all the rewards she was going to find in that area, and she wanted to move on, not step backward.

When Joseph Harris, the production manager for *Hot Spot*, called to introduce himself and fill her in on the rehearsal schedule, Judy listened silently until he had completed his chirrupy message. A strange, sad smile crossed Judy's face. There was a protracted pause, and then softly, mournfully she started to sing: "The party's over, it's time to call it a day. . . ."

But the only positive way of handling the situation was to make the best of a bad deal. In the past few months, Judy had regained some of her equilibrium. She had made a good adjustment to her mastectomy, she felt secure with Gerry, she had found enormous satisfaction in songwriting. She was determined to get through *Hot Spot* as happily as possible and then concentrate solely on the things that really mattered. There was plenty of time; she was, after all, only forty-two.

Judy was unfailingly pleasant and cheerful throughout rehearsals. "*Hot Spot* is not a show that anyone walked away from with pleasant memories," Harris recalls, "but none of the unpleasantness had anything to do with Miss Holliday, not as far as I'm concerned. She was a very nice lady." The show was directed by Morton DaCosta, who had worked with Judy on *Dream Girl* and had later staged such top-grossing Broadway hits as *No Time for Sergeants*, *Auntie Mame*, and *The Music Man*. Judy was fond of "Teck" (DaCosta's nickname) and had confidence in his ability to gloss over *Hot Spot*'s weaknesses. He had a way of making shoddy material look bright and slick, as he had demonstrated with *Mame* and *Sergeants*.

But the DaCosta magic wasn't to work on *Hot Spot*. The show opened disastrously in Washington, D.C. The score was weak, the script was worse, the physical production was tacky, the dances were a series of clichés, and Holliday looked bloated and uncomfortable. (Because of the hormone injections, as post-operative treatment for her mastectomy, she found it harder than usual to lose weight; though by the time the show opened on Broadway, she had slimmed down considerably.) Occasionally a show that opens feebly out of town will still come into New York like a house-on-fire— *Fiddler on the Roof, Hello Dolly!*, and *Forty-second Street* are classic examples—but few such hits opened as feebly as *Hot Spot*, which clearly should have been put out of its misery as swiftly as possible.

The people behind *Hot Spot* were confident that somehow they would be able to transform the sow's ear. So the alterations began. Songs and scenes were deleted, to be replaced by new songs and scenes, which, in turn, were tossed out after a couple of performances. Choreographers came and went; parts were eliminated or added or recast, so that the program had to be corrected for nearly every performance. But the show stubbornly refused to improve: After three weeks of frantic overhauling, it still looked as ramshackle as it had on its first night.

From Washington, the show moved to New York, where it was scheduled to play a week of previews before its official opening. That week started to stretch into infinity as the premiere date was repeatedly postponed. "We were the precursor of those shows of the late 1970s—stuff like *Sarava* and some of the Papp productions—that went on and on previewing in hopes of making some money before the critics came in for the kill," said Joe Harris. On the strength of Holliday's name, however, *Hot Spot* had accumulated a very tidy advance sale.

Changes went on until three days before the premiere, and by this time Holliday was taking an active hand in the decisions made about the production. Encouraged by Mulligan, she had resolved not to be a passive bystander as she had been during *Laurette*; she wanted to play a purposeful part in the fate of *Hot Spot*. She had no illusions that it was ever going to be another *My Fair Lady* or even another *The Bells Are Ringing*, but she was determined that it should be as good as it could be. She didn't want it to be a public disgrace, and, besides, she needed it to run as long and as profitably as possible.

One of her first ideas was to invite Howard Teichmann to revise the script. She and "Tike" (as he was called by friends) had known each other for years, but they had lost sight of each other for a period, and Judy had started to think he disapproved of her. One night, shortly before rehearsals started for *Hot Spot*, she was having dinner at Sardi's and Teichmann was sitting across the room with his wife. He hadn't noticed Holliday, but she had spotted him as soon as she came in. "There's Tike," she said to her escort. "He's ignoring me because he thought I was terrible in *Solid Gold Cadillac* [which Teichmann had written]." She went on and on about this imaginary slight until her escort furtively left the table and informed Teichmann of Judy's distress.

"I thought she had been wonderful in *Cadillac*, and I immediately went over and told her so," recalls Teichmann. "It was a happy reunion, and I wish it had led to something more fruitful than *Hot Spot*."

In calling on Teichmann, Judy was choosing a man who had long and arduous experience as a "play doctor," a theatrical Mr. Fix-it who comes in at the last minute and tries to patch up a failing play (usually without credit but with considerable financial rewards for his anonymity). Teichmann watched the show one evening, and had a few ideas about what could be improved, but on the whole he felt it was beyond redemption.

After the performance, Teichmann visited Judy in her dressing room and outlined some of his suggestions. At one point he seemed to lose her attention and, turning his head, he spotted Gerry Mulligan, only partly visible, standing in the doorway and gesticulating at Judy. Teichmann found Mulligan's surreptitious appearance somewhat unsettling—he seemed to have been lurking about by prearrangement. Teichmann presumed that Judy was relying heavily on Mulligan's opinion, but he couldn't understand why she wanted to keep Gerry's mentorship a secret. Since intrigue of this nature didn't seem at all Holliday's style, Teichmann decided Mulligan must be "a peculiar sort." Actually it was less sinister than that. This was another instance of Mulligan's desire to stay in the background while he was supporting and guiding Judy.

At around the time Teichmann joined the show, Morton DaCosta resigned as director. (Whether he was fired or withdrew voluntarily is not known; there are conflicting reports and DaCosta refuses to talk about Holliday.) To replace DaCosta, the producers, at Holliday's request, selected Richard Quine, director of *The Solid Gold Cadillac* and *Full of Life*, her last pictures for Columbia. It was a highly unorthodox choice since Quine had never directed a Broadway play. He had, however, been a stage actor before going to Hollywood, where he had gone on performing until, getting nowhere as a juvenile lead, he switched to directing. Taking charge of a musical that was already waist-deep in trouble was an enormous challenge for a Broadway neophyte, but Judy adored Quine, and at this point she wanted more than anything else to be surrounded by people she loved and trusted.

Quine flew into New York just in time for a Saturday matinee. By appointment, he met Teichmann at the concessionaire's stand at the back of the Majestic Theatre, where they downed cartons of lemonade for their lunch. "He was bubbling over with ideas," Teichmann remembers, "but I told him to watch the show and see how he felt afterward."

By the final curtain, Quine had turned ashen and he asked Teichmann to tender his regrets to Judy: The show was, in his opinion, hopeless. Independently, Teichmann had reached the same conclusion, and though he would have welcomed Quine's support, he set off alone to deliver the damning verdict.

Judy had taken a suite at the Sherry-Netherland because, as she told Teichmann, she wanted to keep the chaos of *Hot Spot* outside her own home. She was working at least eighteen hours a day, she was dog-tired and trigger-tempered, and she didn't want to work off her frustrations on Jonathan and Helen. As Teichmann was waiting for the elevator, Judy suddenly appeared with a bunch of newspapers under her arm. He asked how she was feeling. *"Farshtinkeh,"* she replied, and though Teichmann didn't know much Yiddish, he caught the drift of her meaning. Her frame of mind was not going to make the verdict easy to accept, but, once inside the suite, Teichmann went straight to the point. He told her that Quine was catching the next plane back to Beverly Hills and that he (Teichmann) really didn't think there was much that he or Quine or anyone else could do to improve the show.

"That, as you can imagine, went down the tubes," he recalls. But after the first shock had worn off, Holliday seemed almost relieved; she admitted that Teichmann was probably right and, anyway, there were no hard feelings.

Other writers were called in to work on the show. Herb Gardner wrote some monologues and comedy material for Judy; Larry Gelbart (one of the authors of *A Funny Thing Happened on the Way to the Forum*) overhauled a couple of scenes; Stephen Sondheim supplied lyrics for a new opening number, "Don't Laugh." But none of the changes made any appreciable difference.

The weekend before the premiere of *Hot Spot*—April 19, 1963—the *New York Post* carried an interview with Holliday in which she said, "You can only live through one or two *Hot Spots* in your life." This was not the way stars usually spoke about a forthcoming premiere, but Judy was in no mood to play games and saw no reason to feign cheerfulness

when everyone knew *Hot Spot* was going to be the bomb of
the season. If at all, it would be remembered as the first
musical within recent memory to open without either a
directorial or choreographic credit—no one wanted to acknowledge responsibility for them.

"I don't mind failure," Judy told the *Post*'s Jerry Tallmer,
"that's part of the business I'm in." The hardships of the
last three years, she implied, had put professional failure in
its proper perspective. What was distressing was the huge
amount of emotional and physical effort that she and so
many other talented people had extended on a project that
was going to wind up as an unmitigated fiasco.

Hot Spot went through the trauma of an official opening
on April 19, as planned, and the reviews were, as expected,
uniformly poor, though there were compassionate words of
praise for Holliday interspersed throughout. (Tallmer's piece
cast her as a victim; perhaps that was the impression she
wished to convey when she spoke to him.)

Howard Taubman, the most benevolent of the New York
critics then wielding power over the Broadway scene, wrote
in the *Times:* "You know [*Hot Spot*] is in trouble when it
requires [Holliday] to do a routine in which she pretends to
be three members of a State Department reassignment committee. What emerges is an ordinary little vaudeville turn.
She manages it neatly enough, but it is redundant. . . . She
does an amusing step a la Russe; she slinks briefly like Mata
Hari; [she affects several accents]; she makes the most of her
scattered opportunities."

This is, beyond a reasonable doubt, indifferent praise for
a leading lady of Holliday's stature. What Taubman clearly
wanted to imply, but was too gallant to state bluntly, was
that Judy had surrendered unconditionally to the vulgarity
of the material. And he was right—it was not a pleasant sight.
Anyone who had the misfortune of seeing Holliday in *Hot
Spot* (or Mary Martin in *Jennie* or Katharine Hepburn in
Coco) will know how dispiriting it can be watching a star

attempting to redeem an unworthy vehicle, particularly if the vehicle is a musical, where joy and communal exhilaration are of the essence.

Thanks to the advance sales, *Hot Spot* managed to run for about five months, finally closing in the early fall of 1963. The burden of carrying the show was so arduous that Judy felt mainly relief at the final curtain, even though the collapse of *Hot Spot* was to leave her in a perilous financial condition. As she had been warned, the IRS now stepped forward with a tax lien of $99,000; and since she had no way of meeting such an enormous claim, the government was threatening to assume ownership of her country home, along with its furnishings and all the possessions of the Dakota apartment.

But this threat was still distant, and Judy had more immediate problems on her mind. Her relationship with Mulligan had started to flounder. After five years, it had reached a plateau where it would either be formalized by marriage or fizzle out—it couldn't survive in this state of limbo. Mulligan, however, couldn't bring himself to make this commitment, and shortly after *Hot Spot* he began to ease himself out of Holliday's life.

Judy was heartsick for many weeks. She was still deeply attached to Gerry and wanted him back, but she realized that there was little she could do to persuade him to return. Much of the confidence she had built up over the past two years now disappeared, though she still managed to muster the determination to keep herself together and move on. She agreed with friends that she must meet other men, though the idea filled her with anxiety. How do you go about telling a man that you've had a breast removed? she asked Anita Loos. "If you wait till you've taken your clothes off, he may tell you to put them back on; if you try to clue him in before, you may scare him away."

Eventually Judy did start seeing a few men, and one (a lawyer who, according to most accounts, was as physically and intellectually drab as most of her other men were colorful) she lured into bed. It was an unsuccessful experiment. Much to her chagrin, he never called again.

Sex was not the only problem nagging at her. *Hot Spot* had left Judy more determined than ever to concentrate most of her energy on developing an alternative or collateral career to acting; but now that Gerry was gone, her songwriting ambitions were in jeopardy. Of course, she could always work with another composer, but a compatible collaborator wasn't easy to find. There was also the possibility that she could go on working with Gerry, but she had serious doubts about how well that would work out.

Not since her final days at Columbia had she felt so desolate and despairing. She didn't know where or to whom to turn. All the exciting avenues that had once seemed to be opening before her now appeared to have narrowed down to dead ends. It took all her fortitude to hold on to her faith in the homily she had repeated to Jerry Talmer: Adversity strengthens.

Chapter Eighteen

A SPECIAL PROVIDENCE

Intensifying Judy's emotional malaise was yet another health problem that had developed during the run of *Hot Spot*. Rouben Ter-Arutunian's sets for the show had consisted mainly of long, hanging strands of rope. They were appropriately evocative of a sleepy third-world republic, but the stomping feet of the D'hum dancers set particles of hemp flying in all directions, and a good many of them came to rest in Judy's throat. At least once during every performance, she staggered off stage coughing and scarcely able to breath.

The condition disappeared once the show closed, and Judy wrote it off as an unpleasant but unavoidable professional hazard. But then suddenly the symptoms started recurring at frequent intervals, and, at Helen's insistence, Judy agreed to visit her doctor. Since she had a long history of throat trouble, it seems peculiar that she was not overly concerned about these symptoms, but apparently she was not. Outwardly she appeared confident that the ailment—whatever it might be— could not be serious.

The doctor ran a series of tests that only served to confirm what he had initially feared. Judy had cancer of the throat.

It was in an advanced stage and the prognosis looked grim. It seemed fruitless to operate.

Because of her propensity to severe depression, the doctor decided not to tell Judy of his diagnosis. Instead he informed her that she had contracted a curable disease, one with roughly the same symptoms as cancer and one that required basically the same treatment. That she believed what she was told is, again, surprising, since most mastectomy patients are aware that they are prone to relapse for a period of at least three years. Judy's friends are not precisely sure when she first realized that she was fatally ill, though definitely there was to come a time when pretense was no longer possible. That time, however, was still many months in the future.

Her deterioration was extremely gradual. For more than a year, she neither felt nor looked terribly ill. Occasionally she was slightly puffy about the face or bloated throughout her body—a side effect of her medication—but because of her lifelong tendency toward overweight, the condition did not seem so unusual. Judy had been warned that she might puff up because of her treatment, a situation she found highly ironic. "It's my luck to have a sickness that makes you fat instead of thin."

Judy had to receive regular medical attention, and she wanted someone to accompany her. But because of an idiosyncratic superstition, she preferred that it be no one who had been with her during her postmastectomy surveillance. That left out Helen, Tessa, and Gerry. So she frequently turned to Cam Walter, an old acquaintance and new friend.

Cam, an attractive blond in her early thirties, was the wife of Cy Walter, the cocktail pianist and accompanist (for the likes of Mabel Mercer) who was for years a mainstay at the posh Drake Room in the Drake Hotel on Park Avenue. Over the years, the Walters had spent an occasional evening with Judy and Gerry—Holliday was a Walter fan, as was Gerry— but it was not until around the time of *Hot Spot* that Cam Walter and Holliday became close.

Escorting Judy to the doctor was not an assignment Cam relished—certainly not at this time, when her husband was also a cancer victim—but it was an obligation of friendship she owed Judy, whom she adored. Along with Helen, Tessa, the most trusted of Judy's business associates, and eventually Gerry Mulligan, Cam was to be one of a small group formed to shield Holliday from the knowledge of how ill she really was, to protect her from anyone who might inadvertently reveal to Holliday the seriousness of her condition.

For a long time the stratagem worked as smoothly as planned. Rita Gardner remembers seeing Judy frequently in this period and never suspected how ill she was. "She looked lovely and she never seemed depressed." Judy still loved to hear Rita sing—everything from Rodgers and Hart to Holliday and Mulligan—and Judy would even occasionally perform herself, usually trying out some of her own material. "She was eager for criticism," Gardner recalls. "She was full of plans and projects for the future."

One of the things she was thinking about was returning to the stage. Continuing her career as a performer was, she had determined realistically, an option that she had to keep open. And unexpectedly she learned of a project that sounded promising. Not long after the closing of *Hot Spot*, Betty Comden and Adolph Green had come to her with the idea for a musical they were planning to write with Jule Styne: If Judy would take on the leading role, it would make for a happy reunion of all the major talents involved in *The Bells Are Ringing*. The basic situation sounded awfully tired—it was to be yet another burlesque of Golden Age movies, and by this time Comden and Green had covered that terrain to the point of near-exhaustion. They were, however, the acknowledged masters of this kind of satire, and the prospect of working with old friends was very appealing to Holliday.

So when the musical went into production in 1964 as *Fade In – Fade Out* with Carol Burnett as its star, Holliday was very hurt. People were talking about Burnett as a new

Judy Holliday, but that wasn't what bothered the original model. Judy appreciated Burnett's talent and realized that the comparison was mutually flattering: Burnett was multidimensional, and audiences responded to her with the same kind of unabashed warmth they granted Holliday. Judy would not have cared if Comden and Green had set out to write a show for Burnett; what enraged her was that they had cavalierly handed a younger and (Holliday suspected) more marketable star a script that was originally earmarked for her.

But her relations with Comden and Green had been seesawing for years, and their erratic behavior was not anything she cared to brood over now. She had more important matters on her mind. According to an old wives' tale, some people instinctively sense that they are approaching death and suddenly begin putting their lives in order, start paring it down to essentials. In Judy's case, the tale seems to have validity. For years she had claimed to care more about who she was as a person than about what she might become as an actress, and now all her remaining energy was directed toward fulfilling herself as a private person.

She began to spend most of her time at her house in the country—and so far, it was still *hers*, the IRS having as yet failed to take possession. The house had undergone one disfiguring alteration over the last year, the result of a misinterpretation of orders. Originally there were two porches —one a lovely, broad veranda with gingerbread columns at the front; the other, just off the kitchen, at the rear, a stooplike construction that was dangerously dilapidated. By phone, Judy had asked a local contractor to remove the porch, and while she later insisted that she had specified which porch, he insisted she hadn't, and of course he had torn down the showpiece and left the eyesore intact.

Judy was distressed, but, since there was nothing else to do, she put up a new front porch, which lacked the charm (and value) of the original. Every time she drove up to the house, she'd mutter a string of curses against the contractor.

This was part of a ritual she went through every time she arrived at Washingtonville. First came the maledictions. Then, jumping from the car, she ran to check on the progress of the tree she had planted at the time of Jonathan's birth. Next, after depositing her bags in the living room, she'd go out to the swimming pool and, picking up a long wooden oar used exclusively for this purpose, gently begin lifting frogs from the water. When the last frog had been removed from the pool and tenderly nudged into the bushes, Judy would invite her guests to go for a swim whenever they wanted, and those who didn't mind a touch of slime went ahead and plunged in.

In the past Judy had managed the house by herself, but now she decided to hire a live-in maid to housekeep—an arrangement that failed to work out as originally planned. Shortly after she started work, the maid announced that she was pregnant; and then, a few weeks later, she came back from a checkup and informed Judy that the doctor had forbidden her to climb stairs. By herself, Judy pulled down a mattress and bed frame from the top floor and placed it on a sun porch for the maid's convenience. Pretty soon the hired hand was spending most of her time in bed and Judy was cooking her meals and serving them on a tray. When Judy was feeling poorly, she'd lie on an adjacent couch; and when visitors dropped by, she'd giggle and announce, "Welcome to the sick bay!"

Judy had her good days and bad days. When she was feeling fit, she was cheerful and funny, often full of mischief. "Let's go down to the parkway and see if there are any seedlings we can swipe," she'd say. She spent hours working in her garden, raising both vegetables and flowers, and through her coaching and artful care, the plants flourished luxuriantly. "That summer she had an almost obsessive need to see life coming up out of the ground," recalls Cam Walter.

Her other major pastime was touring antique shops, tag sales, and auctions. If she learned that an Early American comforter was to be put up for sale, she'd spend the whole week excitedly calculating what she could afford to bid; and if she managed to get it at her price, she'd spend the following week lovingly caressing and examining the material and needlework.

By the fall of 1964, Judy started having more bad than good days. The disease was definitely making inroads, and those friends who earlier had not been precisely certain of her condition now had few doubts. Cam Walter remembers the exact moment when she realized that Holliday was aware she was dying. At a small dinner party one evening, one of the guests told a joke about Judy Garland and her huge homosexual following. The story told of a not-so-bright young man who arrives at Cherry Grove, the predominantly gay community on Fire Island, and discovers all the flags along the marina flying at half-mast. Grasping for an incident tragic enough to prompt this funeral display, the young man screeches, "Good grief! Judy Garland must have died!"

"It wasn't a terribly funny story," recalls Cam Walter, "and telling it at that time was extraordinarily tactless, but a couple of people tried to pass it off with a forced laugh. But I happened to catch Judy's eye and she stared at me just a second before looking away. Her eyes were filled with hurt and despair. It was then that I knew she knew."

Judy's condition was now plainly evident from her physical appearance. She looked ravaged—her eyes were sunken, her face was still puffy though she had started to lose weight, and her hair was thinning, all side effects of chemotherapy. Still, she often dressed up, put on a blush of rouge and a fur coat, and went out to spend a couple of hours at one of her favorite stores. One day as she was Christmas shopping at Bergdorf Goodman's, she noticed two clerks staring at her and heard—or thought she heard—one whisper to the other, "That *used* to be Judy Holliday."

From then on, she avoided places where she might be recognized, and whenever she did go out—usually for an

exploration of the thrift shops along Second and Third
Avenues—she wore dark glasses and an oversize babushka
that obscured most of her face. Often when she returned
from these jaunts, she could scarcely walk because of the pain.
Easing herself onto a couch, she would call for pillows, which
would be piled behind and around her. The softness of the
pillows had a lulling, therapeutic effect: At least for a while
they seemed to absorb all the excruciating agony.

Judy's greatest source of comfort, however, was Gerry
Mulligan, who had returned to her as soon as he learned
that she was terminally ill. The reconciliation caused considerable comment along Broadway, much of it spiteful, since
it was common knowledge that Mulligan was then seriously
involved with Sandy Dennis, an actress who at the start of
her career was frequently and inaccurately likened to Judy.
Many members of the Sardi's set argued self-righteously that
Mulligan should have had the "decency" to "suspend" his
romance with Dennis while he nursed Judy, but this was expecting too much of a man who gave of himself unstintingly.

Nonetheless, the three-way relationship made for a difficult
and at times painful situation. Mulligan was in love with
Dennis, and yet still deeply attached to Holliday. He wanted
to hurt neither, and went to extraordinary lengths to prevent
Holliday from hearing of his romance with Dennis. Many
people feel he was successful in keeping Judy in the dark,
though one story has it that Helen eventually decided to en-
lighten her daughter, but Judy wouldn't listen. "It's all right,
Mama. I know what you want to tell me," she supposedly
said. "It doesn't matter." If true, she probably realized the
terrible anxiety Gerry was going through, and could accept
that he needed someone to comfort him, someone he could
confide in. She really couldn't complain. He was always there
when she needed him. That was enough.

For a while Judy and Gerry went back to their music writing. They completed a song for the film version of Herb

Gardner's play, A *Thousand Clowns*, and Rita Gardner recorded it for the sound track, but most of it was eliminated before the film was released in 1965. (A few bars can be heard during the opening credits.) Cy Feuer, a stage producer, asked them to write a score for a musical version of *Dream Girl*, a project that thrilled Judy as she had never lost her fondness for Elmer Rice's comedy. But before they had made any headway, Judy became too ill to continue. (The musical, retitled *Skyscraper* and starring Julie Harris, opened in 1966 with a score by Sammy Cahn and James Van Heusen.)

Judy's finances were now in very serious straits, more serious than she knew. She'd had no source of steady income since *Hot Spot*, so she was not unaware of the problem, but she was never fully informed of how intolerable the situation had become. Mulligan had quietly started paying the most pressing bills.

By the beginning of 1965, Judy's illness was no longer a secret in show-business circles. Slowly her old friends started dropping by the Dakota for a farewell visit. Max Gordon (of the Village Vanguard) and his wife, Lorraine, came to dinner when Holliday was still well enough to cook and prepare the meal herself. As they were lingering over their coffee, Judy brought out a bottle of fine liqueur Gordon had given her some years earlier. It was still half-full. "Now seems the right moment to finish it," she said with a smile.

One of the last people outside the intimate circle to see Judy before her death was Howard Teichmann. Early in 1965 he called and asked if he could stop by for a visit. Judy hesitated for a moment and then told him she'd be free that evening after dinner. Helen opened the door and quickly disappeared; Jonathan stayed to chat for a moment and then he, too, withdrew, leaving Teichmann alone with Judy.

"Surprisingly, her voice sounded fine, but her face was haggard," he recalled. "About the rest of her, you couldn't tell. She was swathed in one of those all-purpose, voluminous

252 J U D Y   H O L L I D A Y

caftans, making it impossible to tell whether she was overweight or emaciated, but later a sleeve dropped back and her
hand and lower arm looked desiccated."

She was, however, in cheerful spirits. She told Teichmann
that she had been writing lyrics and reading scripts—she was
trying to find a project for the next Broadway season. Then,
as though it were a sudden inspiration, she asked, "Why
don't you write me a play?"

Teichmann was taken aback, but he tried to keep a steady,
noncommittal tone. "Well, it's not all that easy, but if I get
a good idea, I'll certainly let you know." Switching subjects
as tactfully as possible, he told her Shelley Winters had been
after him to turn *Solid Gold Cadillac* into a musical: Shelley
saw herself as a middle-aged Laura Partridge—younger than
Josephine Hull, not quite so young as Holliday in the film
version—surrounded by a board of General Motors directors
who were tottering on the near side of senility. Winters would
be old, but everyone in the cast would be older—it would be
the first geriatric musical.

Shelley and her ideas were always good for a laugh, and
Holliday appreciated the joke, as he had hoped she would.

Teichmann then noticed a flute that was resting on a
coffee table. Following his glance, Judy smiled. "I'm learning
to play," she explained. "It's a new hobby."

Again Teichmann was startled—toying around with a wind
instrument seemed an odd avocation for someone with throat
cancer. "I'm not very musical," he explains, "but I am
curious, so I asked if I could play it, or blow it, or whatever
the hell you do with a flute, and she said, 'Go ahead.' So I
put it to my mouth, puckered my lips, and out came this
absolutely perfect note."

Judy was astonished. "God damn!" she exclaimed. "I've
been practicing for weeks and I've never been able to do that."
(The next day the flute disappeared, and Judy never again
mentioned her ambition to become an amateur flutist.)

By the time of Teichmann's visit, Judy was experiencing

increasingly longer spells of extreme physical duress. Often the pain was so excruciating that Mulligan would have to hold her in his arms for hours at a time, trying valiantly, not always victoriously, to soothe and comfort her. "Judy was an ultrafeminine woman," says Cam Walter, "never more so than at her death." For all her independence, there had always been a part of her that wanted to be held and protected by a man, and Gerry had fulfilled that need more than anyone else, now more than ever before.

Throughout the ordeal, Helen tried to maintain a brave front, but she was confused, alarmed, and angry at what was happening. "This isn't fair," she said to Cam Walter. "This is not the way it's supposed to happen. The mother should die before the child." Unspoken was the all-important question of what would happen to the mother after the child had died.

Eventually the pain became so unendurable and so agonizing to witness that Judy was given heroin. Even then, it was widely acknowledged that heroin was the most effective painkiller for terminal cancer patients, but, irrationally, its use for this and other legitimate medical purposes remains illegal in this country. (The medical profession can be extraordinarily insensitive on this point. One doctor, begged by the daughter of a terminal cancer victim to administer heroin, replied: "Do you want your mother to die an addict?")

Despite its illegality, heroin was in 1966 as easily and expensively available in New York as it is today, and there was no difficulty about obtaining it for Judy. She could afford it, and she had friends who had contacts. A lot of her acquaintances moved in jazz circles, and while they weren't users themselves, they knew how to find out where it could be obtained. Whether or not Judy knew she was taking heroin isn't known. Since she was receiving shots daily, it is entirely possible that she had no notion of what was being injected through her veins.

By March of 1965, Judy no longer had the strength to

leave the apartment, and found it increasingly difficult even to walk from room to room. Two weeks later she was so disabled that she was confined to bed. Most of the day she spent reading, watching TV, talking to friends on the phone, and occasionally entertaining a bedside visitor. Her major concern, however, was Jonathan and his future.

Jonathan had gone through a bad period after the divorce, but now that he was entering his teens, he had become, according to Cam Walter, "cheerful and curious," imaginative, a little withdrawn at times, but "for an adult, great fun to be with." Though he could not have been unaware of what was occurring, Judy wanted him to be fully prepared, by a professional, and she sent him to a psychologist for a series of informal chats.

Judy also felt obligated to foster a reconciliation between Jonathan and his father. Helen was too old to be assigned guardianship, and it would be best that he live with David and Ellen and their children. She'd noticed that Jonathan had started to become more outgoing when playing with Cam Walter's children during the previous year. A real rapport had been established, and Judy wanted him to grow up among people his own age.

But even as she was planning for what would happen afterward, Judy went on reading scripts, and writing and talking about possible stage or TV appearances in the not-so-distant future. "I made a few deals for TV shows," said her lawyer, Arnold Krakower, "though I knew she would never keep them. She needed the encouragement." But who was fooling whom? Once the game was dropped, what was left to be said or done? Nothing much beyond pity, and Judy had already had enough of that. Pretense was preferable to pity, even when it was as well intentioned and artfully packaged as Howard Teichmann's sympathy visit.

Ultimately it mattered not at all whether she was feigning for herself or for her friends. On May 26, she was taken to Mount Sinai Hospital. For several days she remained lucid, though under heavy sedation and unable to speak except in monosyllables. Her admission to the hospital had gone without notice, as had the final stages of her illness: There was to be no death watch by the press. Judy had few visitors beyond Helen, Jonathan, David Oppenheim, Gerry, and Krakower. (Tessa was then working outside New York, and Cam and her children were vacationing for the summer in Connecticut.)

On Friday, June 4, Arnold Krakower spent an hour with Judy in the early evening. She was still fully conscious but unable to speak. He told her that there had been a couple of new TV offers and that during the last week he had taken Jonathan out for dinner and later to a ball game. Judy reached out and squeezed his hand.

Sometime later that night, Holliday lost consciousness. Krakower was the last of her friends ever to communicate with her. Two days later, at 5:00 A.M., Monday, June 7, Judy Holliday died peacefully in her sleep. Precisely two weeks later, she would have celebrated her forty-fourth birthday.

EPILOGUE

Judy's death received front-page coverage from most of the leading newspapers, including *The New York Times*. For most movie and theater fans, the reports came as a shock—outside the show-business world, few people knew Holliday had been ill, and even those who were informed had trouble accepting the early-morning radio reports: If a Judy had died, it must have been Garland. That, too, would have been a shock, but not really a surprise. Some early deaths seem inevitable, almost preordained, but not Holliday's. True, she hadn't done much in the past five years, and the little she had accomplished was not of top quality, but there was no feeling that she had burned herself out or that she had reached the limits of her talent. Certainly she became somewhat lost and confused as she entered middle age, but she had gone on exploring options, extending herself. Unfortunately, before she had discovered her way, she was dead.

The faithful quickly gathered in New York to discuss arrangements for the funeral. Judy had left a will, dated May 17, 1957, but it contained no specifications as to burial procedures. As she was, at most, an agnostic, it was decided that the service should have no definite religious content. Everyone agreed that there should be lots of music—music had always been one of Judy's greatest joys. Gerry suggested he play "The Party's Over" on his saxophone. "No one knew whether he was serious," says Cam Walter, "but we settled for a little Bach and Mozart."

The funeral service was held at Frank E. Campbell at 81st and Madison. Holliday's body rested in a closed mahogany coffin covered with a blanket of roses, carnations, and peonies. Around it were wreaths and bouquets sent by Shelley Winters, Katharine Hepburn, Spencer Tracy, Harold Prince, Vincent Sardi, and Goddard Lieberson.

Among the mourners were Abe Burrows, Sydney Chaplin, David Oppenheim, Howard Teichmann, Morton Gottlieb, Jule Styne, Betty Comden, Adolph Green, and of course, the faithful Mulligan, who, wearing dark glasses, escorted Helen and Jonathan in and out of the Campbell building. Not at all inappropriately, Gerry had been granted the position of first man in Judy's life.

The service was sober and dignified, and it closed with a brief eulogy from the president of the Ethical Cultural Society of New York. Later the same day, at Helen's insistence, a private Hebrew service was held at the Westchester Hills Cemetery.

Judy's will left most of her estate, initially estimated at between fifty and a hundred thousand dollars, to Jonathan and Helen. There were a few small bequests—all jewelry went to Helen, her records to Adolph Green, and so on. The bulk of the estate was then to be divided into two trust funds, for her son and mother, with Jonathan receiving the principal of Helen's trust following her death.

Shortly after the funeral, the U.S. government moved swiftly to take possession of Judy's house and all other properties and personal belongings to offset the balance of the tax lien Judy had been paying off over the last years. "They swept in like vultures," remembers Cam Walter. Some of Judy's

friends drove up to Washingtonville and ransacked the house
for souvenirs—a book or a plate, small items with no mone-
tary value but significant to them as remembrances of Holliday. As the scavengers were pulling out of the driveway, a limb
of a tree fell and struck the hood of the car. "That couldn't
have been Judy," said the driver. "It must have been the wrath
of the IRS."

Jonathan soon went off to live with his father and stepmother. David is presently dean of the School of the Arts at
New York University. Recently he and Ellen separated.

Gerry Mulligan set up housekeeping with Sandy Dennis.
She was pregnant at the time of Judy's death, but was to lose
the baby through a miscarriage. Everyone presumed they
were married, but when they parted company some years later,
they blithely announced that they had never gotten around
to the legal formalities.

Helen returned to the small apartment on West 75th Street
that she had maintained all during the period when she was a
permanent guest at the Dakota. Having lived through her
daughter for most of her life, she now had no idea of how she
should use up the time still allotted her. Many afternoons she
could be seen sunning herself outside her apartment building,
chatting with her neighbors and looking very lost. Occasionally she'd phone one of Holliday's friends and ask, "What
can we do to keep Judy's memory alive?"

Howard Teichmann was one of the people with whom she
spoke. "There wasn't much I could say," he recalls. "It was,
after all, a matter that could only be solved by posterity, by
the next couple generations of filmgoers and how kindly they
looked on her movies."

The forecast looked decidedly unsettled. Judy's best and
most personal work had been done on stage, and that was
beyond recapturing. In 1956 only two of her films, *Born Yesterday* and *Adam's Rib*, had achieved even semiclassic standing, and in one she had played only a supporting role. Worst
of all, a whole new generation of moviegoers had come of age

since her final screen appearance, and for them she was an unknown quantity. At the time of her death, *Newsweek* referred to her as "the nearly forgotten Judy Holliday." The description raised storms of protest along Shubert Alley, but *Newsweek* was reflecting the viewpoint of a wider audience.

The deep sense of sorrow that hovers over Holliday's life and career emanates from the recognition and regret that she wasn't allowed enough time to accomplish all she was capable of achieving. Her story ends on a note of incompletion; far more than Lillian Hellman (who usurped the title for the first volume of her autobiography), Holliday seems in retrospect an unfinished woman.

Even Judy's greatest admirers had to admit that Holliday had not fulfilled all her promise by the time of her death. "When I first saw Judy, I thought she was destined to become the next Laurette Taylor," says Marian Seldes. "I was sure that, as she continued to live and develop as an actress and a person, she would play roles written for her by our best writers. But things went wrong. Life went wrong. She died too young."

In her last months, Judy seemed on the threshold of an important breakthrough in her life, both professionally and personally. It is highly doubtful that she would ever have played the Laurette Taylor roles Marian Seldes envisioned for her, if only because there weren't any playwrights to create such roles; and it's fulsome nonsense to regret (as one journalist eulogized) our missed opportunities to see her as Mother Courage or O'Casey's Juno or one of Chekhov's frustrated heroines. After all, there was still much to be accomplished within her proven range, particularly since at the end of her life she seemed to be reaching some sense of balance between her ambivalence toward acting and her drive toward writing. It appears likely that, had she been granted the time, she would have seen that writing and acting could be combined so that one fueled the other, combining to propel her into promising and fascinating new directions.

Throughout the final months of her life, Holliday expressed a growing confidence in and assurance of who she was—or at least whom she wanted to be—which was retained, however tenuously, through all the emotional and physical setbacks she endured. The spine of strength that many of her friends had spotted when she was a young and seemingly fragile girl —what Betty Comden once called Holliday's "gambler's instinct"; what John Houseman described as her inner confidence that somehow, some way, she would get ahead— had indeed fortified itself over the years. The teen-age Judy Tuvim who had somehow discovered the pluck to face down the jeers of the Village Vanguard regulars in 1939 had grown up to become Judy Holliday, a woman of grit and considerable courage.

As it turned out, Helen needn't have worried about Judy's continuing fame—everything has worked out nearly as well as she would have wanted. Perhaps her daughter hasn't as yet been entered into the first rank of screen greats, but rarely a year passes without another up-and-coming actress being likened to Holliday, and that in itself is some guarantee of immortality. The list extends from Barbara Harris through Goldie Hawn and Lily Tomlin to Gilda Radner. Mary Steenburgen (who won an Oscar for her performance in *Melvin and Howard*) claims to have studied all of Holliday's performances before taking on her first screen role. Nancy Allen recently told a TV talk-show audience that she used Holliday as a model for the character she played in *Blow-Out*. And actors and acting teachers still speak of Holliday's comic technique with a note of awe that reverberates throughout their commentary.

INDEX